CRICKET:
more than a game

CRICKET:
more than a game

Edited by John Sheppard

ANGUS & ROBERTSON

Acknowledgements

The Editor and Publishers wish to thank all those who have permitted copyright material to appear on the following pages: Jack Fingleton for the quotation on page 233 and Allen Synge, The Lemon Tree Press, for the quotation on page 245. William Collins for the quotation by Jack Fingleton on page 214. Associated Press for pictures on pages 72 (left), 98; Australian Information Service, 50 (bottom); Australian News and Information Bureau, 116; Central Press Photos, 11, 13, 14, 34, 42, 45, 60, 70, 72 (right), 76 (top and bottom left), 117, 125 (right), 132 (left), 137 (right), 143, 158, 162 (right), 169 (right), 172 (right), 184 (bottom), 188 (left), 197 (left), 205, 206, 213, 215, 237; Mike Deller, 25 (top); Patrick Eagar, 9, 28 (left), 33 (top), 35, 36, 49, 56, 75, 76 (bottom right), 80 (right), 83, 101 (top), 102 (top), 125 (left), 127, 128 (top), 132 (top), 137 (left), 145, 147, 152, 160, 165, 177 (top), 179, 183, 184 (top), 225, 229 (bottom), 239; David Frith, 20 (bottom), 33 (bottom), 102 (bottom), 177 (bottom), 203, 204 (top right and bottom), 229 (bottom); G. G. R. Hofmeister, 92, 169 (left), 172 (left); Hong Kong Government Information Service, 103, 104; Ken Kelly, 19, 24, 25 (bottom), 41, 81, 90 (left), 128, 155, 162 (left), 204 (top right), 229 (top); Keystone, 43, 107; National Publicity Studios, 50 (top); Press Association, 23, 24, 28 (right), 90 (right), 94, 120, 197 (right), 201; Rigby Pty, 111; John Sheppard, 12; Posy Simmonds, 243; R. Shilton, 139; Sport and General, 80 (left), 124, 129, 178, 181, 190, 212; Sporting Pictures (UK), 193; Sunday Times Colour Magazine, 20 (top); Transworld Features Inc., 230 (top).

Angus & Robertson
London · Sydney · Singapore
Manila

First published by Angus & Robertson (U.K.) Ltd 1975

ISBN 0 207 95642 1

Made and printed in Great Britain by
Hazell Watson & Viney Ltd, Aylesbury, Bucks

Contents

Introduction

As the first word of its title spells out unmistakably, this is a cricket book. 'Well,' you might ask, 'what sort of a cricket book?' My reply would be: 'Should that really matter? If you like cricket and a sufficient number of the writers' names on the front cover appeal to you, isn't that enough? Does it really have to be categorized?'

Sadly, the last of those three questions is rhetorical. After all, most things these days are pushed into one category or another; identifying badges are pinned to their lapels then patted into place. It's a legacy, I suppose, of an era when bureaucrats multiply like amorous amoebae and the filing cabinet explosion comfortably outpaces the human one.

So, the point is taken. In which case, what kind of cricket book *do* we have here? Let's close in on the subject by listing the special compartments that most cricket books can be hived into: tour books, biographies, historical, instructional, general anthology, humour (*The Hundred Most Leaden Cricket Jokes*), esoterica (*Through Alien Cornea: What Cricket Means to the Balkan Peoples, Esquimaux and Indigenous Hawaiians*) and so on. *Cricket: More Than a Game* is very much of a hybrid: it is all these, yet none of them; it is the product of much cross-fertilization.

Part One, sub-titled 'The Cricketing Nations', is the most straightforward. This book was planned, written and designed to be published on the eve of the first-ever cricket World Cup series in England in 1975. Noted writers from the six competing countries—Australia, England, West Indies, New Zealand, India and Pakistan—were asked to contribute portraits of cricket in their different lands. Not potted histories, gentlemen, they were advised. By all means tell us of series and match results but treat them like *fines herbes* or garlic, a soupçon not a tablespoon.

The basic idea has been to have the writers serve up rounded profiles of the cricket they grew up with, its distinctive style, colouring, and personality as expressed through the domestic cricket structures, how young players are coached and discovered, how they rise to the highest levels. Part of their brief has also been to show how the deeds of great players reflect the spirit of their native countries. Who is the archetypal Australian—Miller, Harvey, Bradman, Bill O'Reilly? In what ways did the glories of Learie Constantine and Garry Sobers have significance for their countrymen stretching far beyond cricket? Why, in most eras, is it harder to make an England batting side collapse than any other? Why will New Zealand, after the finest half dozen years in its cricketing history, have to struggle mightily to avoid plummeting back into the cellar during the late 1970s?

These portraits have an X-ray quality; they get beneath the skin to show when the cricketing heart has beaten boldly, when it has frozen in panic, how the insidious dampness of poor administration has sometimes inflicted trench foot on Test teams that have limped to defeat and ignominy.

While the Springboks can only gaze wistfully over the locked bars of their kraal during the World Cup, they can scarcely be ignored. They have contributed too many fine threads to the fabric of cricket for that: the cocked wrists of their pioneer googly bowlers; the grandeur of the Nourses; the bludgeoning bats of Jock Cameron and Graeme Pollock, the miraculous fielding talents of Cheetham's warriors. Louis Duffus, who wrote the South African chapter, has seen almost all of the men and the moments he describes. So, in highly compressed form, Part One is a tour book, biographical and historical.

Biography features strongly in Part Two. This is called 'Arts and Crafts', which may appear at first glance to suggest that it is largely instructional. This is not so, although the young reader will know much more about how to apply himself towards mastering the arts of cricket after reading the words of Benaud, Laker, Ian Chappell and John Snow in particular. Basically each chapter is a personal essay by an outstanding exponent in his special area of cricketing activity.

Richie Benaud describes how his worst and finest hours in Test cricket were only a few hours apart. Jim Laker sums up in one word how bowling to Bradman made him feel; he also wags a stern finger at Pat Pocock, who has now taken over from him as off-spinner for Surrey. Barry Richards tells why he no longer regards himself as an attacking batsman; John Snow defines a 'bouncer' and outlines the reasons why aggression is so important to a fast bowler; Alan Knott predicts that no future England wicketkeeper has much hope of emulating Godfrey Evans by lasting in the Test team until he is almost forty; Ian Chappell explains his misgivings on the English method of selecting Test captains.

Like anything else in life, cricket is not all sunshine and enchantment. It has its shadowy, even murky, patches. And, as with love, it cannot be truly celebrated with booming marches or those perky little up-beat fox-trots that seem to be the only tunes within the range of certain critical keyboards. The greatest passions can be expressed in blues numbers; several are included here; cricket needs them as much as it needs its Cricket *Über Alles* themes. Some of the writers unburden themselves on what they consider are shortcomings in the contemporary game. For instance, any English groundsman who has suffered from a tingling sensation in his ears may learn why when reading Richards and Snow on modern county pitches.

Part Three is a miscellany, a *pot-au-feu* with rich ingredients: venison meat and truffles. Biography is contained here in possibly its finest short form: Jack Fingleton's incomparable portrait of Don Bradman. It underlines the point that Mr Fingleton makes constantly—the matchless value of direct and intimate contact with the game at its highest levels. However, in a frail, imperfect world not every set of fingers that strike a typewriter keyboard in the Press box can have gripped bat or ball in Test matches.

This may be rectified in Elysium, whence John Arlott sends an exclusive interview with Dr W. G. Grace. Admitted on a day tripper's pass, Mr Arlott was granted as much time as the good doctor could allow him. This was not unlimited because Dr Grace bustles around as if convinced that eternity cannot last forever. He bade goodbye to Mr Arlott to go for his daily chat with Mr Stephen Potter, with whom he has struck up a warm friendship.

Is there humour in this section of the book? If the readers think not, Michael Parkinson, Benny Green and Mike Gibson should leave town straight away to gain a start on the vigilantes' posse. However, the Editor is convinced the lynching ropes will stay in their usual resting places, the window seats of suburban semi-detacheds. Finally, Stanley Reynolds offers the book's only item of esoterica, a salute to cricket from an American exile in Liverpool. Mr Reynolds had grown up convinced that each man in the Red Sox, the baseball team of his native Boston, had been directly anointed on his forehead by the finger of God. His conversion to cricket should have brought rejoicing in the game's Vatican at London N.W.8; another infidel saved from perdition.

The Editor gives his eager and grateful thanks to many people: his copy editor, Richard Charkin who staunchly translated many passages from the original 'Strine'; David Frith for his counsel and tireless help in assembling photographs; Irving Rosenwater for determining the range of statistics, then compiling them; Ursula Gross for secretarial help. Gratitude has already been expressed directly to many others who insist their efforts should blush unseen, or untrumpeted.

London   John Sheppard
September 1974

Part One: The Cricketing Nations

Australia: DAVID FRITH

Let's begin by thinking of Australian cricket as a Sidney Nolan canvas: men and boys in puffy caps, tee-shirts and stained, ancient pads, competing on malthoid and concrete pitches in bush towns under gaunt gumtrees, with the heat too much for all but the players and the flies.

Australian cricket is also juvenile Saturday-morning cricketers playing it hard and jovial on matting wickets, perhaps gloveless and with only the front leg padded. It is Saturday-afternoon 'junior' players, from fifteen to fifty, mixing it on the municipal playing area under azure skies, with Test match and horse-racing commentaries blaring from a portable radio lying between the boundary flags that separate one field from another. It is metropolitan club cricketers charting their upward courses—fourth grade one season, maybe second the next, and then first, playing with and against the great names before a smattering of spectators.

It is youths with unrazored cheeks awarded State and Australian XI colours and slaying giants from the outset with scarcely a tremor; their English counterparts are still sending 'fags' to the tuckshop. It is a Sheffield Shield programme (twenty matches, four days each) played at times concurrently three thousand miles apart, on the skid-pan-fast pitch at Perth, the world's newest Test ground, or at homely Woolloongabba, set amid Brisbane's poinsettia and fig trees. The setting may be Sydney with its Edwardian flavour, the concrete mass of Melbourne, or Adelaide's cathedral-backed Oval which brings out the Byron in the commentators.

Australian cricket is green-capped Test players, inoculated with legends, and striving to live up to the characterizations of generations. It is these men, often saddle-brown and sinewy-strong as the flannelled stockmen they were once all thought to be, spurning the word 'humility' as they uncork the clamour of Sabina Park, Kingston or National Stadium, Karachi or the hearty clump of their bats brings impertinent counterpoint to moist sibilence in the stands at Lord's. The awesome rarity of the Lord's air does not squash the lustiness of movement first unleashed in Wycheproof, Nar-nar-goon, Mullengandra or Bowral. Greg Chappell, upright and regal, is at one with his humble compatriot, a watching man, gnarled, indeterminate of age, sleeves rolled well above lean, heavily-veined biceps, hand-made cigarette at the corner of his mouth, crumpled wide-brimmed hat shading fox-terrier-like features, knees and cheekbones level in his bushman's crouch. Cricket remains a simple game to him and he is a lucky man.

In which direction can you look for the archetypal Australian cricketer? Not towards the Don; he was a man apart in so many senses. The untutored swing of the bat may have been his only typical quality or trait. Everything else was too extraordinary to be categorized: the eyesight, the footwork, the confidence, the appetite for runs, the stamina, the ambition, perhaps even the rewards. The final unique touch—he remains the only Australian cricketer to be knighted—was fitting as a just reward, not for its prolonged uniqueness. Altogether, Bradman was towering, awesome but too special.

Searching for the essence, the mind's eye flickers over many figures. It settles for a while on George Bonnor, a man of heroic dimensions—six foot seven, strong, generous and bearded, a great thrower and hitter.

Much of this essence was in Jack Gregory, the darling of crowds in the 1920s, a large, suntanned, ever hatless and sometimes gloveless man. He was a devastating fast bowler with a kangaroo leap, a Tarzan and pioneer of recurring greatness at slip, a batsman whose blade swished with the power that brought him what is still the fastest Test century of all. Some men have radiated 'Australianness' as if it were a form of healthy radioactivity. Such a one was Charlie Macartney, a self-contained man with an iron will and wrists to match. He always took attack joyfully to the enemy; his attitude was that opposing egos and reputations were there to be pulped, not revered. Contemptuously he reckoned he could play most of the crack bowlers of his day 'with a tram-ticket' and they called this nuggety little man 'the Governor-General'.

Herbie Collins was another now-rare 'typical' Australian. 'Lucky' Collins, a Great War digger, craggy of feature, droll and uneffusive, was a gambler off the field and a fighter on it. Saddled with the difficult task of succeeding Warwick Armstrong as captain, he fulfilled the job as well as an ageing team would allow. A fine cricketing brain that later went untapped.

Armstrong himself was a sublime example of that independence of spirit that Australians use not only as if they had taken out the patent on it but as if they had cornered the market as well. Armstrong, 'the Big Ship', had strongest claims for the title of Australia's W. G. Grace, although George Giffen, South Australia's sterling all-rounder of early years, was the man dubbed with it. Armstrong led his team to eight successive victories over England in 1920 and 1921. From the distance he looked like an upended zeppelin. It was said that his bat resembled a teaspoon beside his gigantic frame and that he often made the bowling look like weak tea. He brought the wrath of an Oval crowd on his stubborn head when he absconded to the outfield, left the bowling to arrange itself, and read a stray newspaper 'to see who we are playing'. Super confidence spiked with a dash of disdain.

A classic prototype who rightly thought he was fit to tilt at any man was Bill O'Reilly. 'Tiger', rumbustious, wry, aggressive, glowering, bald, harsh-laughing, awash with Irishness in humour and temper, captor of 102 English wickets in only four series. He was a product of a bush town, as were Bradman and McCabe and Alan Davidson and Barnes, and Gleeson and Bonnor and Walters and Macartney and Tallon and Toshack and 'Terror' Turner and others. Magpies and kookaburras have seen as many wondrous deeds as octogenarian purple-jowled men whose posteriors have grooved hollows down the decades in their Long Room chairs.

Yet, if you stood in an enormous gallery of Australian cricketing portraits and asked, 'What is Australian cricket all about?', many fingernails, from shovel-broad to professionally manicured, would perhaps tap against the same picture. 'That bloke is what it's about.' You would be looking at a man husky and handsome enough to have played d'Artagnan on the screen; the eyes holding an amused and challenging glint beneath a thick, swept-back mane of black hair. A bowling study would show the athleticism of a man who could bowl the fastest ball of the day off four easy paces. A batting study might be an upright square cut classical enough to have adorned an admiring Prime Minister's wall. Keith Ross Miller.

Here was a Paladin who personified his country's playing attitudes. Not for him the English way, bowing to an instinct to grind their way out of difficulties. Miller led frequent charges, especially with the ball. At Adelaide in 1955, England needed a mere 92 to win the match and secure the Ashes. As Australia took the field, vice-captain Miller was asked who would win. 'I haven't a clue. But somebody's in for a nasty half-hour,' he growled.

In twenty balls, that dark pelt flapping, he fired out Bill Edrich, Hutton and Cowdrey. Then, while recovering his strength at extra-cover, he hurled himself under a low drive by Peter May and brought off a staggeringly difficult catch: 49 for four. But his shoulder was damaged, and the vision of victory was to evaporate. Not so at Lord's a year later, when 'Nugget', RAAF hero and one of the great bar-emptiers in cricket history, now in his thirty-seventh year and for years belaboured by a suspect back, bowled thirty-four overs in England's first innings to take five for 72 and thirty-six in the second to take five for 80. As the Australians left the field, one-up but destined to be 'Lakerized' ignominiously for the rest of the series, Miller took a bail from an umpire's pocket and tossed it in a grand gesture to some youngsters in the crowd—very Miller, very Australian.

Miller's career also cast a thin shaft of light on the way that certain cogs in Australia's cricket machinery clicked and whirled. He was never captain of Australia and was never likely to have been. He was, in the administrative eye, intolerably extrovert; he was thought to have hurled one or two bouncers and epithets too many towards the wrong targets. There came a time when the necessity for his appointment might have arisen, for it has been customary to choose the Australian XI and nominate from it a suitable captain. But in Miller's later years, Australia came closer to adopting the English system of finding a captain who might not have been included for his playing ability alone. Victoria's Ian Johnson was the choice, amid general reservations that bubbled up like swamp gas. His Test captaincy record and his personal performances during the period were among the poorest.

Young Ian Craig's appointment in 1957, when Harvey and Benaud were in the side, was a near-parallel. Since then, there has been a reversion to the previous order. Benaud, Simpson, Lawry and Ian Chappell have been world-class cricketers who have undertaken national leadership by right. Only the negative Lawry outstayed his welcome with the selectors.

Lawry personified two characteristics, of being tough and taciturn, that many Australian cricketers have been in the eyes of the world. With Charles Kelleway and Bill Woodfull, he would well serve as part of the national cricket coat of arms. So intransigent was Kelleway that most of his own fellows found him hard to take. Woodfull was the strong, silent type Australia needed in the early 1930s, years of rebuilding and of unique crisis. Lawry, the 'Phantom', with the nose of an echidna, camped at the batting creases around the world right through the 1960s against all the world's top bowlers, ruffling their averages and sometimes their tempers. Tall, lean, gum-chewing (although a lesser figure for connoisseurs of gum-chewing than 'Slasher' Mackay), he could have come only from Australia.

These men were the strata of flint in the native soil, mingling with the rich marl that allowed outwardly-sunnier personalities to bloom. Among the people almost impossible to dislike was loping, rosy-cheeked Bill Johnston, the medium-pace left-armer from Victoria. He radiated his enjoyment with an almost permanent grin and once scampered 38 runs for the last wicket with Doug Ring to beat a panicking West Indies at Melbourne. A freak batting average of more than 100 on the 1953 tour brought from this rollicking tail-ender the succinct comment: 'Class will tell.'

More subtly, the diminutive Lindsay Hassett, Bradman's successor as captain, saw cricket as something less than trench warfare. He was a man capable of plucking off a bobbie's helmet as a fielding aid after muffing an outfield catch and of calling from the crowd on a non-playing day to a colleague who stopped a ball inches from a boundary rope and signalled 'no-four': 'Are you trying to cheat us again, McDonald?' The game was ripe entertainment, too, for Arthur Mailey, the puckish little spin bowler from Sydney who, in the 1920s, tossed up his leg-breaks and googlies, long hops and full tosses, with a prodigality that would be forbidden today; some faceless squib of a medium-pacer would have his place in many teams.

Australian batsmanship has progressed from a raw state through to a modern sophistication, but always with a freedom from inhibition which seems bred in the bone of sportsmen from warm lands. Sometimes the boundaries of rashness are crossed—from sure to cocksure—but gallantry in hitting their way out of trouble has been unsurpassed. In this, Stan McCabe stands alone. He played three classic attacking innings in adversity: 187 not out at Sydney against the fury of bodyline; 189 not out at Johannesburg in 1935–6; and 232 at Trent Bridge when defeat seemed only slightly less avoidable than the follow-on.

McCabe was one of many who represented the perennial strength of the Australian game: adventurous *selection*. He was only 19 and without a century to his name in big cricket when chosen for this first tour of England in 1930. Archie Jackson was another, chosen for New South Wales at 17 and for Australia at 19, when he scored 164 first time out off a strong all-round England attack. Ian Craig was taking a double century for New South Wales off the South Africans at 17 and leading his country in South Africa at twenty-two.

Bobby Simpson was 16 when he first played for New South Wales but had disappointment and exile to Perth that forged him into very tough steel indeed before he became the high-scoring scourge of all bowlers and perhaps the greatest of all slip fieldsmen. Nimble-footed Neil Harvey made 118 in his first Test against England when he was 19, and a record 78 Australian Tests later, earned on retirement a glowing accolade: he was never, never dull to watch. Ron Archer toured England at 19—played an heroic innings at The Oval—and might have been Keith Miller's natural successor as allrounder for a decade but for a crippling knee injury.

These players won their caps with a minimum of fuss, such is the custom. Craig was one of three who had pinned to their reluctant chests the foolish tag 'the new Bradman', which proved deadlier than a gypsy's curse. The tag became a filter of hysterical colours that distorted the stature and achievements of its other discomforted recipients, Norman O'Neill and Doug Walters. Despite this salivating hyperbole, the pressures on young Australian sportsmen are normally endurable because of the abiding mood of practicality and realism that surrounds them. The Press is mostly willing them success; so, too, are the crowds, identifying unashamedly. With fewer players to choose from than their English counterparts, selectors are apt to heap greater faith on their chosen. Benaud was 'carried' for several seasons until the selectors' faith was justified and the public's suspicions dissolved. Lesser patience would have robbed the game of the vibrant and worthy passage of Benaud's captaincy years.

The salute to and trust in youth—sometimes verging on youth for youth's sake—has its obverse side. This is the swiftly-shrivelling tolerance for the mature player who may be having less success than earlier in his career. Some pressmen, whose pens or 'ghosts' function at times with stunted responsibility, urge the faltering player, often noisily, sometimes viciously, to make way for his betters and youngers. The cost to Australian cricket has been considerable. More than one premature retirement—Arthur Morris's comes to mind—has been prompted by the anxiety to avoid this unhappy ending. Besides this secondary point, the need to find security in business has shortened many a playing career. Direct rewards from the game are insubstantial, with the shamefully few testimonials as there have been usually staged in the player's old age, often decades after he has left the game. Only in the 1970s has sponsorship—together with provident funds set up by administration—added to the enticement of playing top-class cricket for a long period in Australia. The fiercely-applied accent on youth has rendered strange the stories of Ironmonger, Blackie, Grimmett and Iverson, who all entered cricket at ripe ages. The explanation is simple enough: they were all spin bowlers, whose skills take time to mature.

Like the society itself, Australian cricket had to start from scratch after the English military and settlers had taken it to the Antipodes to plant it firmly in the dry, red soil. Inevitably the early champions had a British stamp to them. They were coached or inspired by touring English professionals and resident coaches such as Lawrence, Caffyn and Hide. The attitude towards pioneer touring English sides led by Stephenson, Parr and then W. G. Grace himself was on the whole respectful to the point of deference; hands almost strayed to forelocks.

The first signs of temperamental opposition from the 'colonials' came from the likes of F. R. Spofforth, 'the Demon', tall, bushy of brow and quick to anger. At Lord's in 1878, a haughty and undiplomatic member wound up his disparaging commentary on the visiting Australians by expressing surprise that they weren't black like the last lot—ten years before the first Australian team to Britain consisted of aborigines. Spofforth, almost speechless with rage, took ten MCC wickets for twenty in the match, drowning mingled fury and humiliation in the most telling form of vengeance.

Spofforth's torment of English batsmen did not end there: he was by far the most feared adversary throughout the 1880s until the amazing little C. T. B. Turner burst on the scene, taking 101 English wickets in a mere seventeen Test matches. Spofforth was also a forgiving man; he was to end his days quietly, prosperously and popularly in the Old Country.

Australia did not settle down as a Test-playing eleven until the mid-1890s. Then, specifically in the 1894–5 series, the team under George Giffen played five Tests, all thrilling encounters, against Stoddart's side. The grounds filled, men and women converging by coach, steamer and on horseback to experience the ambivalent joys of a look at the pale men from Home while cheering on their own national side. The young country, unpolished and vigorous, was proving its fibre.

Through nostalgia and immigration, this dual-natured spirit subsists still although sentiment barely remains. The white-hot iron that cauterized sentiment was the 1932–3 conflict. When Douglas Jardine unleashed his fast leg-theory bowlers at Bill Woodfull and his men, public exasperation and a seething sense of hurt were so intense that Anglo-Australian relations were stretched almost to

Upright and regal: Greg Chappell, classically cover-driving at Lord's in 1972 during his innings of 131, has a shared spirit with his ungainly bush cousins.

snapping. 'Bodyline' offended the Australian's unbuffed but deep sense of fair play. It took him, and is taking him, a long time to forget.

Australia picked up the pieces after the Hitler war with a ferocious appetite for success; her dominance, established between the wars, was unquestioned. The Don faded so brightly in 1948 (although the mechanics of that triumphant tour sent frissons through Australian cricket for almost a decade), the national pride was touched with confidence bordering on arrogance. This is the major quality separating the Australian approach to sport from that of the English, which can be so apologetic in victory, almost masochistic in defeat. (Some members of the England team were baffled and upset at widespread comments after rain had robbed them of a Lord's win over the 1974 Pakistan side which had collapsed miserably on a dampish pitch. Comments that a win would have been 'unjust and regrettable'—leaking covers had damaged the pitch—offended the competitiveness of the England players.)

Rich Australian confidence and irreverence were never more clearly personified than in 1948 by Sidney George Barnes, the shrewd, tough, thickset batsman who, after a snub from authorities at Lord's, vowed to make a hundred there against England. Ignoring several proffered handshakes, unworried by a first-innings duck, 'Bagga' made 141 in the second. Although his shoulder was not rubbed smooth by regular contact with turf accountants—an almost un-Australian trait—Barnes had backed himself for his hundred with eight pounds to the tune of fifteen to one.

While the feathers were preened, chivalry was not absent. The visiting MCC teams of 1946–7 and 1950–1 were shown much sympathy and some affection ('Lettuces with hearts as big as Freddie Brown's' was one Sydney barrowman's cry), but irony glinted sometimes at the edges. The next side, four years on, had to be taken far more seriously. The root of the many-layered hostility from barrackers was the shock of Tyson's speed; the typhoon blew in without warning. Other causes of dyspepsia were Hutton's coldly-cynical slow over-rate and the tissue-paper resistance of too many Australian batsmen.

Curdled stomachs and frayed souls were both put back in prime working order by the sparkle, gaiety, sportsmanship and unrelenting excitement of Worrell's West Indians in 1960–1, possibly the most joyous of all Test series anywhere. Teeming transistor-addicts on shop floors, televiewers and onlookers (a world record 90,000 of them crammed into the vast bowl of the MCG one day) savoured the genius of Sobers and Kanhai, the spectacular athleticism of Wes Hall and the lovely willingness of both sides to play with unfettered good fellowship. With a grace seldom accorded the 'Poms', they recognized the visitors were unlucky not to win at Adelaide, when the unflappable Mackay and rabbit last man Kline held out for ninety minutes, and to be deprived of the final Test by a margin no wider than Wally Grout's bail. The unforgettable tied Test had triggered the hysteria (Benaud's plunging neckline made him the sex symbol of the season); the ticker-tape farewell through Melbourne streets gave it a finishing touch as warming and pretty as golden wattle. That series was worthy of a reprise of Philip Lindsay's words penned after he saw the boy Bradman proclaim his genius against his first English opposition: 'And light of heart that evening did I stroll home while the stars of the Southern Cross seemed to twinkle more brightly even than usual.'

Australian teams in that series contained many classical exponents of the art at which Australian cricket has always been supreme—fielding. It had Simpson at slip, Benaud at gully and close-up, Davidson the amazing 'Claw' and O'Neill, his bazooka throw from covers perhaps the strongest ever. Simpson followed the Gregory tradition and heightened it for Ian Chappell and Keith Stackpole; O'Neill was the link in time between Harvey and Sheahan at cover. Add to them from other years Ernie Jones, a fearless ball-trap at mid-off, Boyle or Barnes at short leg; Pellew, Burke or Bradman patrolling the deep: in an all-time line-up of these players it would be hard to work out where the next run might come from. Baseball as a winter sport for many Australians has obviously put the fizz in their throwing arms. Crowds love it and give it heavy applause. Too much, it seemed,

Bobby Simpson, greatest in a long line of fine Australian slip fielders, puts paid to Fred Titmus at Old Trafford, 1964.

A Sunday social match on one of Sydney's many municipal parks. Cricket means sere grass, parched earth, chilled beer in 'esky' portable fridges, alfresco lunches of prawns and steak sandwiches.

for Trevor Bailey, who thought the response overdone, a word that Australians themselves had cause to use about at least two aspects of Bailey's play. But national pride in outfielding and throwing is sustained by applause and hardly an Australian has a poor arm. He simply dare not.

Australian *cricketers* may have their own characteristic methods—batsmen generally strong off the back foot and ever ready for attack; bowlers either with sharp speed or capable of accurate wrist-spin. But the *spectators* have a unique conduct. They reckon their entrance money makes them members of an unpaid choir. Much of the barracking is good-humoured, often springing from a well-informed source. Sometimes rancour activates the bellowing, with visitors not always the targets.

The most raucous and famous barracker was 'Yabba'—Stephen Gascoigne, rabbit-hawker of Glebe, Redfern and Balmain. 'Whoa, he's bolted', he shouted when J. W. Hearne managed a single after twenty minutes' immobility. 'You'll have to wait till the tea interval like the rest of us', when an umpire raised his hand to signal a bye. 'Call Nurse . . . (a well-known abortionist). She'll get 'em

out.' A generation later, a spiritual descendant loudly advised an English batsman who was padding away excessively to 'tie ya bat t'ya leg—then ya might get
some runs.' Sadly the television age of canned laughter and music has also
dragged response down to canned commentary—the mass and witless banging
together of empties.

Barrackers' abuse can drop to depths of irrationality. I once heard a middle-
aged man screech out after Davidson landed a short one under an English batsman's ribs: 'That'll teach you Pommie bastards to join the Common Market.' He
was as boorish, and may have been as lubricated, as the lout who grabbed a fistful
of John Snow's shirt when he unwisely moved within grabbing distance at
Sydney's Paddington end after having felled an Australian batsman. And, although the invective of 1897–8 fell short of the 1932–3 barrage, it did almost
drive England's leader, Andrew Stoddart to tears. Lord Harris and his team
barely escaped injury when a mob stormed the field at Sydney in 1878–9, in-
censed at an umpiring decision and an English professional's reference to their
'convict origins'. A couple of the tougher pros sprang to His Lordship's defence
with cricket stumps.

Despite the random barrages of beer cans, and the stupid invasions of the
ground to whack successful players' backs, Australia's cricket grounds are for relaxation; men here were bare to the waist many years before the informality was

*Jack Gregory, a great allrounder. The essence
of 'Australianness' was in his lean, open
features and bounding frame.*

permitted at Lord's. In the early 1970s a girl who also doffed shirt and other upper covering briefly made the cricket secondary as a compelling attraction.

Shirtlessness is one part of the egalitarian and easy outlook that has made cricket in Australia free of the class divisions of the English game. Australians could never comprehend the 'apartheid' of amateurs and professionals. Inter-state rivalries have varied from serious to frenetic; there was a 'withdrawal of labour' in 1912; at least one touring side left Australian shores split by religion. But Australian cricket has been reasonably free from internal tensions; the national team normally is bound together with a unity that is the envy of other countries.

Perhaps the one local resource never effectively tapped has been the aborigine. So few of them have shown an interest in the game. So few have reached first-class standards and all have been fast bowlers. There was Jack Marsh in the 1890s, illiterate, sometimes called for throwing (indignant, he concealed a splint on his arm) and proud of his ability to bowl like 'plurry hell'. A lovely dandy, he used to ride the tram to the Sydney Cricket Ground, wearing his blue New South Wales cap and holding an open newspaper, usually upside-down.

(Left) Hounded into early retirement? Critics eager to impale Arthur Morris for later stuttering efforts against Alec Bedser too quickly ignored former glories. Few left-handers came better.

(Right) The D'Artagnan of his tribe: Keith 'Nugget' Miller: imperishable deeds of resistance and the day's fastest ball off four easy paces.

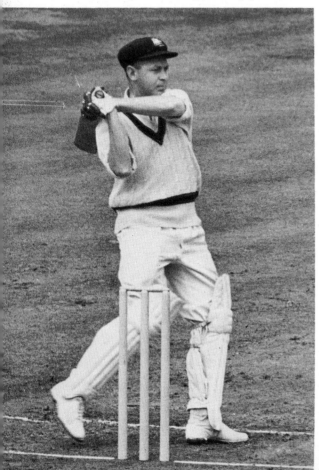

Between the wars there was the small and wiry Eddie Gilbert, who came from an aboriginal settlement near Brisbane and who had to be cajoled into wearing boots. His delivery off a few paces was deadly fast for a few overs until his stamina gave way. But there was a question mark too about his action; the knowledge that his leverage of the ball developed out of boomerang-throwing tending to be used in evidence against him. He eventually returned to a twilight existence, took to drink, and was placed into care at the age of forty, unable to speak.

Australians relish size and heroism and have much to relish in both spheres: three of their own—Trumper, Macartney and Bradman—scored pre-lunch centuries against England; the two highest-ever scores, both topping 1,000, were made by Victoria, who within weeks of one of them were toppled for 35—tall poppy levelled, the Australians loved that; Ponsford is the only man to have twice scored more than 400 runs; Bradman's long-standing world record of 452 not out still the best for quality of opposition; O'Reilly mooted as the finest bowler ever to draw breath; Corinthian murmuring of English style and artistry crushed with four names: Trumper, Kippax, Jackson and McCabe. Australians ask rhetorically: was there ever a more exquisite wicketkeeper than Bert Oldfield or a more efficient one than the laconic Grout? Or as shrewd a captain as Benaud—unless it was M. A. Noble? Or a more skilful and visually exciting fast bowler than Ray Lindwall? Was Sobers, the West Indian monarch, that much more talented than Davidson, who was capable of 140 runs and eleven wickets against class in a single Test?

The questions may be harder to phrase in future years when Australian teams will contain players with names looking like something from an oculist's eyechart. The wide brown land has absorbed teeming thousands of European migrants, and second-generations are taking to the game of cricket in its rising popularity. The first five of the batting order in 1990 may read: Battalino, Poppercrese, Bailenhopper, Padinski and de Blonger. They will play with all the native nerve and dedication of Simpson, McCabe, Bradman, Miller and the Chappells. Tradition will demand it.

AUSTRALIA IN TEST CRICKET
(All statistics up to 14 February 1975)

SUMMARY OF RESULTS

	Played	*Won*	*Lost*	*Tied*	*Drawn*
v England	220	86	71	0	63
v South Africa	53	29	11	0	13
v West Indies	35	19	6	1	9
v New Zealand	7	4	1	0	2
v India	25	16	3	0	6
v Pakistan	9	5	1	0	3
	349	159	93	1	96

MOST APPEARANCES

R. N. Harvey	79
W. M. Lawry	67
R. Benaud	63
R. R. Lindwall	61
G. D. McKenzie	60

MOST RUNS

	Tests	*Inns.*	*N.O.*	*Runs*	*H.S.*	*Av.*
D. G. Bradman	52	80	10	6,996	334	99·94
R. N. Harvey	79	137	10	6,149	205	48·41
W. M. Lawry	67	123	12	5,234	210	47·15
R. B. Simpson	52	92	7	4,131	311	48·60
I. M. Chappell	56	100	6	3,922	196	41·72
I. R. Redpath	54	97	10	3,690	171	42·41
K. D. Walters	47	80	8	3,633	242	50·45
A. R. Morris	46	79	3	3,533	206	46·48
C. Hill	49	89	2	3,412	191	39·21
V. T. Trumper	48	89	8	3,163	214*	39·04
C. C. McDonald	47	83	4	3,107	170	39·32
A. L. Hassett	43	69	3	3,073	198*	46·56

MOST RUNS IN A SERIES

		Tests	*Inns.*	*N.O.*	*Runs*	*H.S.*	*Av.*
D. G. Bradman v Eng.	1930	5	7	0	974	334	139·14
R. N. Harvey v S. Afr.	1952–3	5	9	0	834	205	92·66
D. G. Bradman v Eng.	1936–7	5	9	0	810	270	90·00
D. G. Bradman v S. Afr.	1931–2	5	5	1	806	299*	201·50
D. G. Bradman v Eng.	1934	5	8	0	758	304	94·75
D. G. Bradman v India	1947–8	5	6	2	715	201	178·75

HIGHEST INDIVIDUAL INNINGS

334	D. G. Bradman	v England	Headingley	1930
311	R. B. Simpson	v England	Old Trafford	1964
307	R. M. Cowper	v England	Melbourne	1965–6
304	D. G. Bradman	v England	Headingley	1934
299*	D. G. Bradman	v South Africa	Adelaide	1931–2
270	D. G. Bradman	v England	Melbourne	1936–7

MOST WICKETS

	Tests	Runs	Wickets	Av.
R. Benaud	63	6,704	248	27·03
G. D. McKenzie	60	7,328	246	29·78
R. R. Lindwall	61	5,251	228	23·03
C. V. Grimmett	37	5,231	216	24·21
A. K. Davidson	44	3,819	186	20·83
K. R. Miller	55	3,906	170	22·97

MOST WICKETS IN A SERIES

			Tests	Runs	Wickets	Av.
C. V. Grimmett	v S. Afr.	1935–6	5	642	44	14·59
W. J. Whitty	v S. Afr.	1910–11	5	632	37	17·08
A. A. Mailey	v Eng.	1920–21	5	946	36	26·27

BEST BOWLING

9–121	A. A. Mailey	v England	Melbourne	1920–21
8–31	F. Laver	v England	Old Trafford	1909
8–43	A. E. Trott	v England	Adelaide	1894–5
8–53	R. A. L. Massie	v England	Lord's	1972
8–59	A. A. Mallett	v Pakistan	Adelaide	1972–3

1,000 RUNS AND 100 WICKETS

	Tests	Runs	Wickets
R. Benaud	63	2,201	248
A. K. Davidson	44	1,328	186
G. Giffen	31	1,238	103
I. W. Johnson	45	1,000	109
R. R. Lindwall	61	1,502	228
K. R. Miller	55	2,958	170
M. A. Noble	42	1,997	121

CAPTAIN IN MOST TESTS

R. B. Simpson	29
R. Benaud	28
W. M. Lawry	25
W. M. Woodfull	25
D. G. Bradman	24
A. L. Hassett	24

* not out.

England: JOHN ARLOTT

The character of English cricket is strong but not simple. Like that of a person, it is produced by a wide variety of experiences. In most children character is relatively simple; in the adult it is complex, moulded by events which are rarely all of a kind, but, like the resulting individual, may at times seem contradictory. Cricket has been—and is—both juvenile and adult; carefree and grave; prosperous and impecunious; disreputable and moralistic; simple and involved; plebeian and patrician; corrupt and honourable; parochial and universal; physical and imaginative. All these phrases have left their imprint on the game as, on a man, adversity may leave his brow furrowed from care, happiness his face scored with laughter-wrinkles.

More than any other game cricket reflects the social setting in which it is played; it varies not only according to period but also according to place. That is why there is an instantly perceptible difference, not merely between English and Australian or Indian and West Indian cricket—but between that of India and Pakistan who, as lately as 1946, formed a single international team; between the West Indian territories; and even between neighbouring English counties.

These distinctions exist because of differences of background and of history; as Indian history is uniquely India's, so is Indian cricket. The longest cricket history is the English. As a result, its character has been created by more, and more varied, influences than any other. Only its life-story explains its harmonies and contradictions; its consistencies and vagaries; its attractions and its disappointments; its pleasures and discomforts.

If one word must distinguish English cricket from all other, it must be 'professional'—yet many of its most memorable and important phases have been purely amateur. Similarly, wherever one looks, there are contradictions. It began, surely enough, as a children's game; but it has also been performed in an extremely adult vein. It was originally a rustic sport; but soon after that it was both urban and sophisticated. It can be, and often is, played in a carefree fashion; but it can also be grimly efficient. In some of its phases it has been romantic; in others coldly practical. Some of its greatest executants have been described, accurately or not, as spontaneous performers; others equally capable have been summed up as coolly technical.

Ultimately it is a happy amalgam of paradoxes. One wet day at Lord's, long after play had been abandoned, Beverley Lyon sat in his box, sipped at his port

Face in repose, wrist cocked for action, Dennis Lillee at Trent Bridge, 1972. Lillee later blasted the pensive non-striking batsman John Edrich from Test cricket for two years.

ARCHIE JACKSON

Proudly on display inside the pavilion at Sydney Cricket Ground, a portrait of a 'favorite son', the late Archie Jackson.

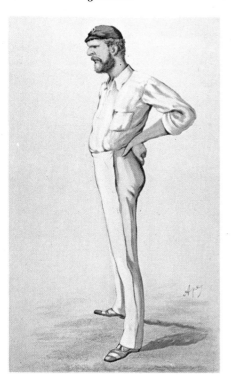

(Left) George Bonnor—all six foot seven inches of him. His powerful hitting and throwing helped to carve Australia's cricket traditions. (Right) Melbourne Cricket Ground in the nineteenth century had a sylvan aspect, such a contrast to the modern concrete colossus, which is hard on players' nerves and feet.

and said to Percy George Fender, one of the few captains who ever matched him in quickness of wit, 'Cricket grew up as a game for twenty-two decent men to play among themselves; it was never meant to be a vehicle of international competition, a spectator sport, or headline news—otherwise it would not have a code of laws any thinking man could drive through in a coach and four.'

The professional characteristic has always been strong. When the game first grew to eminence, in the eighteenth century, the outstanding performers were the rural professionals first of Sussex, then Kent and then Hampshire. In the early 1970s, the English teams under Ray Illingworth's captaincy made shrewd use of their assets while concealing their weaknesses. They won or drew Test rubbers against stronger sides until eventually, in 1973, the far more powerful West Indies touring team broke through the façade and beat them overwhelmingly. For those who had peered beneath the surface of the English performances for some seasons before, those defeats were neither surprising nor an indication of collapse, but simply evidence of the skill with which the flaws had been papered over for years. Then, immediately afterwards, the team under Denness in the West Indies was virtually outclassed and, on form, certain to be beaten. Yet it avoided defeat after the first Test by a series of dogged retreat actions and, against all earlier probability, won the last Test to achieve an incredible tied result in what had been, until then, a completely one-sided series.

This quality of tenacity, linked to deep tactical understanding, the judgment which picks the precise time to turn defence into attack, to exploit an opponent's weakness or a turn of weather or pitch, is, above all, the mark of the professional player. It is founded in his appreciation of the truth that knowledge of the game and its tactics can, if properly applied, often outweigh physical playing ability.

In football and tennis, for example, it is common to speak of an experienced player 'using his head to save his legs' against a younger opponent. In cricket the matter goes further than that; wise bowlers do, in fact, 'think out' batsmen. When David Harris, the greatest bowler of the latter part of the eighteenth century, grew old, he was so crippled by gout that a great chair was brought on to the field for him to rest in between deliveries; but he was still capable of bowling men out to win matches played for a thousand guineas a side.

Harris, by his peculiar method—in effect top-spun near-shoulder-high under-arm—used to make the ball bounce unpleasantly. 'It was but a touch, and up again and woe be to the man who did not get in to block them, for they had such a peculiar curl that they would grind his fingers against the bat.' By contrast there was Wilfred Rhodes, who took well over four hundred more wickets than anyone else who ever played, and who was a killer on a sticky wicket. Rhodes used to deceive batsmen into destroying themselves on good batting pitches. At the most elementary level, by variation of flight and, therefore, apparently of length, he would persuade a batsman to drive at what he took to be a half-volley but which was sufficiently short of that for his stroke to lift it to catchable height.

Rhodes batted well, too. When he first played for England he went in last. Thirteen years afterwards, he and Jack Hobbs set the record, which still stands, for an English first wicket partnership against Australia. He scored 39,802 runs, took 4,187 wickets and held 708 catches. He was the prototype of the 'senior pro'; indeed in many ways he personified English professional cricket. After he ceased to play, he went to coach at Harrow, a foreign and, at times, puzzling setting for one of his somewhat puritanical—or at least purist—standards.

It is told that one afternoon he was bowling there in the nets to a typical young Harrovian of aggressive batting tendencies who three times in succession came down the wicket and pulled good length balls far and wide to midwicket. The fourth beat him through the air, passed through his stroke and, as he stood stranded, hit his middle stump. The young man threw back his head and roared with laughter. Thereupon Wilfred Rhodes, in the manner of one lamenting another's sin, said: 'Nay, nay, Maister Smith—yon's no laughing matter.'

A vignette of Rhodes, and of the professional cricketer, remains sharp almost forty years afterwards. Now in his fifties, he was bowling in a net for the batsman's benefit, not his own. As the ball was tossed to him, he assessed its arc so early as to raise his arm and catch it almost without watching it. It settled with a slight rustle into his toughened palm. The tool of his trade, he turned it into his spinner's grip with the familiarity of a cobbler taking up his awl or a mason his chisel. In a comfortable, economical rhythm, he walked back to exactly the spot where he had begun his previous approach—indeed, all his previous approaches for forty years. He came up again, putting his feet down in the same spot, bringing his arm from behind his back and over, only a little lower and more stiffly than he had done more than half a million times before. It all looked monotonously alike— the batsmen of almost half a century had been lulled into thinking that—but it was not. He was too proud to bowl less than well. The player in the net, pushing forward, was now a little soon with his stroke; now hurried into it; eventually drawn forward and beaten—in play he would have been stumped. Rhodes said nothing; perhaps there was the hint of a smile on that almost expressionless yet peaceful face, but no other reaction. The batsman nodded acknowledgment of being beaten, then lobbed the ball back. It settled again with a rustle into the craftsman's hand; and he bowled once more.

Many of the earliest cricketers of whom we have knowledge—the Hambledon players of about 1760 onwards—were village craftsmen; cobblers, saddlers, builders, potters, or small farmers who did much of the farm work like hurdle- making, pen-building, repairs to saddlery and tools themselves. They were the first organized cricket professionals. Their backers, like Sir Horace Mann, the Duke of Dorset, the Earl of Tankerville or Lord Winchilsea, often took the country cricketers on to their estate staffs as gamekeepers or gardeners to ensure first call on their playing services. It was an oddly feudal and uneconomic arrangement.

A few of the patrons captained their teams in some games, but 'grand matches' were entrusted to the professionals. These were often played for as much as a thousand guineas a side—a vast sum by present-day values—with far more depending on side bets. Yet the players were paid no more than five pounds a game, out of which they paid their own expenses.

This state of affairs lasted through the Regency period, while cricket, in one of its most profound formative stages, moved away from the rural centres to an altogether more sophisticated London setting. Hitherto major matches had been played on or near the country estates of Kent, Sussex and Hampshire, where the leading cricketers lived and worked. Now they were brought from all over the country to London. Many of them had never seen the capital nor experienced city life before; and now they were playing in a single match for the backers' wager of more money than they would earn in a lifetime.

It is little wonder that there was widespread and justified gossip about young countrymen unable to resist the blandishments of the 'legs' who jingled gold sovereigns under their noses at the cricketers' London house of resort, The Green Man and Still, in Oxford Street. The bookmakers—one of them John Gully, former heavyweight champion of England and subsequently an M.P.—sat outside the pavilion at Lord's and it soon became obvious that many results were in contradiction of form and the odds. The whole matter was forced to official

Wilfred Rhodes, puritanically professional, an assassin on a sticky wicket and too proud ever to bowl less than well.

Denis Compton personalized England's national euphoria for cricket just after the Hitler war. Later his candour as a commentator also swept across the approved, 'correct' line.

notice when a group of players began to quarrel on the steps of the pavilion. The allegations of 'selling' matches coincided so closely with unexpected turns in crucial fixtures that they could hardly be doubted. As a result, a number of the leading cricketers of the day—including William Lambert, the outstanding all-round player of the period—were banned from the game. It was many years, however, before the standards of Victorian respectability caused the exclusion of bookmakers from cricket grounds; they did not return, with official approval, until 1972.

The third major change of the first quarter of the nineteenth century was the development of bowling from underarm to roundarm. Although some contemporary reactionaries forecast the destruction of the game, when the 'new' bowling was legalized, it also opened up fresh vistas for batting and fielding.

From this point onwards, cricket became a national, and a spectator, sport. It soon grew up in the northern cities of the Industrial Revolution. There Nottingham was the early major power, followed by Yorkshire—at first virtually Sheffield—and Lancashire.

Cricket is at its purest at small club level. The bowler is from White Waltham club; the batsman with the late backlift is from Waltham St Lawrence, playing in the Haig National Village Cricket Championship.

The special place: Every cricketer, from Adelaide to Zanzibar, yearns to tread the turf at Lord's. Pale blobs among Tavern crowd in foreground are unclad English backs, sacrilegious to some.

By the middle of the century, cricket once more broke fresh sporting ground with the first of the touring teams. The All-England XI was founded by William Clarke, a one-eyed Nottingham bricklayer who had married a widow of a land-lord of the Trent Bridge Inn, and turned the meadow at the back of the house into a cricket ground. He himself was a great lob bowler who, as a matter of history, took a wicket with the last ball he ever bowled. After several years of organizing cricket in Nottinghamshire and bringing it to a high standard, he founded the All-England XI. It played matches up and down not only England and Wales, but Scotland as well, against local elevens, sixteens or even twenty-twos. It did, in fact, consist of the best eleven cricketers in the country, plus two or three 'spare' men to loan to the opposition to even up the match. It included on merit two amateurs in Alfred Mynn, the huge fast bowler and hitter, and Nicholas Wano-strocht, a schoolmaster who, to avoid giving offence to the parents of his pupils, played under the pseudonym 'Felix'. These men, by example, spread the in-structional gospels of the straight bat and length bowling. They appeared in towns which have never seen a first-class cricket team since. To the considerable profit of William Clarke, they drew huge crowds and aroused immense enthusiasm for the game all over the country.

In 1854, for instance, they played against a Gloucestershire XXII captained by a Doctor Henry Grace and including his son Edward. They were the father and elder brother of W. G. Grace who, precisely on his historic cue, had been born in 1848. He, who was to create a fresh, major aspect of the character of cricket, was barely seventeen when he scored 170 for South Wales against Sussex; eighteen when he made 224 not out for England against Surrey; and for thirty years he was the most towering figure cricket—or any other sport—has ever known. He came into the game in the day of roundarm bowling, tearaway, slinging fast bowlers and rough pitches. He once stopped four shooters in a single over of a Gentlemen v Players match at Lord's. He tamed the crude slingers so completely that a whole generation of length bowlers grew up whose purpose was to curb his mastery; and he lived to play and emphasize his stature in the age of overarm. He created the modern technique of batting, combining back and for-ward play, attack and defence, on good wickets and bad, as no one had ever done before—and few since. More than once his season's aggregate or average was twice that of the next man in the table.

He created, broke and reset virtually every batting record in the cricket of his time; yet, on his figures, he would have been outstanding by his bowling alone. He was an immense personality too and the first of the great drawcards of sport. He filled cricket grounds wherever he went, from village field to Lord's; in the United States, Canada and Australia.

He became the eminent Victorian of cricket and during his reign—if only partly through his influence—cricket grew from a slightly disreputable game into one associated with moral rectitude. In the same period, Test cricket—England v Australia—began; and the towering grandstands were built at Lord's, The Oval, Leeds, Sheffield, Old Trafford, Trent Bridge, Melbourne and Sydney.

Although Grace earned much money from the game, especially through testimonial funds, he was pre-eminently an amateur figure. As captain and opening batsmen of the Gentlemen's XI for many years, he first broke the dominance of the professionals; and, under his leadership, two generations of amateur cricketers grew up who played a considerable part in the game from about 1880 to the outbreak of World War I in 1914. This has been called the Golden Age of Cricket—and with considerable justification, for in that period the game was at its most splendid and many-faceted best. The core of professional skill had been diligently fostered. It was strongest in Yorkshire, Nottinghamshire and Lancashire; but was also firmly rooted in the MCC 'bowling staff' as it was called. In all these 'schools', instruction was thorough, discipline strict; the social climate still substantially feudal. The Hon. Robert Grimston and Lord Harris at Lord's, and Lord Hawke in Yorkshire, ruled cricket as complete autocrats.

Meanwhile, the public schools and Universities provided a constant stream of players of high, varied and sometimes idiosyncratic skills. MacLaren, the captain and record-breaking batsman of Lancashire; Jessop, the most consistently spectacular of big hitters; R. H. Spooner, a superb stylist; Bosanquet, who invented the 'googly' and defeated Australia with it; C. B. Fry, the most versatile of all games players; R. E. Foster, another double international; and—appropriately in a period when the Delhi Durbar made history—the Indian, Ranjitsinhji: would all have been outstanding and, in their different ways, unique in any generation.

Meanwhile, among professionals, there were the two amazing Yorkshiremen, Hirst and Rhodes, beyond doubt the finest pair of all-rounders ever to play in the same team; Jack Hobbs, successor to Grace as the greatest batsman in the world; S. F. Barnes, arguably the finest bowler of all; Tom Richardson, the legendary fast bowler, and his brilliant colleagues, Lockwood and Lohmann who completed such a fine bowling combination for Surrey; Woolley, whose spectacular batting overshadowed his highly capable bowling and slip fielding. The Australian Victor Trumper came to England and established himself among the great; the South Africans perfected the googly and used it to rout England. It was a romantic era which ended with a flourish of characteristically Edwardian splendour never quite recaptured after World War I.

The inter-war period in most fields of entertainment saw the introduction of 'star appeal'. W. G. Grace had been recognized as a giant in his time, but, otherwise, cricketers had never been subjected to this new publicity—of interviews, 'ghosted' books, commercial recommendation, sponsorship and sensationalism. Those twenty years contained the remarkable last phase of Jack Hobbs; the rise

Jack Hobbs. A sprig from cricket's Golden Age, he was successor to W. G. Grace as the world's best batsman. Here (June 1933) he was still molesting bowlers most civilly.

For several seasons, Ray Illingworth's honest professionalism prevented the sawdust from dribbling massively through the loose stitching of a fairly average England team. Here umpire Bird cautions him about an England bowler's follow-through.

of the Australian record-breakers, Ponsford and Bradman; Hammond, McCabe; the entry of the West Indies, India and New Zealand into Test cricket; and, as could barely have happened in an earlier age, the so-called 'bodyline' Test series in which the English fast bowlers destroyed the Australian batsmen on their own pitches and provoked such heat as to cause international discussions at ministerial level.

It was now that English cricket began to be consciously intellectualized, or at least, professionalized. Although amateur talent was not so high or so extensive as it had been before 1914, it still existed at an appreciable level of ability. Now, however, many of the best amateur players—men such as P. G. H. Fender, M. J. Turnbull, R. E. S. Wyatt and R. W. V. Robins—studied tactics and techniques with a profundity that was virtually professional.

After World War II, the game resumed in an atmosphere of nostalgic euphoria personalized by Denis Compton in the south and Len Hutton in the north. The 'pop' age dawned in a period of English dominance over Australia in Test cricket whose heroes were Laker and Lock; fast bowlers Trueman, Statham and Tyson and those durables, Bailey and Evans.

Then, suddenly, that generation had faded; their successors had less public appeal. We were now in the 'affluent society' with the motor car releasing the former captive audiences of urban workers. Cricket fell upon hard times. In 1966, when England's footballers won the World Cup, soccer finally superseded cricket in the majority public imagination. Its higher wages attracted young players who might have gone to cricket, and several counties were only a single step from bankruptcy.

Despite legislative contortions to make county cricket more attractive, it simply did not draw the crowds to make it viable. It was rendered solvent by the introduction, among the counties, of the overs-limit form of the game which had existed at club level for many years. First the Gillette Cup, then the John Player League, the Benson & Hedges Cup and the Prudential Trophy one-day international matches, drew fresh audiences.

The logical consequence of the one-day prosperity is the 1975 competition for what will be called, despite anything the authorities may say, the Cricket World Cup. The gate money and sponsors' payments from such competitions, Test receipts, radio and television fees, effectively subsidize the County Championship —the form of play the players themselves prefer. In a technological age, they are now, more than ever before, preoccupied with technique.

Simultaneously with the game's solvency, county cricketers followed almost every other employee in Britain in achieving representation to discuss any differences with authority; the formation of The Cricketers' Association in theory, if not everywhere in fact, removed the feudal atmosphere from the game.

So much for the English cricket which formed its history on the high plateau of performance—cricket played at its highest level. There are, however, important depths completely apart from the first-class game which yet have major effects on its character. While much competitive play—among the minor counties, in the leagues of the north and midlands, the powerful London clubs—is in varying degrees related to the first-class game, there are still strata which reflect the basic urge which first caused men to play cricket. It is at its purest at small club, village, and even knockabout, level, where the standard of performance is often such that it is barely recognizable as the game the professionals play. That, after all, is where it was born; and at a pinch—if it ever ceases to be a spectator sport—that is where it will infallibly continue to exist.

It is one of the most important aspects of the character of cricket that it compels the affection—amounting sometimes almost to an obsession—of men who play it only badly. Their devotion is carried beyond their own efforts into support of their local team, their county or their country, with an intensity which long outlasts their own playing days.

There are, too, a relatively large number of people whose addiction to the game is reflected in watching matches, compiling statistics, collecting in the wide field of cricketana, or studying its history, with a devotion hardly found in any other sport.

Except at Test matches and some one-day games, the number of spectators has dwindled. Yet there is a far larger spectatorship for major matches than ever before. There was an appreciable audience for cricket commentary on radio; but that for televised cricket is altogether more devoted and, from the nature of the medium, more informed. So, where at the height of enthusiasm in the pre-broadcasting era, 30,000 people at most might watch a Test match, now the figure for television is more than 3,000,000 so that a considerable proportion of the population is as closely involved with the play as the people at the ground. Indeed, because of the siting of the cameras and their capacity to go into close-up, the television viewer generally has a better view of crucial phases of play than any spectator present. This is a difference of knowledge rather than of emotion, but it is nevertheless highly significant; the game is now more truly national than it was at the apparent height of its popularity.

It is expressive of the character of English cricket that it has bred and nurtured art to a far greater extent than that of any other country; or than any other sport in this country except, perhaps, hunting. At least half-a-dozen paintings, notably a landscape by Paul Sandby, of fine quality are based on, or include, cricket; and there are fifty more of genuine artistic competence: as well as forty or fifty prints of real merit. Some capable poets, too, have devoted at least passing attention to the game. It has, though, been best served in prose. Writers as capable as Mary Russell Mitford, Edmund Blunden, Siegfried Sassoon, Horace Annesley Vachell, A. G. Macdonell, Sir Arthur Conan Doyle and Richard Hughes wrote understandingly about it.

Some who devoted their specific attention to it have, beyond all question, not only enriched the game, but added a significant dimension to its character. The first of them was John Nyren with Charles Cowden Clarke as his amanuensis: he was followed at a considerable remove in time by such evocative and sensitive writers as Sir Neville Cardus, Dudley Carew, Alan Ross, Harry Altham, J. M. Kilburn, R. C. Robertson-Glasgow—of all of whom it could be said that their writing is sufficiently 'universal' to satisfy readers with no interest in cricket. This is the English game's aesthetic streak. Then comes the long and wide procession of those who have reported the game in the Press—where for many years considerable space was devoted to it—forming the opinions of the majority who cannot watch for themselves. Thus more than a foible of cricket's character must be attributed to those who have written about it.

Finally, it is—and always has been—the subject of unending conversation; arguments range through the merits of different generations; of one player or one team against another: interpretations of the laws, or any other aspect of an activity profound enough to stimulate thought and talk at many levels.

Such are the threads and depths of character behind the familiar, weather-beaten, and apparently indestructible, face of English cricket.

ENGLAND IN TEST CRICKET
(All statistics up to 14 February 1975)

SUMMARY OF RESULTS

	Played	Won	Lost	Drawn
v Australia	220	71	86	63
v South Africa	102	46	18	38
v West Indies	66	21	19	26
v New Zealand	45	22	0	23
v India	48	22	6	20
v Pakistan	27	9	1	17
	508	191	130	187

MOST APPEARANCES

M. C. Cowdrey	109
T. G. Evans	91
W. R. Hammond	85
K. F. Barrington	82
T. W. Graveney	79
L. Hutton	79
D. C. S. Compton	78
J. B. Statham	70

MOST RUNS

	Tests	Inns.	N.O.	Runs	H.S.	Av.
M. C. Cowdrey	109	179	15	7,459	182	45·48
W. R. Hammond	85	140	16	7,249	336*	58·45
L. Hutton	79	138	15	6,971	364	56·67
K. F. Barrington	82	131	15	6,806	256	58·67
D. C. S. Compton	78	131	15	5,807	278	50·06
J. B. Hobbs	61	102	7	5,410	211	56·94
T. W. Graveney	79	123	13	4,882	258	44·38
G. Boycott	63	110	14	4,579	246*	47·69
H. Sutcliffe	54	84	9	4,555	194	60·73
P. B. H. May	66	106	9	4,537	285*	46·77
E. R. Dexter	62	102	8	4,502	205	47·89

MOST RUNS IN A SERIES

			Tests	Inns.	N.O.	Runs	H.S.	Av.
W. R. Hammond	v Aust.	1928–9	5	9	1	905	251	113·12
D. C. S. Compton	v S. Afr.	1947	5	8	0	753	208	94·12
H. Sutcliffe	v Aust.	1924–5	5	9	0	734	176	81·55

HIGHEST INDIVIDUAL INNINGS

364	L. Hutton	v Australia	Oval	1938
336*	W. R. Hammond	v New Zealand	Auckland	1932–3
325	A. Sandham	v West Indies	Kingston	1929–30
310*	J. H. Edrich	v New Zealand	Headingley	1965
287	R. E. Foster	v Australia	Sydney	1903–4
285*	P. B. H. May	v West Indies	Edgbaston	1957
278	D. C. S. Compton	v Pakistan	Trent Bridge	1954

MOST WICKETS

	Tests	Runs	Wickets	Av.
F. S. Trueman	67	6,625	307	21·57
J. B. Statham	70	6,261	252	24·84
A. V. Bedser	51	5,876	236	24·89
J. C. Laker	46	4,101	193	21·24
S. F. Barnes	27	3,106	189	16·43
J. A. Snow	42	4,609	176	26·18
G. A. R. Lock	49	4,451	174	25·58
D. L. Underwood	47	4,063	172	23·62

MOST WICKETS IN A SERIES

			Tests	Runs	Wickets	Av.
S. F. Barnes	v S. Afr.	1913–14	4	536	49	10·93
J. C. Laker	v Aust.	1956	5	442	46	9·60
A. V. Bedser	v Aust.	1953	5	682	39	17·48
M. W. Tate	v Aust.	1924–5	5	881	38	23·18
G. A. Lohmann	v S. Afr.	1895–6	3	203	35	5·80

BEST BOWLING

[b]10–53	J. C. Laker	v Australia	Old Trafford	1956
9–28	G. A. Lohmann	v South Africa	Johannesburg	1895–6
[a] 9–37	J. C. Laker	v Australia	Old Trafford	1956
9–103	S. F. Barnes	v South Africa	Johannesburg	1913–14

[a] = first innings
[b] = second innings } of same match.

1,000 RUNS AND 100 WICKETS

	Tests	Runs	Wickets
T. E. Bailey	61	2,290	132
R. Illingworth	61	1,836	122
W. Rhodes	58	2,325	127
M. W. Tate	39	1,198	155
F. J. Titmus	49	1,311	146

CAPTAIN IN MOST TESTS

P. B. H. May	41
R. Illingworth	31
E. R. Dexter	30
M. C. Cowdrey	27
M. J. K. Smith	25

* not out.

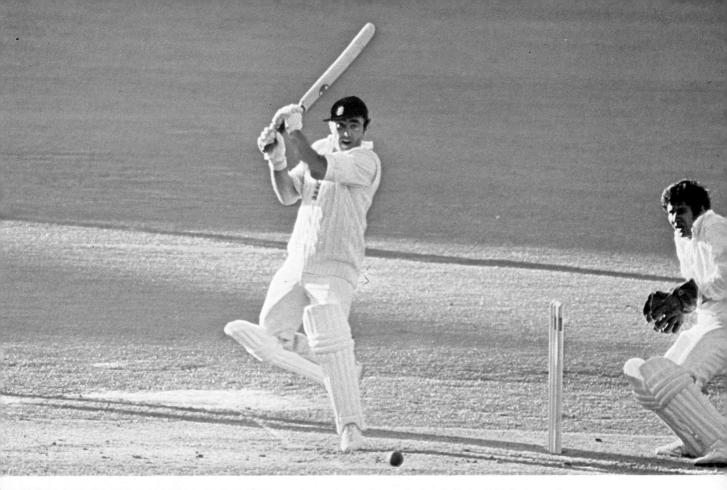

The professionals' professional, John Edrich, instantly recognisable despite the askew cap and attenuated shadows in 7 p.m. sunlight at Lord's against Pakistan in 1974.

(Overleaf left) Among many other things, John Arlott says, English cricket is 'plebeian and patrician'. Dexter's category was clear: ramrod posture, St James's Street vowels helped him to his title: Lord Edward.

(Overleaf right) Emulating the Everton Weekes square cut: a 1980s hopeful among the sugar cane of Barbados; pads and gloves are too great a luxury.

R. E. Foster, a double international, and cricket's least reluctant debutant; his 287 in his first Test at Sydney in 1903–04 remains the twelfth highest personal innings in Test history.

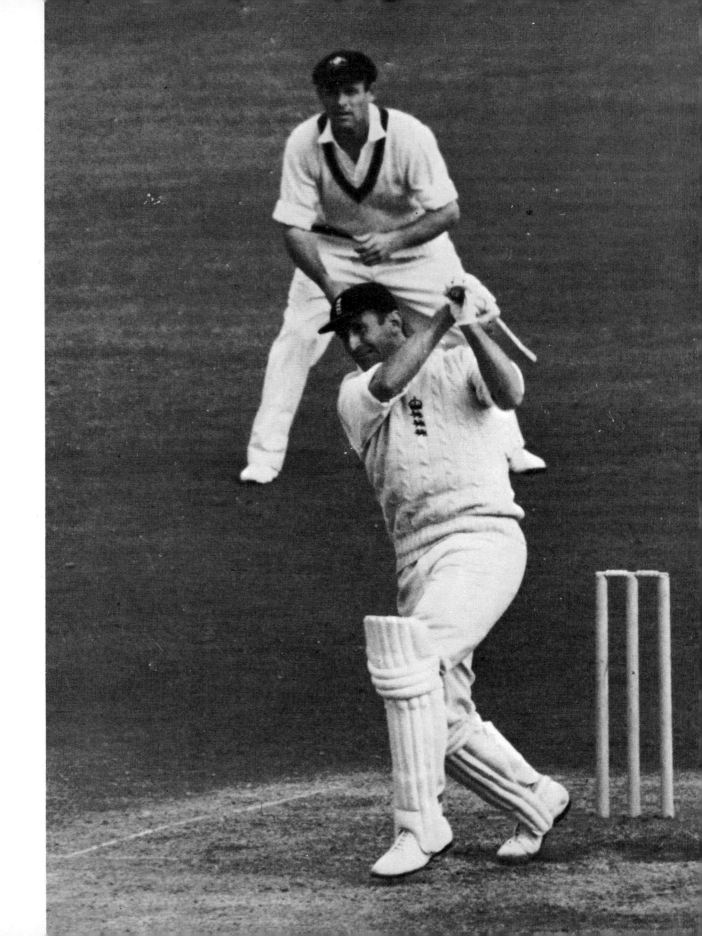

If only he could have lasted forever. Garry Sobers, one of the few modern monarchs who still carried a broadsword into battle.

A beach game at Accra Beach in Barbados continues zealously until the rising tide or inky darkness blots it out for the day.

West Indies: TONY COZIER

Dialogue in a Barbados schoolhouse.
TEACHER: Here's a simple sum, Reuben. What do four and four and five and five make?
SIX-YEAR-OLD REUBEN: Four thousand four hundred and fifty-five is the number of runs that Mr Everton Weekes made in forty-eight Test matches for the West Indies.
TEACHER: Not what I was after, but absolutely correct.

That short scene is shot through with dramatic licence, but does make its point. For moppets in Barbados and every other part of the West Indies, the agonies of learning addition, multiplication and division are worthwhile because through them youngsters can tot up Test scores and work out cricket averages. That this knowledge will later help them to make their way in the world is an afterthought that they will consider when they have to focus on such secondary matters.

These priorities are inevitable. Throughout the West Indies, cricket is imbibed with mother's milk. In no other part of the planet does the game seep into the consciousness at such an early age or thrust itself so vigorously and enduringly into the lives of the population. In the Caribbean, cricket's domination over all other aspects of life is legendary. Those who moan about the game are the kind of people who complain that their oranges contain too much juice or that their mangoes are too sweet. Any man who could not instantly give Sobers's statistics to three decimal places or who opines that Venkataraghavan must be a high priest of transcendental meditation would be arrested as a Cuban agent or asked sympathetically how long he had been inside. His ability, or lack of it, to give a run-by-run description of Worrell and Weekes at Trent Bridge in 1950 would decide his fate.

What is the secret behind this intense obsession with the game? One broad reason is that almost the entire male population of the West Indies islands are able to play—and play to a high standard. This active, rather than passive, connection enabled the West Indies to establish their credentials at international level faster than other countries.

The urgent quest for the snappy headline has oversimplified descriptions of West Indian play. The rasp of machettes being sharpened was loud throughout the islands after a smart Fleet Street sub-editor, in 1950, dubbed Goddard's triumphant tourists 'calypso cricketers'. The phrase was too shallow: it implied an approach solely of carefree abandon, almost of irresponsibility. What made it rankle the more was the strong, if incomplete, vein of truth the label carried. In many respects, it is not a wholly inaccurate summary of the cricket and the players from these islands.

For years, a host of reasons have been put forward for the attitude of West Indian cricket—for there is no doubt the attitude has grown to form an easily recognizable identity. Perhaps the best answer can be found in the people themselves and in their general way of life. No matter what difficulties are strewn before him, the West Indian gets as much enjoyment as he can from life. He has a hair-trigger sense of humour; solemnity is an impediment. In many of the islands, notably Trinidad, the annual carnival bubbles and surges with bacchanalian revelry; it is no accident that the steel band and calypso originated in this area.

Nor is it any accident that West Indian cricketers have fashioned the reputation they have done down the years. The aim of every young West Indian cricketer is universal but pursued more zealously than elsewhere: to hit the ball harder and bowl it faster than anyone else. Experience at higher levels may temper this ebullience, but this natural instinct is never lost, or completely submerged. For those lacking the physique or strength to burst the ball at the seams or pound the bat from the batsman's hands, the talent to improvise helps out. Massive or immensely strong men such as Walcott and Lloyd and Weekes through force stung palms and dented pickets. Those of slighter frame devised their own methods: hence the delicacy of Worrell's late cut or the unorthodoxy of Kanhai's falling sweep. A four's a four for all that.

No player feels the chafing against the grain of his nature more acutely than a West Indian contained for over after over; no player feels less delight in stock bowling—steady, economical, medium-pace, tick-tock stuff. Other men can jog around sturdily and usefully like pit ponies; the West Indian craves the padding grace and striking power of the panther. An Australian friend, in the West Indies for the first time, watched couples on a nightclub dancefloor moving rhythmically to the calypso beat. His first reaction, he said, was an understanding of the grace of Wes Hall running in to bowl, Sobers pouncing on a short-leg catch and Kanhai at the wicket.

The evidence that cricket reigns is obvious and everywhere. A drive through Kingston or Georgetown, for instance, on any day of the year will reveal young boys—and some with greying whiskers—playing cricket in some form or other. They are in action on the streets, in park space no matter how cramped or narrow-chested, and on open land. In Barbados, during the season, almost a hundred excellently organized club games are played every Saturday on near-ideal pitches, each one contested with the serious intent of a Test match. And this on an island the size of the Isle of Wight.

Nor has a chronic shortage of facilities contained cricket's popularity or the zest for playing and watching it. When Bourda, the small ground in Georgetown, hosts a Test match, hundreds make a daily round trip of up to two hundred miles from Guyana's sugar areas to see the game. A fan has to be in one of the queues outside the ground from as early as four a.m. to be assured of a seat in the arena, which holds only 13,000. Here at Bourda, and at Kingston's Sabina Park, dozens of intrepid fanatics watch hour after hour perched precariously on the branches of breadfruit or samaan trees outside. When Bridgetown's Kensington Oval was overflowing its 15,000 capacity during the 1974 Test against England and all gates were closed, several ignored warnings over the public address system and swung into the ground, Tarzan style, by way of a high tension cable. For most spectators, accommodation is hardly 'mod. con.'—they are crushed, rocked, pummelled and jostled for six hours under broiling tropical sun. Frail old parties are at a big disadvantage.

However, inconvenience is also a way of life for players on some islands. In Dominica, for many years there was only one ground suitable for competitive club cricket. Yet there were eight teams. It meant that you played your game one weekend (and even this was uncertain on an island with an eighty-inch annual rainfall), then hung around for another month for your turn to come up again. Yet Dominica has managed to produce a crop of outstanding players in recent years, including Grayson Shillingford, one of the first Windward Islands men to win a West Indies Test cap.

Trinidad, home of a succession of notable cricketers—Learie Constantine, Roach, Ramadhin, Stollmeyer, Gomez, Julien—also plays much of its club cricket under testing circumstances. Open space in the capital, Port-of-Spain, is severely limited and the expansive Queen's Park Savannah has always been, by necessity, the centre for most outdoor activity. It simply cannot meet the demand and many cricket fields must overlap: one game's fine-leg is another's deep mid-on. Trinidadian club cricketers tell stories of bolting horses running across the bows of an advancing fast bowler (the Savannah is also the racecourse site) and of kites suddenly descending in mid-pitch—children have no other room for their kite flying.

Despite all this congestion and turmoil, cricket has flourished, and keeps on doing so, for a myriad of reasons. Firstly, perhaps the most obvious: the climate. A bounty. A blessing. It is never too hot or too cold to play this game. While it may be very wet in the rainy season, there is always enough intermittent sunshine for budding Test players to set up an improvised pitch in the street, in someone's backyard, anywhere. The weather also allows the preparation of hard, true pitches which have encouraged the long-established West Indian tradition for strokeplay and for fast bowling. Sadly, Test pitches in the last decade have been over-prepared; they have become slow and lifeless. But for Saturday afternoon games—the backbone of the sport—they are what theorists call ideal: fast, bouncy, and true.

Beyond the sheer physical excitement of playing, the West Indian youth has another powerful spur, one that does not touch so strongly on the flanks of youngsters in England, Australia or New Zealand. In underdeveloped territories, where wages are generally low and unemployment often embarrassingly high, cricket has been the one easily available avenue to fame and fortune. The lad from a poor, humble family can earn, through his ability on the cricket field, a job off it he might never have had. Apart from the adulation, the game could bring him—and indeed his family, his village, his island, his race—a new feeling of self-respect. These motives and incentives remain as high as they ever were.

Two stories of great players illustrate the rags-to-riches theme. Learie Constantine, seemingly powered by 100,000 volts at whatever he did on a cricket field, began as a boy playing in Port-of-Spain streets swatting a coconut tree bat or pelting down a lime or cork ball at savage speed. On the West Indies 1928 tour of England—its first official Test series—his team was overwhelmed but he did a wonderful tour double of 1,381 runs and 107 wickets. The following year, he joined Nelson in the Lancashire League, the first in a long line of West Indian professionals there. After his scintillating career ended in 1939, he settled in England, became a barrister, was a noted figure in community work, was awarded a seat in the House of Lords and was High Commissioner for Trinidad and Tobago. He died in 1971.

Garry Sobers, one of a family of six children whose merchant-seaman father was killed by a German torpedo in World War II, showed while still a stripling that he was placed on this earth to outperform all others as an allround cricketer. His astonishing deeds and his demeanour throughout twenty years of almost continuous play brought him a spattering of world records and respect from the noblest and most demanding opponents. He rightly became the highest-paid professional as well. One school of thought says that colonial experience stripped indigenous peoples of their self-respect. If so, it is no wonder that the West Indies revere their cricket and the extraordinary feats of such as Constantine and Sobers.

During the past two decades, an aspiring young cricketer has not been starved of chances to emulate them, even if he starts at the bottom rung of the ladder. That rung may be in his village team in a sugar estates competition or in a championship such as that run by the Barbados Cricket League. Most likely the ground he plays on will be small and inadequate and funds so low that gear is of poor quality, second-hand, almost non-existent—or all three. The Barbados League has done an extremely important job in organizing more than ninety clubs; so, too, have the sugar estates in Guyana, Jamaica and Trinidad. In these matches finesse may be slight; courage is not. A batsman will saunter out gloveless and wearing only one pad to tackle with aplomb bowlers of tearaway pace. The important ingredients are there: teams of eleven men each, fine weather, competitive cricket and essentially good pitches.

*'ew Ball? Fast bowler?
Both are there to be hit,
nan. Kanhai's brutality
to Chris Old at
Edgbaston is what
Vest Indians would call
a captain's innings.*

The Hallelujah Chorus: Barbadians, Trinidadians, Guyanese emotionally united in exile into West Indians in full throat at Old Trafford; Sobers was a marvellous binding agent.

Outstanding players in these rural leagues will soon be noticed in urban areas whose clubs comprise, generally speaking, the more readily recognized championships. Small club teams in Barbados produced—along with Sobers—Nurse, Griffith and Weekes. In Guyana, the small village of Port Mourant, in the sugar belt on the east coast, was the cricket kindergarten over the last generation of four great players: Butcher, Solomon, Kanhai and Kallicharran.

No less vital have been the major secondary schools. As everywhere in all sports, schoolboy performances catch appraising eyes. In the West Indies, like Australia, a rocket-path to the heights can swiftly follow. Jeff Stollmeyer, perhaps as lustrously-silken a batsman as the West Indies has produced, later a Test captain, journeyed to England with the 1939 touring party just out of Queen's Royal College, Trinidad, as did Gerry Gomez, that solid allrounder. In 1963, less than a year out of QRC, wicketkeeper Deryck Murray, repeated the trip. Derek Sealy, a seventeen-year-old wicketkeeper/batsman, made the first tour to Australia in 1930–1 when a student at Combermere School, which Worrell was attending when he first played for Barbados. Opening batsman Robin Bynoe broke off his studies at Harrison College in Barbados to tour India and Pakistan in 1958–9. From these two starting points, the tiny upcountry ground or manicured schoolfield, the young player advances along the rising corridor through major club team, territorial team and, his greatest possible ambition realized, into the Test eleven.

In the late 1960s, when the West Indies side was skidding downhill, cricket authorities were worried that a dual exodus—emigrants UK-bound seeking a better living and young players lured into county cricket—would shrink their pool of players to a dangerously low level. Inevitably the haemorrhage made local clubs—the backbone of West Indian cricket—more brittle. Standards fell visibly, especially in Barbados which at one point was feeding a dozen of its leading players a year into the English counties. With the immigration door to Britain forcibly banged shut and the other almost closed, club strengths and competitions were expected to rise again during the late 1970s.

From the outset, cricket in the West Indies belonged to the people, even when some of those people belonged to other people. Research has yielded the first

A seminal figure in bringing stature to West Indian cricket, hope and dignity to his people. Glimpses of 'Old Electric-Heels' peep through the ermine in 1969 as Lord (Learie) Constantine—Britain's first coloured Life Peer—takes his place in the House of Lords.

official reference: a meeting of the St Anne's Club in Barbados in 1806. Yet it is thought that cricket was played on a few of the islands long before then and that the Garrison at Barbados had a field long before the Duke of Wellington's oft-echoed dictate of 1841 that all British military establishments should have a 'cricketing ground'. At that time the Caribbean game was a social occasion, the preserve of the white elite; after all, slavery was not abolished until 1833.

By the 1890s, descendants of former slaves had reached a good standard; they proved they were needed. When Barbados and British Guiana protested in 1893 about Trinidad's including black players in its team for a three-way tournament, the protest was quickly choked off. Commonsense had breached the rigid racial barriers that had extended well into the nineteenth century; shrewd people knew the whites were too few to build and sustain a substantial international team, Black players impressed four visiting English teams during this decade, so it was not surprising that one third of the first representative team that 'Plum' Warner's brother, R. S. A. Warner, brought to England in 1900 was black. Because of this good start, cricket has been a fine positive force for race relations in the Caribbean, although it took until 1960 for a black captain, Frank Worrell, to be appointed.

The main impetus for cricket until official recognition in 1928 were regular series against England, home and away, England showing the flag, the West Indians showing their strokes and growing efficiency. That team to England in 1928 received the princely sum of thirty shillings a week 'to cover incidental or out-of-pocket expenses', while the professionals, such as they were then, got three pounds a Test with no talent money. Incentives for the others included thirty shillings for a first-class century and fifteen shillings for five wickets in an innings.

The arrival of Constantine, the harbinger, at Nelson in 1929 ushered in the next significant phase: the comparatively rich and rewarding era of professionalism for West Indians in the Leagues. Now their best players could really absorb knowledge of the toughest playing conditions while earning good money, always an enticing prospect for any youngster with little education and few commercial hopes.

It was a good life: while belts loosened, defences tightened. Dozens came over learning to cope with the ball that swayed eerily towards them under pewter skies, bit into rich, heavy turf then darted who knew which way: towards the bat's edge or tried to scuttle through the gate; eggshell blue-skies and palm fronds were indeed six thousand miles away. The education of the Leagues school was a potent thrusting force towards the pinnacle. A great many of the players who helped in the spectacular rise of West Indian fortunes after World War II played in the leagues, warming and lightening the greyness for discerning crowds at Accrington or Enfield or Todmorden.

In more recent times, the horizons broadened even wider. The English County

More embers than blaze as his twilight closes in, Wes Hall can still singe, as Colin Milburn finds out, clean bowled for one playing for Western Australia v West Indies in 1968.

Championship, needing blood transfusions to survive, opted for the O (for overseas) positive type. Naturally the leading players—Sobers, Kanhai, Deryck Murray, Lance Gibbs, Clive Lloyd—had some of the first and plumpest contracts waved at them. The promising—John Shepherd, Van Holder, Kallicharran, Geoff Greenidge, Gordon Greenidge, Lawrence Rowe among others—followed and prospered. In 1974, Gordon Greenidge played an innings of 274 not out for D. H. Robins's XI which his Hampshire teammate, Barry Richards, declared must have been one of the greatest in history—fair recommendation from a fair source.

For West Indies the 1930s had belonged to Constantine, his huge and ferocious fast bowling partner, Martindale, opening batsman Roach, but above all to George Headley, 'the Black Bradman'. This impeccable batsman had scored a century in each innings against MCC at Georgetown in 1929–30, averaged 97 in a four-Test series in 1934–5 and again scored centuries in both innings of the Lord's Test in 1939.

While barrage balloons drifted over Lord's and England's cricketers wore khaki or navy blue, exciting talents were sharpening in the Caribbean, notably the W plan—Worrell, Weekes and Walcott—who blossomed into possibly the most feared and explosively brilliant middle-order batting trio in cricket history. They delivered a two-nil home blow to the solar plexus of a strangely-anaemic MCC touring team in 1947–8, cleaned up India in 1949, then presented the *coup de grâce*: the 1950 victory over England in England.

Seemingly out of nowhere, a pair of virtually untried youngsters—one tiny, one elongated—spun England into tangled disarray. Ramadhin and Valentine, two names forever bracketed in history, in song and legend. Fifty-nine wickets between them. The three Ws, the dependable Rae and Stollmeyer softening the opposition with lance, rapier, broadsword and battleaxe. Impromptu calypsos billowed across London, euphoric countrymen swooped and snake-danced across the venerated turf at Lord's. Back home, massive headlines such as: 'West Indies Humble England' made the reading feast of a lifetime. Never before or since have so many joyous people gathered at Bridgetown as came to greet the boat carrying back the returning heroes.

During the 1950s, the West Indies stumbled against Australia down under in 1951–2 and in England in 1957. But Walcott led the run-rampage against Australia in 1955 with five centuries in the series and Sobers, just into his majority, slashed Len Hutton's name from the world record list with 365 not out against Pakistan. To the man cutting cane in Jamaica or tallying bananas in Grenada or building a new road in Guyana, it was clear evidence that his people had come of age and were more than ready to govern themselves.

It was hardly coincidence that the most celebrated period in the annals of West Indian cricket—the early 1960s—ran parallel with complete independence of the four main territories: Jamaica and Trinidad and Tobago in 1962, Barbados and Guyana in 1966, and the appointment of the first black captain, Worrell, for an overseas tour.

The man and the hour were perfectly blended. Had Worrell failed—and many a sniper was crouched behind the parapet with finger curled eagerly around the trigger—the marksmen's contention that a black man was incapable of leading would have been a psychological set-back for both West Indian cricket and life. Instead, Worrell offered glorious dawn, noon, and sunset as captain. The dawn—the 1960–1 series against Australia, tied Test and all—was an incomparable five months of cricket's history. Of course the tie was a fluke. But Worrell prompted all the way flair, enjoyment, responsibility and application from his troops. Here was a mature, experienced man with a calm and dignified approach and keen appreciation of his players. He was never flustered, never raised his voice, a rare quality in the Caribbean. No single independence speech in any Caribbean island is more keenly remembered than his whispered call to Wes Hall at Brisbane, with the scores level: 'No no-ball now, Wes, or you can't go back to Barbados.'

Worrell as leader was the crucial factor, the final delicately-forged piece that made the machine complete. As far back as the 1930s, Constantine told the noted cricket writer, C. L. R. James, that all West Indies needed was a captain. The importance of leadership is more pronounced with the West Indies than with most other sporting teams. A group of highly talented individuals does not necessarily comprise a successful team, particularly when they are by nature volatile. Add to this the insular divisions of a peculiar geographical set-up, and fragility under stress is easy to comprehend. The combination has split West Indies apart in the field many times.

So, for all its vitality and zest, West Indian cricket has been continually taunted with the charge that it has reacted poorly in time of crisis. In most cases, the evidence is irrefutable. Time and again they have slid from seemingly unassailable positions only to be denied victory, or suffer numbing defeat. In 1974 a severely-limited English team wriggled out of tight corners in two Tests in the Caribbean, then levelled the series in the fifth when West Indies collapsed inexplicably. Even with the strongest of teams, the West Indies seem to get careless after winning series, as happened against Pakistan in 1958, Australia in 1965 and England in 1966.

After the Worrell-Benaud series—when West Indians again walked eight feet tall—they scored these victories to establish themselves as world champions: England 3-1 in England in 1963; Australia 2-1 at home in 1965; England 3-1 in England in 1966 and India 2-0 in India in 1966–7. These were their strengths: the all-round genius of Sobers, the batting artistry of Kanhai, Nurse and Butcher, Hunte's reliability, the searing pace of Hall and Griffith, the bewitching off-spin of Gibbs. The brouhaha about Griffith's alleged 'chucking' stabbed at West Indians as if a member of their very families had been attacked.

The grey canopy of twenty Tests without a win lifted with the pummelling of England up there in 1973. But, during these doldrums the game was besmirched with a revival of the internal bickering, rampant insularity and petty jealousies that had previously degraded Caribbean cricket. Geography and politics have been twin curses. Save for the years 1958–62, life span of the West Indies Federation, West Indies had not been a political entity during all its years as an international cricketing identity. Even the federation did not include Guyana. For cricket purposes, the Caribbean territories with British colonial histories have been grouped together and remained thus united for almost eighty years. Several efforts at integration in other areas failed; none has endured as long.

Win or lose, the outstanding player has been accepted as 'West Indian' outside his native island. Trinidadians and Guyanese have not cared that Headley played for Jamaica and that Sobers was born in Barbados. However when the West Indies are struggling, especially in a home series, all hell can break loose if a home favourite is omitted for an ordinary, unestablished player from another territory.

'W' for Wallop, Wonderful and Woe (to bowlers). The most potent middle-order batting trio in history: the late Sir Frank Worrell, Clyde Walcott and Everton Weekes.

With total crowd support often flowing only from success, an out-of-form, failing Jamaican in a Barbados Test can feel most uneasy. Sun and alcohol, disappointment and parochial irritation combine into a deadly mixture. The three most notorious crowd disturbances—at Georgetown in 1954, Port-of-Spain in 1960 and Kingston in 1968—erupted when the West Indies were floundering; wrath was not directed against the opponents, England in each case.

It is salient that the West Indies have generally done well in England since World War II. The uplifting support comes from immigrant spectators who classify themselves as West Indian, rather than Barbadian at Kensington Oval, Bridgetown, or Guyanese at Bourda Oval, Georgetown. These insular circumstances, plus the archaic system of having a representative from each main territory on the selection panel, have not always meant the best team has been chosen. Sometimes, good players have been sacrificed to satisfy local demand or through

Fortunately for New Zealand, Glenn Turner's livelihood is scoring runs for Worcestershire and his country. His county colleague, John Parker, is NZ's only other professional player.

(Above) New Zealand's cricket victories are few but her settings are unsurpassed for charm. Wellington's Basin Reserve shows why the game rivals confession as balm for the soul.

(Left) Inheritors of diffidence and swagger. NZ captain Bevan Congden (left) and Australian skipper Ian Chappell shake before the First Test at Melbourne in 1973. Too seldom has Australia sought cricket competition across the Tasman Sea.

bartering of names between selectors. On the whole, however, the system down the years has been so well administered and organized throughout the area that the odds on a talented individual coming to the fore have been good and, of late, excellent.

These days, more and more cricket is being played throughout the Caribbean. Modest sponsorship has arrived and the senior (Shell Shield) and junior (Benson and Hedges Trophy) are run on a regular basis. Previously there was no annual league at either level, just spasmodic matches between the various territories. For example, before the Shell Shield started in 1966, Trinidad had played Jamaica only once in the twenty-one years since the end of the last war. The smaller islands in the Windward and Leeward groups, neglected mainly through organizational problems in the past, have entered as a combined team and have done enough to suggest that many future stars will come from Antigua, Dominica, St Kitts and St Vincent. Two Antiguans are already proving this: Andy Roberts with 119 wickets heading the English Championship bowling in his first season with Hampshire; batsman Vivian Richards giving a jewel-like glitter in his debut season with Somerset. Youth series have been played against Australian and English teams in the West Indies and youth teams have visited England twice in the 1970s.

Some claim there may be too much cricket: West Indies played eight Tests in 1973 and ten in 1974, with many players drawn from overcricketed English counties, and playing Shell Shield and other matches around the world. Predictably many have felt the strain. Exhaustion made Sobers announce his retirement from county cricket in August 1974, a few weeks after he turned thirty-eight.

Yet it is inconceivable that, for a West Indian, there will ever be such a thing as too much cricket. He has always been, is and will always remain an unabashed lover of the game; his appetite will never be satisfied.

WEST INDIES IN TEST CRICKET
(All statistics up to 30 September 1974)

SUMMARY OF RESULTS

	Played	Won	Lost	Tied	Drawn
v England	66	19	21	0	26
v Australia	35	6	19	1	9
v New Zealand	14	5	2	0	7
v India	28	12	1	0	15
v Pakistan	8	4	3	0	1
	151	46	46	1	58

MOST APPEARANCES

G. S. Sobers	93
R. B. Kanhai	79
L. R. Gibbs	66
F. M. Worrell	51

MOST RUNS

	Tests	Inns.	N.O.	Runs	H.S.	Av.
G. S. Sobers	93	160	21	8,032	365*	57·78
R. B. Kanhai	79	137	6	6,227	256	47·53
E. D. Weekes	48	81	5	4,455	207	58·61
F. M. Worrell	51	87	9	3,860	261	49·48
C. L. Walcott	44	74	7	3,798	220	56·68

MOST RUNS IN A SERIES

		Tests	Inns.	N.O.	Runs	H.S.	Av.
C. L. Walcott v Aust.	1954–5	5	10	0	827	155	82·70
G. S. Sobers v Pak.	1957–8	5	8	2	824	365*	137·33
E. D. Weekes v India	1948–9	5	7	0	779	194	111·28

HIGHEST INDIVIDUAL INNINGS

365*	G. S. Sobers	v Pakistan	Kingston	1957–8
302	L. G. Rowe	v England	Bridgetown	1973–4
270*	G. A. Headley	v England	Kingston	1934–5
261	F. M. Worrell	v England	Trent Bridge	1950
260	C. C. Hunte	v Pakistan	Kingston	1957–8
258	S. M. Nurse	v New Zealand	Christchurch	1968–9
256	R. B. Kanhai	v India	Calcutta	1958–9

MOST WICKETS

	Tests	Runs	Wickets	Av.
L. R. Gibbs	66	7,673	265	28·95
G. S. Sobers	93	7,999	235	34·03
W. W. Hall	48	5,066	192	26·38
S. Ramadhin	43	4,579	158	28·98
A. L. Valentine	36	4,215	139	30·32

MOST WICKETS IN A SERIES

		Tests	Runs	Wickets	Av.
A. L. Valentine v Eng.	1950	4	674	33	20·42

BEST BOWLING

9–95	J. Noreiga	v India	Port of Spain	1970–71
8–38	L. R. Gibbs	v India	Bridgetown	1961–2
8–104	A. L. Valentine	v Eng.	Old Trafford	1950

1,000 RUNS AND 100 WICKETS

	Tests	Runs	Wickets
G. S. Sobers	93	8,032	235

CAPTAIN IN MOST TESTS

G. S. Sobers	39
J. D. C. Goddard	22

* not out.

New Zealand: DICK BRITTENDEN

From missionaries to mercenaries . . . from too little cricket to too much . . . from the floating of a company for a first English tour to a packed house, including a streaker, in the Auckland Test with Australia in 1974 . . . these have been strands in the unravelling yarn of New Zealand cricket down the years.

In the process much has been lost and much gained. The cloak of the cavalier, which distinguished the New Zealand team in England in 1927, has been replaced by a veneer of sophistication. A large part of this change has come from the determination of the Board of Control to improve New Zealand standards through more tours and Tests. Figures suggest the plan is working: of New Zealand's eight victories in 114 Test matches over forty-five years, five have been won since 1968. New Zealand remains a junior partner in the Test company, but now England is the only country New Zealand has not beaten at least once. And that historic breakthrough was very nearly achieved in two of the three matches in England in 1973.

New Zealand's forced growth in international cricket may be measured by the swiftly-increasing number of her commitments. In ten years before World War II, New Zealand played fourteen Test matches. Then came six Tests in the 1940s, thirty-two in the next decade, forty-three in the 1960s, and an additional nineteen to the end of March 1974.

While this comparatively heavy programme has improved New Zealand's modest record, and has brought a distinct hardening in attitude among top players, it has posed fresh problems. New Zealand is a small country, with a population not much above three million. Cricketers number some forty thousand. The time has passed when having an employee play an occasional Test match or go on tour brought pleasure to both employer and player. Since the early 1970s, many top players have had much difficulty in obtaining leave. Some have had to withdraw from teams because their firms no longer want part-time workers. A few have lost their jobs by going on tour. Others have declined to tour because they could not afford to be by-passed for promotion while they were away.

Allowances for players have risen but they still do not compare with the ruling rates for Test teams in most other countries. New Zealand has been discovering it was not big enough to match the finances of the major cricketing countries. For a first full-scale tour of Australia late in 1973, the team was without six top players from the tour of England earlier that year: not all stayed home because of business commitments, but it was a significant and costly loss for a struggling Test country.

The structure of New Zealand cricket also makes international survival difficult. The game is based on Saturday club competitions in metropolitan centres
and in country areas. Public interest in these club championships is low; attendances can be counted in scores.

Many New Zealand club grounds are as aesthetically appealing as Britain's best.
Cricket in Christchurch has had its home among the oaks and elms of Hagley Oval
for over a century; it is as serene and restful and pleasing a place as one might wish
to see.

In the country, many matches are played with the sea rustling or pounding in
the background; a batsman defeated and deflated by a full toss can seek solace in
the surf not many yards beyond extra cover.

New Zealand cricket architecture, however, is almost always strictly utilitarian:
clubs cannot afford to spend much money; they don't have it. Whilst New Zealand
often enjoys a buoyant economy, many cricket clubs have to survive through
weekly raffles or the sale of beer after play; a fortunate few have done extremely
well financially through regular bingo sessions in hotels.

Competition cricket is keen but friendly. From the senior grades come the
candidates for Plunket Shield teams and first-class cricket. But cricket, like rugby
football in New Zealand, has an almost Teutonic regard for organization; there
are match and bonus points down through the several grades. Even in special
competitions for more mature players—many of them former Test or provincial
representatives—points are zealously pursued.

This earnestness applies, too, in country cricket. But playing conditions vary
considerably. There are some turf wickets in country areas, but most are matting
on concrete or one of the new synthetics. Often rural cricketers travel enormous
distances for their games. They make match days family occasions; picnic and
swimming parties, huge spreads of sandwiches, cream sponges and the like. Often
matches are on a limited-overs basis, start early and finish in time for the farmers to
tend to their flocks or herds. Country players rarely have time for practice. City
ones, in recent times, can seldom be bothered. The contemporary New Zealander
has enough money for a car, a golf club membership, a set of surf skis. Access to
counter-attractions is easy, on good roads, in a country where one is seldom far
from a beach. Consequently, not many put in consistent practice.

The structure of the game, however, gives young players every chance to advance.
Youngsters below their teens have inter-school mid-week matches; adult clubs
organize Saturday morning cricket. At secondary school level, there is the incentive of a recently-organized interchange of visits with Australia, on a national basis.
Players under twenty can compete in a week-long, inter-provincial tournament
during the long Christmas holiday period and a similar contest exists for players
under twenty-three. From there, it is up into Plunket Shield and Test cricket.

In the schools, coaching has become a distinct problem. Schoolteachers, brought up on a jealously-guarded forty-hour week, are not now willing to spend time with youngsters coaching after school. There are exceptions, naturally, but the number of school coaches has shrunk drastically. As ever, promising boys still get tuition. A long line of English coaches has voyaged down, with the apple-cheeked men of Sussex predominant; A. E. Relf, almost seventy years ago; John Langridge, Bert Wensley, Jim Parks snr. The latest in a long line is Martin Horton, of Worcestershire and England. He has been exceptionally successful as national coach, with his main mission the moulding of coaches. In years ahead, his campaign will do much to arrest the decline in school coaching numbers.

New Zealand cricket has a very visible and staunch core of supporters. Their staunchness has been tested: for years they had little more to enthuse over except individual feats of arms. Their persistent hopes have been better rewarded in recent years, but the country does tend to blow hot and cold about cricket. One day raptures, the next ridicule. Playing England at Auckland in 1955, New Zealand struggled to score 200. But, at lunch on the third day, England was also in the mire, at 7 for 183. Many people, including visiting English pressmen, thought England would have a desperate fight when batting fourth; New Zealand had a chance of winning a Test match for the very first time.

The prospect was too enchanting for a Christchurch businessman to resist. He rushed from his office to the airport and climbed aboard an aircraft bound for Auckland, six hundred miles away. In those distant days, the national air service used DC3s, comfortable craft, but not very fast. About the time the plains of Canterbury were sliding past the wingtips, the pilot announced that England were out for 243. When they were over the rugged Kaikouras, he said New Zealand had lost two quick wickets. By the time they were crossing the Cook Strait, the game was all but over. For this was the day New Zealand established one of its Test records—the lowest score of twenty-six.

This travesty brought out the scoffers in hordes. But, just a year later, when at the same ground New Zealand won its first Test, the nation briefly went cricket crazy. So it has gone on until, of late, teams have produced more reasons for solid support. In 1969, New Zealand won its first Test rubber; then gave England those bad frights in 1973. It has now chalked up a victory over Australia and was robbed of another in Sydney by rain.

The tide of events has stimulated a new approach from the New Zealand cricketer. There have always been players of talent, but usually too few at a time to make much impression against strong Test sides. Doubtless, standards of abilities have levelled among the cricketing nations. Because this has coincided with sharp improvement from New Zealand, the feeling of being clumsy country cousins has ebbed from the home players.

These days, the New Zealand Test player does not overestimate his ability. He

May 31, 1973: Glenn Turner scores his 1,000th run in May. Historic but costly. He so drained the well that he scored few runs when most needed—in the Test matches.

is wise enough in the ways of cricket to appreciate his own and his country's shortcomings. But he can also see that an MCC tour blazer or a large green Australian cap no longer means invulnerability. While that first win against England has still eluded, New Zealand has stacked up enough success to know that it will come sooner or later. Self-disparagement was a fault in earlier years. New Zealand had several chances of winning Tests against the mother country, but was too diffident and timid to take the chances.

At last the public has begun to realize the prospects too. New Zealand and Australia played two series back-to-back in 1973–4. The Australian tourists flew over for the second series after two resounding victories in the first, but memories of their lucky escape in Sydney lingered in New Zealand minds; fans were eager to see what would happen on home pitches. Record crowds swarmed to each Test venue; each day at Auckland, weekend attendances were more than 30,000, a proper reflection of public interest.

The path to maturity has indeed been rocky. When Plunket Shield cricket began on its present basis more than fifty years ago, the scoring rate, averaged throughout each season, was seventy runs an hour. The rate declined for several reasons: cricketers began to take themselves more seriously; prospects of Tests and tours appeared. So the game became more tight-fisted. In the 1950s, the Shield scoring rate slipped below forty an hour over the whole series. With this lack of aggression went a loss of the personalities who had enlivened the game.

The stolid approach was encouraged by selection policies that whirled players in and out of New Zealand teams with dizzying speed. To date, some one hundred and thirty players have appeared in Tests for New Zealand; half of them have averaged between one and five matches. During the 1960s there was no further need for revolving doors in Test dressing rooms. The selection committee of the time decided to retain chosen players, demonstrating their faith in them. This mirrored the Australian style of carrying a good player through a personal drought. Since New Zealand has become less eager to dispense with a player after a failure or two, it is no coincidence that team performances have improved.

The Test player does not wait a long time for the tap on his shoulder, but still has his difficulties. His first-class season, if he appears for his province in every match, lasts fifteen days. There are six teams, each playing the others in three-day games. Australia, with only five Sheffield Shield teams, has a season of thirty-two days. The Australian plays, as a rule, on faster pitches. Too low, too slow is the common criticism of New Zealand pitches; it has generally been justified. At Dunedin, Christchurch and Auckland, Test grounds are also used for rugby football; groundsmen have a fierce task getting their grounds ready for cricket. The Wellington ground belongs to soccer in winter. This gentler football code does not churn grounds as much as rugby heavyweights ploughing about in winter mud.

Now and then players thrive on a really good pitch, but lack of steady hot sunshine tells. Climate has helped New Zealand to discover a steady stream of talented seam bowlers: A. R. McGibbon, Dick Motz, Bruce Taylor and others have rightly been compared with the pre-war bowling of Jack Cowie, regarded in 1937 as the best of his kind anywhere. But spin bowling has declined. With seamers so successful it is a spendthrift captain who uses spin. It is a sorry business.

Climate plays its part, and here the Australian is by far the more fortunate. New Zealand has a pleasant summer, sometimes a hot one, but the hard, white light of Australia seems to develop and mature players more quickly. National character also tells. New Zealanders have a diffidence the Australians find hard to understand. Modesty may not be as apparent in the New Zealander as it was, but his confidence cannot begin to compare to that of the Australian, whose cricketing heritage strengthens an immense belief in himself.

The slowly-growing confidence is reflected in recent New Zealand performances. Sheer application in 1972 allowed them to draw against the more talented West Indies. The following year in England, New Zealand steeled itself to the immense task of scoring 479 by totting up 440 at Trent Bridge. At Lord's it created a New Zealand Test record of 551 for nine. When Australia ran up a colossal 511 for six at Wellington early in 1974, New Zealand replied with 484. This, it must be conceded, was on a pitch which reduced the most erudite bowler into a day labourer. But, not so long before, a New Zealand side confronted with so huge a total, would almost certainly have crumbled; that twenty-six record would have been at risk.

Because he is very much a part-time player, the New Zealand representative seems to get more enjoyment from his tour than most others. He is seldom blasé. There is still a hint of adventure in it for most of them—office workers, sales representatives, teachers; New Zealand has only two full-time professionals, Glenn Turner and John Parker, both of Worcestershire.

Yet, for all its advances, New Zealand suffers a creaking cricket machinery. Until sponsorship increases, or employers begin to seek cricketers for their payrolls, giving them as much time off as they need, the selection of full-strength teams will continue to be a torment. The supporters' clubs that have been formed in recent years can contribute only a few hundred dollars a year to the game.

Other problems have always lurked nearby, some more than a little bizarre. There are no recorded instances of bottle throwing, crowds surging truculently onto pitches, bonfires lit in grandstands—the diversions enjoyed in some other cricket countries. But beyond New Zealand, no mention has been made of a game stopped by . . . rifle fire. This was in Taranaki in 1866, when British soldiers were engaged in battle with the formidable Hau Haus. Rangers and troops paused in their pursuit for a cricket match; with a rum ration at stake, this match in no way resembled country house cricket.

The players were armed, the batsmen's guns being held by the umpires. This was more a matter of convenience than an insurance against lbw dismissals. It became a very tense, close game. The troopers scored 100, the rangers reached 90 for nine. . . . . A ball was hit a vast distance and the fieldsmen chasing it went to ground as the Hau Haus, hidden in nearby scrub and clearly disenchanted with the quality of the cricket, let loose a hail of bullets. Spectators and players drove off their attackers. Although the odd Maori sniper continued to loose off an occasional shot, the game was resumed. In these circumstances, the rangers' last pair could be forgiven for being parted at 93. The incident may help to explain why the Maori race has not taken kindly to cricket. Maoris have shown a marvellous flair and seething enthusiasm for the faster-moving rugby but have taken little part in New Zealand cricket.

When cricket first began here, transport problems meant that it had to be localized; after the first inter-provincial match in 1860, few such games were played over the next twenty years. With the few roads so rough, players often travelled in tiny coastal steamers; on lesser journeys their coach rides were distinctly uncomfortable.

While local matches were few, New Zealand very early began to receive touring parties of high quality. George Parr had a team in New Zealand in 1864, with a Grace in it, and Julius Caesar. Sponsor of this tour was a Dunedin publican, Mr Shadrach Jones, the first and, so far, the last of the country's cricket impresarios. In 1877–8 the fifteen of Canterbury beat an Australian party, a considerable feat because normally twenty-two players were fielded against so strong a touring team. The victory went to administrative heads. The following summer a Canterbury team that visited Victoria lost everything: form, fortune and finance. The players were stranded in Australia until enough money was collected in Christchurch to bring home the chastened warriors.

By the turn of the century, some fifteen tours had been made by teams from England, Australia, Tasmania, New South Wales, Queensland, Fiji and the Melbourne Cricket Club. The first New Zealand team was assembled to play New South Wales in Christchurch in 1894. Later that year, the New Zealand Cricket Council was formed. One of its early tasks was to organize a tour of Australia in 1898–9. Even in those days, they could not gather together the strongest team. Fifteen years later a second tour was made with somewhat better results. But, it was not until 1927 that New Zealand could send its best team to England. The council had so little money that a limited liability company, 'New Zealand Cricket Ltd', was formed, with ten thousand shares at one pound each sold up and down the country. These investors received an ultimate share of only a few shillings in the pound but the investment had been sound.

This team was captained by Tom Lowry (today a highly successful farmer and racehorse owner) who could be described as an early counterpart of Hampshire's

A batsman of rare charm and courage, Bert Sutcliffe performing one of cricket's delights that left-handers contrive more sweetly than batsmen who stand the other way.

breezy Colin Ingleby-Mackenzie. Strong in build and resolve, he was a hard hitter and a fearless character aggressive in outlook and sometimes in manner. Lowry had captained the Cambridge XI and played some cricket for Somerset, allegedly while wearing a brown homburg hat. He was a successful batsman although he once finished behind R. C. Robertson-Glasgow in the county batting averages.

English cricket authorities were thought to be dubious about more than the quality of this first-ever New Zealand party; they seemed to hold suspicions that the players might have boomerangs in their cricket bags.

Although many games were second-class, this was a full tour. It started with a frenzy of hitting: New Zealanders' 586 for nine in 320 minutes at Holyhead. The bowling was rubbish but this display set the tone for the tour. Two days later, they played MCC at Lord's, a match in which 1,502 runs were scored. On the second day, Lowry, and the exceedingly aggressive C. Dacre—later to bat with distinction for Gloucestershire—made 115 in forty-five minutes. Both scored dazzling centuries.

Lowry was one of six batsmen who topped 1,000 runs in the 26 first-class fixtures. Dacre was another. A third was C. S. Dempster, who showed outstanding quality on his two tours of England and for several seasons with Leicestershire. Apart from leg-spinner W. E. Merritt, the bowling—and the fielding—were indifferent. But the batting had a rollicking air that has never been recaptured. The nearest approach to it was the 1949 team, perhaps New Zealand's strongest batting combination. In that golden summer, eight batsmen scored more than 1,000 runs —a record for a touring team—and the side lost only one match, so nearly equalling the record of the triumphant 1948 Australians. The graceful, gentlemanly Bert Sutcliffe scored 2,627 runs, a tour total only exceeded by Bradman. And there was the charm of Martin Donnelly to further distinguish a happy summer.

The touring party in 1973 had heroic leadership by Bevan Congdon. His two centuries in three Tests could have shaped potential victories; his granite determination showed how much New Zealand cricket had hardened.

Now there had been a tour of the West Indies, two of South Africa, three of India and Pakistan. A Test series was won, for the first time, in Pakistan in 1969. Yet the old phrase must prevail: cricket is more a projection of character than of mere results. The most striking example of this was on the South African tour in the early 1950s, when New Zealand wrote one of the most stirring passages in not just their own but the entire history of cricket.

They were at Ellis Park in Johannesburg. On the morning of the second day, word was received that the fiancée of Bob Blair, the side's fastest bowler, had lost her life in a train disaster which claimed one hundred and fifty people. Blair stayed in his hotel room when the players went to the ground.

After taking the last two South African wickets, the New Zealanders went in to face a very young and very vigorous Neil Adcock. They were regularly struck by the ball rearing from a lively, even dangerous pitch. Two retired hurt. Lawrie Miller departed, coughing blood. Sutcliffe sustained a fearful blow behind an ear. At hospital he fainted twice. John Reid took five sickening blows in his twenty-five minutes of batting.

Soon after lunch, New Zealand's score stood at 59 for five, with two batsmen *hors de combat*. Unexpectedly Miller came in again. He left at 82 for six. Then Sutcliffe emerged into the white light, his head turbanned in bandages, his face pale as parchment. All brilliance and bravery, he attacked, hitting seven sixes in an innings of 80 not out. But the most poignant moment came with the fall of the ninth wicket. The players began to leave the field, Sutcliffe included.

They stopped; and the silence was immense when Blair emerged from the gloom of the tunnel. Sutcliffe went to meet him, put a compassionate arm about his shoulder. Then, the most touching, unforgettable gesture: Blair brushing his glove across his eyes before taking his first ball. The pair batted together for ten minutes. They scored 33, Blair adding a six to Sutcliffe's soaring, graceful hits. New Zealand cricket may sometimes have been short of finesse; it cannot boast about its Test record; but this day above all—and there have been others—showed what it can provide in courage and character.

The game in New Zealand flourishes. It is played keenly and in a proper spirit. There is little of the deliberate intimidation of batsmen by conversational fieldsmen which Australians say is commonplace in their club cricket, and even in interstate games. Public interest has never been stronger. At Test times, crowded pubs are often hushed, the plastic beer hoses idle, for minutes at a time. When New Zealand was fighting for imperishable fame at Trent Bridge and Lord's in 1973, across the world a nation was awake and listening.

It will need more Test successes for the present fervour to survive. To win them, the recent rate of tours and Tests must be maintained. And there is the rub. But cricket in New Zealand is played, at the top level, competently and creditably.

NEW ZEALAND IN TEST CRICKET
(All statistics up to 30 September 1974)

SUMMARY OF RESULTS

	Played	Won	Lost	Drawn
v England	45	0	22	23
v Australia	7	1	4	2
v South Africa	17	2	9	6
v West Indies	14	2	5	7
v India	16	2	7	7
v Pakistan	15	1	5	9
	114	8	52	54

MOST APPEARANCES

J. R. Reid	58
B. E. Congdon	48
B. Sutcliffe	42
G. T. Dowling	39
R. C. Motz	32
V. Pollard	32

MOST RUNS

	Tests	Inns.	N.O.	Runs	H.S.	Av.
J. R. Reid	58	108	5	3,431	142	33·31
B. E. Congdon	48	91	6	2,853	176	33·56
B. Sutcliffe	42	76	8	2,727	230*	40·10
G. T. Dowling	39	77	3	2,306	239	31·16
G. M. Turner	27	49	6	2,196	259	51·06

MOST RUNS IN A SERIES

	Tests	Inns.	N.O.	Runs	H.S.	Av.
G. M. Turner v West Indies 1971–2	5	8	1	672	259	96·00

HIGHEST INDIVIDUAL INNINGS

259	G. M. Turner	v West Indies	Georgetown	1971–2
239	G. T. Dowling	v India	Christchurch	1967–8
230*	B. Sutcliffe	v India	New Delhi	1955–6
223*	G. M. Turner	v West Indies	Kingston	1971–2
206	M. P. Donnelly	v England	Lord's	1949

MOST WICKETS

	Tests	Runs	Wickets	Av.
B. R. Taylor	30	2,953	111	26·60
R. C. Motz	32	3,148	100	31·48
J. R. Reid	58	2,837	85	33·37
R. O. Collinge	23	2,224	83	26·79
H. J. Howarth	24	2,683	77	34·84

MOST WICKETS IN A SERIES

	Tests	Runs	Wickets	Av.
B. R. Taylor v West Indies 1971–2	4	478	27	17·70

BEST BOWLING

7–74   B. R. Taylor v West Indies   Bridgetown   1971–2

CAPTAIN IN MOST TESTS

J. R. Reid   34

* not out.

India: K. N. PRABHU

India's cricket, especially the Test matches, can be broadly classified, like novels on library shelves, into three categories: thrillers, classics and light entertainment. A further category is the 'heavies', almost entirely reserved for Test series against Pakistan. These series are special; they have a flavour of their own, not always smooth to the palate. About them, a native from either side of the border might answer critics as Yorkshiremen are said to mutter to outsiders about Roses matches: 'And what is it to thee?'

India's only visit to Pakistan, in 1953, could have prompted the question: 'What is it to anyone?'; it was hardly worth the notice. The five Tests, three of them on matting wickets, were a travesty of cricket, a futile exercise in statistics. Though India had the batting, with Umrigar, Manjrekar and Ramchand scoring consistently, they lacked the drive and imagination needed to break the deadlock. Indian spinners Gupte, Mankad and Ghulam toiled with limited success against Hanif, Imtiaz and Alimuddin, while the Pakistanis banked on their pacemen, Khan Mohammad, Fazal and Mahmood Hussain. With rival captains Mankad and Kardar content to play for draws, the teams rightly earned the title of 'the dull dogs of cricket'. (The 1963–4 series of five drawn matches against M. J. K. Smith's MCC team could perhaps be classified as a 'heavy'.)

Another grouping, now mercifully defunct, was the period of 'almanac' years during the forties when the domestic content was purged of drama and adventure; the game was often reduced to the sterile statistics of huge batting scores, of which more later. In those years, numerous batting records were set up on pitches as cruel and unyielding as Victorian landlords; the bravest bowlers felt their hearts turning to dust.

In literature, classics can be hewn from tragedy. In cricket, those which linger most vividly and resoundingly in memory stem from success. But not always. Amid the debris of the 1952 team in England, when the ambitious Trueman proved his worth and manhood in scything through the visitors, Vinoo Mankad's performance at Lord's was classically heroic. It earned him the title of 'Magnifico'. He scored 72 and 184. He took five for 196 in 73 overs and then bowled 24 overs for 35 runs. Robertson-Glasgow summed up Mankad's game neatly when he wrote: 'His batting has talent, patient or fervid according to need. His bowling has cool genius. It is accurate, simple of movement but subtle in design, able to wring spin from obstinate surfaces; consistent in variety; nearly inexhaustible. Mankad in attack is instantaneous, timeless in defence; in both most courageous. He is the cat that springs and the cat that walks.' Extraordinary tribute for a player in a team so overpowered; it lost even that Test match.

Classical, too, were the centuries at Old Trafford in 1936 by Mushtaq Ali and V. M. Merchant, another disastrous tour which was punctuated by dissensions, unholy wrangles and the amazing despatch back home of Lala Amarnath before the first Test, despite splendid allround performances. These two innings drew the richest purple from Cardus's pen. Mushtaq and Merchant were noted figures in India's age of elegance that stretched from the thirties—despite the run-mountains of the immediate postwar years—to include the 1946 tour so dear in memory because it brought back the sunlit joys of international cricket after six years of Hitler and other undesirables. That summer was made glorious by the batting of Merchant, Hazare, Modi and Pataudi senior and by the bowling of Mankad and Amarnath.

But the true classics of success were India's three winning series in the span of two years: 2-0 over the West Indies in the Caribbean early in 1971; 1-0 over England in England the following summer; and 2-1 over England at home in 1972–3. They were historic not only as the richest passage in Indian cricket history but also because the unexpected and shattering brevity of this exultation had a ripe 'Indianness' about it. The numbing 3-0 defeat on English soil in 1974 was like having an eldest son who had brilliantly passed his Bar examination, won his first case resoundingly, then suffered some inexplicable amnesia which emptied his head of accrued knowledge. The setbacks put an edge to the words of a noted contemporary Australian cricketer who had said: 'The Poms are the hardest country to beat at cricket. They never give up; someone has always got his head down and is grafting away at you. They seldom give you the feeling you can skittle them that the Indians sometimes offer.'

In 1974 how distant seemed that misty August morning at the Oval in 1971 when Chandra, his shirt tails flapping in the breeze, took six for 38 to prostrate England for 101 and enable India to return home with the Golden Fleece. That bounty had an even warmer lustre in the cold season of 1972–3, largely through Chandra's record 35 wickets at 18·91 apiece. Yet Lewis's touring team, dismissed as a 'second eleven', proved good enough to push India all the way. India never really recovered from the trauma of defeat at Delhi—Wadekar's first as captain—but he managed to maintain his run of good luck. The matches at Calcutta and Madras could have gone either way. Greig harassed the Indians on the field and entertained others off it. India's spin attack, honed sharp by the fielding of Solkar, Abid Ali and Venkat in the close-in positions, cast a spell over the leading England batsmen. By the way he handled his men, by his carriage and bearing, Tony Lewis restored to English cricket the image it had presented when India first took to the game.

To borrow a simile from Cardus: 'Gandhi and Gunga Din would have been satisfied.' Perhaps the reversals of 1974 are put into perspective when one considers that Bedi, for Northamptonshire, and Venkat, for Derbyshire, had between them bowled more than 1,600 overs in county cricket the previous summer. Familiarity had perhaps bred something. What a contrast in their ceaseless toil and presentation of their wares to the Australian Clarrie Grimmett, who would not even bowl to his Australian teammates at the nets; he knew they would be rivals when they changed the green for other caps.

Like the books, cricket thrillers have worn many jackets, some of them lurid. Among these was the first West Indian tour in 1948–9 when Goddard responded to Phadkar's unwise bouncers at Madras by unleashing Trim and Jones. Then India were robbed of a chance of drawing the rubber at Bombay, with six runs left for a win. The drawn series against Simpson's 1964 Australians had its tense moments: a close affair at Madras and Chandra giving India a chance to win at Bombay with four for 50 and four for 74. The five-match series with Dexter's 1961 tourists excited and entertained. Barrington (594) and Manjrekar (586) hit record aggregates for their respective sides; Borde and Durrani gave India the initiative for a good win at Madras. In Australia in 1967–8, the tourists did not win a Test, but skipper Pataudi's glorious knocks of 75 and 85 at Melbourne drew unabashed superlatives from commentator Frank Tyson and spectator Lindsay Hassett.

As light entertainment for the visitors, India in 1956 eased the bruises of Johnson's homeward-bound Australians, who used the series as a decompression period from Laker and saw the first pure gleams of mastery from Benaud. The same year, John Reid's New Zealanders were untaxing entertainment for India, Mankad and Roy scoring a record 413 for the first wicket at Madras, Sutcliffe and Reid replying massively for New Zealand. Eight years later, another team led by Reid provided interesting finishes in most of the Tests. Perhaps the best of the entertainments was the 1951–2 series against Nigel Howard's nondescript MCC party in which only Graveney and Statham would perhaps have been good enough for selection against Australia. The match at Chepauk had the overtones of a classic for India. With centuries by Roy and Umrigar to back them, Mankad and Ghulam enabled Hazare to claim the honour of leading India to their first Test win against England.

In all countries, what has been bred in the bone manifests itself in the character, attitude and style of the cricketers. From Nayudu and Naoomal to Wadekar and Venkat, the players have reflected India's changing mores and styles. Those who toured England in 1932 batted with an extravagance that belonged to those spacious times. Watching them, Cardus was moved to write: 'Yesterday we saw more cutting and driving during any one hour of the day than we had seen on the same field all season. It was impossible to take one's eyes off the action for fear of missing a beautiful hit.'

If Archie MacLaren represented the best of cricket's Golden Age, Nayudu was no less a true representative of his times. Like W. G. Grace, he was a legend in his lifetime. Every schoolboy tried to imitate him. His reputation as a hitter of sixes was sustained to the very end of his career; he retired when he was near sixty. Old timers recall a picture of him examining a ball found in a waterspout at Folkestone. It had been lodged there the previous season by another big hitter, H. B. Cameron, of South Africa. Perhaps, in his reflective study of that battered ball, Nayudu was working out the extra loft and velocity it would have needed to have cleared the stands. Unlike the bowler himself, he would have dearly relished Sobers's historic attack on Malcolm Nash of Glamorgan in 1968.

Players of the Nayudu era in India had no formal schooling in the arts and crafts of the game. They were born free and lived free. At this nascent stage, there was no place for sophistication. Observers of those days marked the absence of googly bowlers and spinners of class. Consequently, the Indians were at home against pace bowling. The team of 1932 was applauded for exploding the theory that 'the bowling of today cannot be cut with safety'. It was not to be wondered that India's chief weakness was against leg-break bowling and Cardus wrote with prophetic insight: 'When they have mastered the trick of it, the best team in England will have to look out.'

Till the forties, India's cricket was largely a matter of doing what comes naturally. The accountants and theoreticians had not arrived on the scene. The game was largely a weekend affair. It was run by the princes and the gentry, with the Roshanara tournament, at Delhi, and the Moin-ud-Dowla, in Hyderabad, drawing the best talent in the land. The wickets were fast and the lesser games were played on coir matting which encouraged bowling above medium pace and the enterprising stroke-player.

With the gradual dissolution of the princely houses, Indian cricket was to become more formal and disciplined in character, though from time to time a Mushtaq Ali and a Mankad would defy the rational laws of batting. Visiting teams also influenced the character and technique of the players; now there was more to cricket than 'having a dip'. There could have been no better exponents of the new schools than the two Vijays, Merchant and Hazare. Here was form and style, trim and disciplined to meet all needs, all situations, all wickets. Indeed, after the 1936 tour, with England facing a shortage of opening batsmen, Cardus wished he could paint Merchant white and take him to Australia as Warburton.

If the English summer of 1947 was taken up by the race between Compton and Edrich to outdo Hayward, the immediate post-war years in India witnessed a similar duel between Hazare and Merchant on the flawless Brabourne wicket. When Hazare scored an unbeaten 316 for Maharashtra against Baroda, Merchant bettered it with an unbeaten 359 for Bombay against Maharashtra. A knock of 288 by Hazare against Holkar eclipsed the 278 by Merchant against the same team.

On and on it went: B. B. Nimbalkar, with 443 not out, and K. V. Bhandarkar put on 455 for Maharashtra's second wicket against a weak Kathiawar attack on the flawless Poona wicket. (It was fitting that John Jameson, one of the two players who later broke this record, 465 unfinished with Kanhai for Warwickshire against Gloucestershire at Edgbaston in 1974, was born in Bombay.) Kathiawar, who had made only 238, conceded the match as Maharashtra, at 826 for four, had not reached the point of satiety, like the characters in the film *La Grande Bouffe*, who set out to gorge themselves to death. Later the Indian Board—by this time, the groaning Board—introduced a rule to prevent such walk-overs. That season of 1948–9 was remembered not only for the visit of the first West Indies team, but for the tall scores registered in the Ranji Trophy. In the semi-final between Bombay and Maharashtra as many as 2,376 runs were scored for 38 wickets, eclipsing the 2,078 for forty wickets by Bombay against Holkar in 1944–5 (of which Denis Compton, then on Army service in India, scored 249 not out for Holkar).

It was, however, too good to last. Crowds had begun to tire of these soulless exercises in statistics. The wickets pampered the batsmen. Even the fainthearted and the mediocre could get away with it. A batsman's talent was measured not by his technique but by the tenure of his innings. Nimbalkar's bid to beat Bradman's highest was seen in its true perspective, for it was 'no contest' between two poorly-matched sides. It is true there was no dearth of talent. But a professional element had crept in which was to be the bane of Indian cricket.

Amarnath, the first to venture in the Lancashire League, was an 'original'. Against Jardine's 1933–4 visiting team, he had hit 118 in his first Test appearance at Bombay, prompting E. H. D. Sewell to write in *The Times of India* that he was as good a batsman as Duleep. Like his mentor, there was no suppressing Amarnath's indomitable spirit. But others who followed were not immune to the dour, businesslike approach to the game. A certain air of caution had begun to creep in— a marked disinclination to take risks, a tendency to run for cover, or play safe at the least sign of danger. Thus these times could be called 'the age of endurance'. There was an air of disenchantment and it left its mark on cricket, which became largely functional.

This helped to push Indian cricket towards its nadir: the 1959 tour of England, which brought their game into disrepute. They lost all five Tests and won only six of thirty-three matches. It was a depressing experience. D. K. Gaekwad never looked the part of a captain. Much had been expected of leg-spinner Subhash Gupte, hailed as the best in the game, but the wickets were not to his liking. However, there were faint glimmers of hope: players like Baig, Contractor, Jaisimha, Borde and Nadkarni promised well for the future. Baig, summoned up from Oxford University, joined the select band who have scored a century on their first Test appearance with 112 at Manchester. But the Indians were no match for

Cowdrey's England, with Barrington giving hints of the scourge of bowlers he was to become; Alan Davidson's hamstrings may still twang at the memory of him.

Summing up that series *The Times* cricket correspondent wrote: 'If India are to do better next time, they will have to get down to making more of the ability they have. In the field there is room for vast improvement.' Luckily for India, their next series was against Benaud's Australians on their first full-length tour. Considerate as he was intelligent, Benaud restrained Davidson, Lindwall and Rorke from triggering off a fusillade of bumpers as Alexander's West Indians had done the year before. Mainly through Benaud's fairness and exceedingly high popularity, a new spirit was swiftly pumped into Indian cricket. At the end of the series, Benaud swapped ties with his opposite Ramchand, much smaller token than the riches the admiring crowds would have offered had they been theirs to give.

With the princes out of the picture by the fifties, the business houses had taken over. During an English summer, players like Manjrekar (who never quite fulfilled his early promise of becoming another Merchant), Umrigar and Gupte were given a lien on their jobs while they played in the Lancashire League. While this added to their proficiency, it also made for staleness. Gupte, whose flight and spin had bewitched the West Indians on their own grounds, was never quite the same bowler, barring brief spells against West Indies in 1958 and England in 1961. On their return, these players had no respite as they had to fulfil commitments in a crowded domestic programme.

There was a dramatic change in the sixties. A new generation of cricketers had arisen. They had worked their way from school and college to claim the attention of the national selectors by their performances in the Ranji Trophy. Players like Contractor and Engineer, Pataudi and Baig, Wadekar, Sardesai, Venkat, Bedi and Prasanna introduced a new element of assurance and disciplined performances into our cricket. It was sophisticated, yet there were hints of the esoteric past. Pataudi showed his verve with the remark that E. W. Swanton quoted in his autobiography that he knew he could bat with only one eye 'when I saw the English bowling'. Under Pataudi, a new spirit was manifest in our cricket, exemplified by his dynamic approach to batting and fielding. Unlike other occasions, the three Tests of 1967 were lost without dishonour. Pataudi's 148 at Leeds was the mainspring for India's 510, her highest Test score against England; the 'Tiger' had bold and unmistakable stripes.

India seems to be unique among major cricketing nations in that cricket here is a game for all seasons. In some part or the other of this sub-continent, it is played right through the year, in the bracing cold of North India, the monsoon of the west coast and in the pitiless scorching summer of the plains. But the official season lasts from November to March. This is the best part of the year, marked by festivals, vivid sunsets and a nip in the air. Divisions between north and south are even more marked than they are in England. In the north and east, while hockey and

V. M. Merchant showing Hutton slow on the bend at The Oval in 1946. Merchant could be classical and merciless; Cardus wanted to paint him white as a 'ring-in' for MCC's 1936–7 tour.

football are popular, cricket is just another game. In the south, it is a leisurely pastime. But in Western India, Bombay particularly, cricket is a religion.

Bombay man is a real fanatic. This accounts for Bombay's supremacy in the Ranji Trophy and the large number of Test players turned out in this city. A Bombay suburb, Shivaji Park, has been to Indian cricket what Pudsey was to English cricket years ago. It has provided Wadekar and Gavaskar, Manjrekar, Ramakant Desai and others who have been the mainstay of the city's and the country's cricket.

In Bombay, cricket is played throughout the year, even at the height of the monsoon; perhaps this explains the number of technically proficient batsmen produced. Besides, Bombay's cricket-besotted followers—comparable in ardour to Liverpool and Manchester football fans—could match their counterparts on the Hill at Sydney or Bourda Oval in Georgetown. John Woodcock of *The Times* once wrote that the noise at the stadium, when a new batsman took guard, reminded him of the whine of a jet ready to take off.

Nowhere in the world do so many film stars and elegantly-garbed women attend a cricket match. And it is here that Abbas Ali Baig, after a match-saving innings against Benaud's team in 1959, had the rare and gratifying experience of being embraced and kissed by an ecstatic teenager, better surely than the back-pummelling from freckled youngsters that Ian Chappell once had to endure on one of his own cricket grounds, losing his cap into the bargain.

It must be admitted also that nowhere in the world do so many people suffer in the cause of cricket as they do in Bombay. In the cheaper stands they are herded and penned within eight-foot high barbed wire fences. Watching cricket within these miniature 'stalags', without toilet or refreshment facilities, can be sheer torture. Any little incident is enough to provoke the mob, like the one in December 1969 when Venkat was given caught at the wicket, although the Australian wicketkeeper Taber was not among those who appealed.

Eden Gardens of Calcutta has been another trouble spot. The average Bengali takes his sport seriously. But he can be volatile and emotional when it comes to dealing with the police and authority. And it was authority that bungled on New Year's Day of 1967 when the popular stands, burst by overcrowding, spilled onto the field, to be sent back reeling by a ruthless cane and tear gas charge by the police. The boil-over of the crowd did not stem from any incident on the field of play.

Eden Gardens is apt to raise the spirits of visiting seam bowlers, for the humid smog from the Hoogly hangs over the ground for a good part of the day. Bengal abounds with seam bowlers, but rarely do they get a chance to exploit their skills on the slow turners elsewhere.

Talent has been concentrated mainly in the west and south; Bombay's main challenger has been from the south. When Bombay lost on the first innings to Mysore in the Ranji Trophy semi-final of 1973–4, it yielded the primacy after fifteen long years. Mysore went on to win the championship by outplaying Rajasthan. The inherent weakness of the competition is exposed by the fact that Rajasthan barely managed to survive the league rounds.

It is interesting to search for parallels. Bombay's Ranji Trophy record reminds one of the equally impressive achievements of Surrey and Yorkshire, New South Wales and Victoria. Bombay, too, has always played the game 'tight', like the Yorkshire teams of old. With so many Test players in its side, Bombay has an efficient, professional approach about it. Even when most of the stalwarts were away—as in 1961 in the West Indies, 1967–8 in Australia and 1971 in the West Indies—they were able to ward off all challengers.

From the days of Merchant and Modi, down to Wadekar and Gavaskar, their batting has been their main strength; Bombay cricketers are raised in a tough school. They play a large part of their cricket—the Kanga League—on wet wickets during the monsoon season. And for their commercial firms, they compete in numerous tournaments.

How the West was stunned. B. S. Chandrasekhar clings to a return catch from John Snow at The Oval in 1971. Chandra won this match, then bemused England throughout the next series.

Indian cricket reached its apogee in 1971 with successive series wins over West Indies and England. To celebrate, municipal authorities at Indore built a sixty-foot-high 'Victory Bat' with players' names in Hindi.

The northerners are the sturdy race. Their martial virtues have been celebrated in narrative and song by Kipling. According to tradition, the north has been the seed-bed for India's fast bowlers. But most of the 'quickies' of recent times have come from the west and east where conditions favour seam bowlers. After partition of the land, the north has not produced fast bowlers of the type of Nissar, Nazir Ali and Jehangir Khan or attractive strokeplayers like Amarnath and Wazir Ali.

Now, with its headquarters in Delhi, cricket has become more a social occasion. Each morning, play is interrupted for introduction of dignitaries. During Tests, women keep knitting away—like so many Madame de Farges awaiting the fall of heads. But the scene itself is tempered by kindlier images. Hampers of food are set out, music oozes from transistor radios washing over the festive scene until the cool, pearly haze settles over the minarets of the Jumma Masjid.

In the south, the game is something of an intellectual exercise. After all, it is the south that gave us Venkat, Prasanna and Chandrasekhar. They have supplanted Gupte and Mankad, who had made spin bowling a western speciality. The ground at Chepauk, when the late Con Johnstone presided over it, was very much like the Saffrons. But the soft Kentish tones have now been crowded out by the harsh outlines of giant superstructures to house the Test match crowds. But, to the Tamilian, cricket is essentially the game with the lovely name. He is ever ready to bestow due praise on the opposition. In 1959, a crowd of enthusiasts presented a silk shawl to Benaud. Only an overzealous umpire prevented Australia's popular captain from completing the over with the gift draped around his shoulders. When Lewis's men were hard pressed, they were egged on with rousing exhortations from Churchill's speeches. It was the south which gave us Ramanujam (protege of G. H. Hardy, the great mathematician), whose love for cricket has been described so admirably in C. P. Snow's *Variety of Men*.

Kanpur has, of late, lost its Test status. Green Park was always a seething cauldron. Ringed in by steelhelmeted police, with a student crowd as volatile as *aficionados* of the bullring, watching and playing cricket here was always an adventure. Kanpur's enthusiasts can never be said to be partial. They have pelted and felled home players, as well as visitors, with fruit and stones.

Now the Test honour goes to Bangalore. This garden city deserves it. For Bangalore has always been associated with good cricket and cricketers: Chandra, Prasanna and Viswanath. It is proud, too, of another 'native son'—M. C. Cowdrey.

In recent years there has been, as usual, a clamour for more reform of the Ranji Trophy tournament. Down the years, the Ranji Trophy has undergone many modifications. It has been enlarged to include teams from the Railways and Services and the new States formed with the reorganization of the country. From 1956 it has been played regionally on a league basis, with the qualifiers from each of the five zones—north, south, east, west and central—taking part in knock-out rounds. From 1970–1, the scheme has been enlarged to provide for two qualifiers from each zone to compete in the last rounds of the tournament. But these reforms have failed to upset the cricket balance of power in the country. It has been urged that the powerful teams be separated from the 'also rans', and greater prominence be given to the Duleep Trophy, which is a stiffer and keener contest. In the season of 1973–4 a new force was manifest in our game when North Zone, led by Bedi, caught West Zone on a lively wicket at Poona and their batting had enough staying power to win the Duleep Trophy for the first time.

While the sad summer of 1974 seemed to underline the cynical statement that the only certainty about Indian cricket is its 'inglorious uncertainty', the country's cricket is now capable of taking this setback in its stride. Schools and colleges are regular recruiting grounds and, under a sound administration, the game has begun to prosper. Its heart too, is sound. For, along with the educated and sophisticated, we have originals who would do credit to the hornyhanded artisans of the past.

Among them is one of India's most talented allrounders. The story goes that, when he was out shopping during the off-day of a Test match, he passed a pet shop. When one of his mates expressed surprise at the variety of food for pets, this player remarked: 'Why not? Aren't they also human beings?' You must expect the unexpected response in a country whose cricket has drawn a froth of ecstasy and scorn in succeeding breaths; where the silken raiment of success and sackcloth hang side by side in the dressing-room lockers.

INDIA IN TEST CRICKET
(All statistics up to 30 September 1974)

SUMMARY OF RESULTS

	Played	Won	Lost	Drawn
v England	48	6	22	20
v Australia	25	3	16	6
v West Indies	28	1	12	15
v New Zealand	16	7	2	7
v Pakistan	15	2	1	12
	132	19	53	60

MOST APPEARANCES

P. R. Umrigar	59
C. G. Borde	55
V. L. Manjrekar	55
V. Mankad	44
P. Roy	43
Nawab of Pataudi, jnr.	42
F. M. Engineer	41
R. G. Nadkarni	41

Bishan Bedi, slow left-arm for India and Northamptonshire, he has been asked to spin an almost-new ball as glazed as a toffee apple.

(Above) And you thought Calcutta was crowded! After scoring the winning run against England at The Oval in 1971, Abid Ali has his potential claustrophobia tested by a foam of Indian fans.

(Right) Sunil Gavaskar faded somewhat after a sensational debut series for India against West Indies, then recovered his form. Saturday-afternoon players can but dream of such footwork and wristiness.

(Below) 'Patient or fervid according to need.' Vinoo Mankad in 1952, when his allround performance at Lord's was 'classically heroic'.

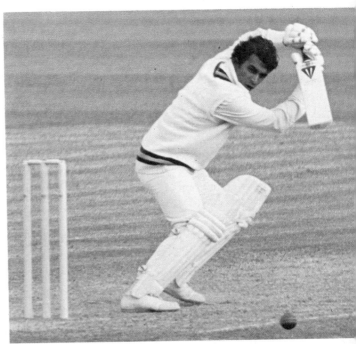

MOST RUNS

	Tests	Inns.	N.O.	Runs	H.S.	Av.
P. R. Umrigar	59	94	8	3,631	223	42·22
V. L. Manjrekar	55	92	10	3,209	189*	39·13
C. G. Borde	55	97	11	3,062	177*	35·60
Nawab of Pataudi, jnr.	42	76	3	2,698	203*	36·95

MOST RUNS IN A SERIES

	Tests	Inns.	N.O.	Runs	H.S.	Av.
S. M. Gavaskar v West Indies 1970–71	4	8	3	774	220	154·80

HIGHEST INDIVIDUAL INNINGS

231	V. Mankad	v New Zealand	Madras	1955–6
223	P. R. Umrigar	v New Zealand	Hyderabad	1955–6
223	V. Mankad	v New Zealand	Bombay	1955–6
220	S. M. Gavaskar	v West Indies	Port of Spain	1970–71

MOST WICKETS

	Tests	Runs	Wickets	Av.
V. Mankad	44	5,236	162	32·32
S. P. Gupte	36	4,402	149	29·54
E. A. S. Prasanna	30	3,933	137	28·70
B. S. Bedi	35	3,934	131	30·03
B. S. Chandrasekhar	26	3,109	112	27·75

MOST WICKETS IN A SERIES

	Tests	Runs	Wickets	Av.
B. S. Chandrasekhar v Eng. 1972–3	5	662	35	18·91
V. Mankad v Eng. 1951–2	5	571	34	16·79
S. P. Gupte v N.Z. 1955–6	5	669	34	19·67

BEST BOWLING

9–69	J. M. Patel	v Australia	Kanpur	1959–60
9–102	S. P. Gupte	v West Indies	Kanpur	1958–9
8–52	V. Mankad	v Pakistan	New Delhi	1952–3
8–55	V. Mankad	v England	Madras	1951–2
8–72	S. Venkataraghavan	v New Zealand	New Delhi	1964–5
8–79	B. S. Chandrasekhar	v England	New Delhi	1972–3

1,000 RUNS AND 100 WICKETS

	Tests	Runs	Wickets
V. Mankad	44	2,109	162

CAPTAIN IN MOST TESTS

Nawab of Pataudi, jnr.   36

* not out.

Pakistan: ZAKIR HUSSAIN SYED

In 1971, the Pakistan hockey team returned home after winning the World Cup and with it the Grand Slam—they had earlier won the Asian and Olympic titles. They were given an historic welcome but this was as a zephyr to a hurricane when compared with the welcome the Pakistan cricket team received in 1954 when they came home from England after drawing the series in their first official encounter. The joyously-received victory at The Oval established cricket as the number one sport in Pakistan—a fact which even hockey administrators have grudgingly come to accept. At the time, many people considered the Oval victory a fluke, but later victories over Australia and the West Indies confirmed the great potential of Pakistani cricketers.

During those early years, the Pakistan cricket team was built around Hanif Mohammad the batsman, Fazal Mahmood the bowler, Imtiaz Ahmad the wicketkeeper and, above all, Abdul Hafeez Kardar the captain. There were other useful cricketers in the teams and touring parties but not many who would have been coveted by selectors from other countries.

Hanif Mohammad was the little master whose youthful eyes had sometimes peered at opposing bowlers from beneath the brim of a solar topee. 'Mr Concentration' he came to be called—both a tribute to his skills and a lament at the leash he was so often compelled to wear at the crease. For almost two decades he was most of the vertebrae in the spinal column of Pakistan's batting. As long as Hanif Mohammad was still batting the Pakistanis could expect miracles. He was as reliable, as constant as a nuclear-powered clock; his dismissals between thirty and a hundred were amazingly low.

Yet, despite his greatness, he was often the target of criticism for his slow scoring. Such comments could scarcely have been more unkind. Hanif was one of the greatest stroke-players in the world, as many a bowler would testify, but he was forced to curb his stroke-playing on many occasions to keep his team's innings alive. His immersion in the job of scoring runs was almost total. Hanif was once dismissed, for a very high score, in a Quad-e-Azam trophy match, caught at silly mid-off. He refused to move. The opposing captain later told me Hanif had stood his ground *not* to contest the decision but because he could not immediately process the thought that his long innings was finally over.

Fazal Mahmood, as long as he played international cricket, was the deadliest seamer of his type. If the wicket gave the slightest help, his curling leg-cutters must have evoked in batsmen's minds that oft-quoted vision of a striking cobra. Once he was on top, there was no escape, even for batsmen of the calibre of Neil Harvey. Most of Pakistan's early victories were carved by his bowling. He was the first Pakistan bowler to take ten wickets against England, India, Australia and the West Indies. His value to Pakistan cricket can be determined from one set of figures: twelve for 99 v England at The Oval, 1954.

At a time when the fielding of most of his team-mates was only of average club standard, the consummately efficient Imtiaz Ahmad was a great inspiration and example. He was never spectacular but was brilliant when it counted most for a wicketkeeper—he rarely missed a catch. And, mind you, wicketkeeping was not his only virtue; he was one of Pakistan's leading batsmen in his day and possibly—here McCabe's admirers may quibble—the finest hooker the game has seen. When he was a Test player, the hook shot was considered by many of the most talented batsmen as a dangerously risky shot. So it was all the more marvellous to see Imtiaz step outside his off stump and hook bumpers from Trueman, Hall, Griffith, Gilchrist, Lindwall and Davidson with admirable ease and confidence. Cricket enthusiasts everywhere adored his style of play. Even today, long after his retirement, he is perhaps the most popular cricketer Pakistan has produced.

However, more than any other single individual, it was one person, A. H. Kardar, who was responsible for developing early Pakistan teams into fighting units; he forged a tradition for those who followed to grasp like a battle pennant. When administrators were looking for a suitable person to replace Mian Saeed Ahmad, the ageing cricket captain, many eyes swung towards Kardar. Not everyone was keen; his appointment brought a number of frowns. But very swiftly this tall Oxford Blue justified his appointment. He was a man with the strength of natural leadership in his bones; even selectors dared not disagree with him; he was the 'skipper' to all, including governors and ministers. The power he achieved through this deference was a blessing because Hafeez Kardar could field the teams he wanted—and produce results. In later years, his decision to go into politics was widely welcomed. People who knew him personally or had followed his career more distantly were not surprised at his success in the 1971 elections and later his place in the Punjab Cabinet as a senior minister.

Another reason for the early success of Pakistan cricket was the sound organizational structure which the newly-formed nation inherited at the time of independence. Lahore was one of the leading established cricket centres in the subcontinent. Here were played two grades of cricket—club and university.

Club cricket was extremely fiercely contested as, like the English county system, it had a weight of tradition. Fanatically loyal to their clubs, players brimmed with pride when turning out for them. It was all amateur stuff. Most club matches were played at Iqbal Park in the shadow of the famous Badshahi mosque and the Lahore fort, two of the finest examples anywhere of the Great Moghul architec-

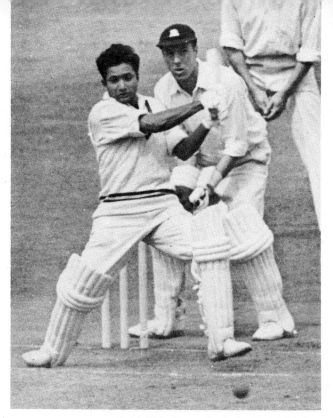

(Left) 'Mr Concentration'. Hanif Mohammad casting aside his usual compulsory restraint with a satisfying slog against England in 1962.

(Right) In 1971 Northamptonshire dropped Sarfraz Nawaz from its list. Three years later he could achieve 3 for 51 and 53 against England at Leeds, with hints of better to come.

ture. Crowds of more than ten thousand were not uncommon (players in Sydney grade cricket, turning out for, say, Mosman v Western Suburbs, might well blink at that figure). Some spectators travelled from very distant areas to enjoy a match between the Crescent Club and the Mamdot Club or the Lahore Gymkhana and the Friends Club. While the players sweated their guts out in the middle in 120°F temperature, the animated crowd entertained itself by drinking *sherbat* (soft drink), or eating *haleem* (a very spicy meat dish) and *kulfi* (the Pakistani version of icecream).

During those periods when the Pakistani Test calendar was sparsely filled, these club matches were the ultimate competitions; they were played throughout the year without a break in schedules. The credibility of the success of these competitions becomes stronger when it is realized that they had no organized financial base. Cricket lovers ran and financed most of the clubs. The most renowned of these patrons were Chacha Sharif Churchill, A. Rable Nizami, Q. D. Butt and Qureshi. They transported their teams to matches in *tongas* (horse-drawn

The assertiveness and correctness of Wasim Raja, one of his country's newer batsmen, were two reasons why Pakistan in the mid-1970s faced the future with confidence.

passenger carriers), gave them lunch and, at the end of the match, presented a simple prize to each of the most outstanding performers.

University cricket was restricted to a younger age group. Government College, Lahore and Islamia College, Lahore almost invariably reached the final of the University Cricket tournament. Like the old-time battle of the Roses in England, the clash between these two rivals was considered the match of the year. Supporters of both colleges, tooting on bugles and trumpets and pounding drums, swarmed along to ensure the finale to their tournament had all the bubbling excitement of a last night at the Proms in London's Albert Hall. Every over was as tense as a sitar string. Observers could justly say that any player who did well under the prodigious pressure of this match had the nerves to acquit himself well in Test cricket. Consequently, almost ninety per cent of Pakistan Test teams down the years comprised players who had emerged unsinged from the drama of 'the great University match' at the University grounds. The Lahore Gymkhana ground, one of the oldest Test centres in Pakistan, was the other major scene of cricket activity. Surrounded by centuries-old, huge banyan trees and the lush green of Lawrence Gardens, it is one of the few grounds in the entire sub-continent with a turf wicket.

Unfortunately, popularity has drained away from both club and university cricket for a number of reasons. Financial support from individual patrons has dried up; one individual, no matter how rich, cannot afford nowadays to run a club singlehanded. While the introduction of more departmental clubs has swelled the numbers, the standard of the cricket played has declined. Initially, in Lahore, there used to be, say, fifty good first-class cricketers playing against each other regularly. Now there are almost four hundred pretty average club cricketers in various teams; the edge has gone from the competition. This is regrettable because the deterioration of club cricket means the weakening of one more nursery and there have never been many of these in Pakistan. Dwindling interest from heads of the institutions has made university cricket more anaemic; with indifference at the top, players do not have the incentive to work hard at their cricket. The final between the traditional rivals had been reduced to an ordinary match; again the parallel with Roses matches seems sadly retained.

So Karachi began to overtake Lahore as the established and pertinent cricket centre. Cricketers from Karachi and Lahore have shown marked differences in their approach to the game. The Karachi players have tended to be more defence-oriented and technically superior to their counterparts from the Punjab, who are aggressive and attacking by nature. Crowds loved this style of play immensely but the consistency of Punjabis in first-class and Test cricket has not matched the dourer approach of Karachi players.

By 1960, Karachi was entrenched as an additional cricket centre, but Pakistan cricket in general was on the decline. More than anything else, the inefficient

They also serve who only kneel and pray. A tranquil, private moment for a Pakistani supporter at Lord's 1974. Rain later saved his team from miserable defeat.

organization of the Board of Control for Cricket in Pakistan (BCCP) was responsible for this rapid downhill slide. The BCCP had no permanent headquarters. It consisted of Ghulam Mustafa, the full-time assistant secretary, and his trunk of files and records. The Board moved to wherever its president was posted. Most presidents were non-professionals who gained their appointment largely through their prominent status in society. Without a permanent secretariat and burdened with 'part-time' presidents, the BCCP could not function as an effective instrument to promote and improve the game in Pakistan. There was no planning and no system.

The Board was responsible for organizing just one tournament a year at national level and struggled pitifully to do this satisfactorily. Players had few chances to play first-class matches; sediment gathered in the conduits to block younger players from emerging; established players, no matter how unfit or out of form, began to take their places in the national team for granted. Without a system of elimination, newcomers had no incentive to improve; they had to show extraordinarily brilliant talent to clear a path towards the top. More by providence than anything else, such fine talents did come along: Mushtaq, Intikhab, Majid, Asif Iqbal, Syed Zaheer Abbas, Wasim Bari, Sadiq Mohammad, Javed Burki, Pervez Sajjad and Salim Altaf. The irrepressible thrust of their talents crashed them through into international cricket, not poised and responsible manipulations from the Board; these have been sadly lacking. This gulf was the major reason that the Pakistan team, while containing many brilliant players, could not be welded into a unified force to match the results of lesser, yet illustrious, predecessors.

This brings me to another very important point. Not a single cricketer from Pakistan, with the possible exception of the great Hanif Mohammad, has been fortunate enough to have received serious professional training in his early years. That most of these players mentioned above have matched the best in the world emphasizes the natural talent that abounds in Pakistan. Also, not inhibited by restrictions which can develop through relentless coaching, Pakistani cricketers thoroughly enjoy every minute of every game. It is their intense enthusiasm which has appealed to spectators everywhere. On very few occasions have Pakistani cricketers deliberately or cynically mauled the spirit of the game through the way they have approached a situation or match. One could conceivably argue that they have not produced the results in Test matches that the experience many of them have received in the steeliness of the English county game should have brought about. To me, for one, this is not a major tragedy; results purely as results should be secondary.

It is inevitable that I should study in depth the almost unbelievable contribution the Mohammad family has made to Pakistan cricket over two decades. Elsewhere cricketing families have been prominent: the Harveys of Australia; the Pollocks of South Africa; the Richardsons of England; Ranji, Duleep and the two Nawabs of Pataudi of India. Other than the Mohammads, the family clusters in Pakistan have been more profuse than in other countries.

There is the Khan family (Burki, Majid and Imran), the Rana family (Shafqat, Sultan and Azmat) and the Ahmed brothers, Saeed and Younis. Imposing as their records are—and the Khans have provided two Pakistan captains, Burki and Majid—the Mohammad family of Wazir, Hanif, Mushtaq and Sadiq towers above them all. Almost half of the Test centuries scored by Pakistan have flowed from the bats of this one family. Since Pakistan came into Test cricket, as least one member has been in every side.

To me the most astonishing thing about them is the way that each differs so strongly from the others in style of play and approach to the game, which, in itself, is surely proof of cricketing genius. Wazir was methodical; Hanif a perfectionist to the very core; Mushtaq dashing and solid and Sadiq flamboyant. The younger brothers have been the luckiest; the elders have invariably helped them along. Hanif nursed Mushtaq into a permanent place in the Test side, while

Mushtaq has guided Sadiq in the job of establishing himself. Hanif, having scored a superlative century against West Indies in the Dacca Test of 1959–60, withdrew from the Lahore Test so that Mushtaq could get a chance. As the youngest, Sadiq is the last of the line, but there is no doubt that he will try to coach Hanif's son Shoaib into the Test team before he retires. So the caravan of Mohammads could go on forever. Had an English family contributed such a concentrated and magnificent rôle to its country's cricket, the father would have been granted an earldom and the mother an independent damehood at the very least.

Even their considerable and unbroken impact has not prevented Pakistani cricket from having an emaciated look; it is starved for success. Wickets have been a perennial problem. The placid turf pitches at Lahore and Karachi have daunted bowlers and thwarted results in all levels of cricket; the Dacca pitch has never woken from its habitual slumbers to permit anything but drawn matches. Compared to them the Pindi club strip was a rare oddity: not only was it the only pitch which helped bowlers at all, it was so good for spinners they feasted on it. Pindi was used only once for a Test match—against New Zealand. The projected five-day Test was over in three. A definite result and the interesting activity of falling wickets proved distressing to some—the pitch has been condemned ever since.

The sway of bat over ball in Pakistan has all but crushed the spirit of many bowlers; they have found it agonizing to keep pounding away against such massive odds. This has helped to explain why Pakistan teams bat so deep but top-class bowlers have been so scarce.

The authorities were not blind to this handicap. Some years ago they decided to experiment, to change their lifeless monsters into spinning wickets. Then, in 1970, a lowly-rated New Zealand team defeated Pakistan at Lahore, a win that gave the visitors the series, an historic win for them. Immediately the experiment was jettisoned as if it was a contaminated thing. Life was expunged from the pitches; the bowlers were back on their imposed treadmill.

The defeat by New Zealand had a traumatic effect. The authorities felt they had to seize on radical measures to check the downhill trend. The President asked Abdul Hafeez Kardar, by then a member of the Punjab Legislative Assembly, to take over as president of the BCCP. His mission was to start immediately to put the ruling body onto a sound and rational footing. He established the first-ever BCCP headquarters at Gaddafi Stadium, Lahore, together with a fully-fledged secretariat. The number of national tournaments was increased from two to four. The Pentangular tournament, launched in 1973, was an unqualified success.

This tournament was the first of its kind since Independence. In it, Pakistan's top teams played each other on a league basis, producing an astonishingly high standard of cricket. Thriving on the benefit of being able to play more than one first-class match a year—as had previously been their lot—some young players turned in splendid performances. A vital factor of the tournament was that it, at last, allowed the BCCP to make a true assessment of the country's cricketing resources in terms of talent.

The Board's new administration began regularly to announce the schedule of tournaments a year in advance, then carry them out successfully—a gratifying improvement. Patterned on MCC ground staffs, two cricket nurseries, at Lahore and Karachi, were launched. Cricket patronage began to blossom in the government. A guiding force was the Prime Minister, Mr Bhutto, once a keen player and still an ardent follower of the game.

All these concerted efforts began to bring benefits. For instance, the senior players on the successful tour of England in 1974 felt a new kind of pressure for their places. After a very long time, the well-established players realized that failure could put them swiftly out of the team. Getting back might be very difficult with a flow of new talent, of whom Wasim Raja and Imran Khan were the standard bearers, gathering momentum in the country's revitalized structure.

With much talent already available, growing numbers burgeoning in the wings, a fresh sense of purpose, Pakistan's cricket future, at this vantage point of the mid-1970s, had never looked brighter. The Test team was at last harnessing a greater percentage of its residual powers; the unbeaten England tour of 1974 was striking evidence of this. Gone was the brittleness of earlier years, the habit of wilting under pressure, sometimes with victory looking close at hand. Its self-confidence, stemming in part from the toughening experience so many players were having in English county cricket, made Pakistan a match for all countries. Its top players were both battle-hardened, yet, at this point in time, the Test side had perhaps the youngest average age of any.

PAKISTAN IN TEST CRICKET
(All statistics up to 30 September 1974)

SUMMARY OF RESULTS

	Played	Won	Lost	Drawn
v England	27	1	9	17
v Australia	9	1	5	3
v West Indies	8	3	4	1
v New Zealand	15	5	1	9
v India	15	1	2	12
	74	11	21	42

MOST APPEARANCES

Hanif Mohammed	55
Imtiaz Ahmed	41
Intikhab Alam	41
Saeed Ahmed	41

MOST RUNS

	Tests	Inns.	N.O.	Runs	H.S.	Av.
Hanif Mohammed	55	97	8	3,915	337	43·98
Saeed Ahmed	41	78	4	2,991	172	40·41
Mushtaq Mohammed	36	63	5	2,452	201	42·27
Imtiaz Ahmed	41	72	1	2,079	209	29·28

MOST RUNS IN A SERIES

	Tests	Inns.	N.O.	Runs	H.S.	Av.
Hanif Mohammed v West Indies 1957–8	5	9	0	628	337	69·77

HIGHEST INDIVIDUAL INNINGS

337	Hanif Mohammed	v West Indies	Bridgetown	1957–8
274	Zaheer Abbas	v England	Edgbaston	1971
240	Zaheer Abbas	v England	Oval	1974
209	Imtiaz Ahmed	v New Zealand	Lahore	1955–6
203*	Hanif Mohammed	v New Zealand	Lahore	1964–5
201	Mushtaq Mohammed	v New Zealand	Dunedin	1972–3

MOST WICKETS

	Tests	Runs	Wickets	Av.
Fazal Mahmood	34	3,436	139	24·71
Intikhab Alam	41	3,865	102	37·89

MOST WICKETS IN A SERIES

	Tests	Runs	Wickets	Av.
Khan Mohammed v India 1954–5	4	349	22	15·86

BEST BOWLING

7–42	Fazal Mahmood	v India	Lucknow	1952–3
7–52	Intikhab Alam	v New Zealand	Dunedin	1972–3
7–74	Pervez Sajjad	v New Zealand	Lahore	1969–70
7–80	Fazal Mahmood	v Australia	Karachi	1956–7
7–99	Mohammed Nazir	v New Zealand	Karachi	1969–70

1,000 RUNS AND 100 WICKETS

	Tests	Runs	Wickets
Intikhab Alam	41	1,389	102

CAPTAIN IN MOST TESTS

A. H. Kardar   23

* not out.

South Africa: LOUIS DUFFUS

The timing of South Africa's expulsion from Test cricket had a harsh and unpalatable irony for her supporters.

On that March day in 1970 when the South African players trooped off the field behind Mike Procter—joyously acclaimed for his best Test bowling of 6 for 73—it was very likely the strongest cricket team in the world. Certainly it was the most scintillatingly exciting and adventurous.

Its 4-0 massacre of Bill Lawry's Australians had capped the finest and most triumphant half-decade in the country's eighty-one years of international cricket. In that five-year span, South Africa had won eight of the nine Tests that produced a result, including a series against England.

Lacking an outstanding spin bowler, these teams were not ideally balanced, but consider their merits: an excellent attack of fast and medium pace, led by Procter and Peter Pollock; perhaps the finest-ever crop of allrounders in a single squad—Trevor Goddard, Eddie Barlow, Procter again; splendid fielding highlighted by unforgettable displays from Colin Bland and two capable leaders in Peter van der Merwe and Ali Bacher.

Above all, the dominant force in their cricket was total dedication to attacking batting, a spirit that stood out in sharp contrast to their predecessors. And this positiveness was the nub of the irony. The background to what South Africans called their Champagne Era (1965–70) was long years of teams lacking in ability struggling with a dourness that made these final successes all the more glorious. Generations of a predominantly defensive strain had been transformed into one of exhilarating aggression. But, alas, there was no certainty that when, some day, the country came back from the wilderness, its players would not revert to cautious methods to re-establish themselves at the highest level.

It is puzzling to try to determine why it should have taken South Africans, bred from people who had courageously braved so many dangers—from drought to Zulu spears—so long to inject boldness into their cricket. Possibly the inferiority complex, formed from their earliest cricketing experiences, became so ingrained that it needed several generations—and some exceptional influences—to shake it off. But, as late as 1966, a visiting captain, Bobby Simpson of Australia, was able to say that South African cricketers were 'afraid to win'. Simpson might have had in mind the strangely slow scoring that denied South Africa a glowing chance of victory in the final Test at Sydney in 1963–4. There had been many other occasions when men in Springbok caps 'either feared their Fate too much or their deserts were small'.

As happened in so many countries around the world, it was largely members of British military garrisons whose off-duty recreation launched cricket in South Africa. One famous link with soldiery lit up South African cricket for half a century. Dave Nourse came out from Croydon as a bugler boy with the Pietermaritzburg garrisons. He settled in the country, played in forty-five Tests and sired an even more illustrious player in Dudley Nourse.

South Africa's natural debt to England was unbounded and carried heavy interest charges. The game could not have become so firmly established in the Union without the English teams that came out in succeeding summers, and which, until well into the twentieth century, played in minor matches against teams often containing fifteen, eighteen and up to twenty-two members.

These visiting English teams were never fully representative; it was not until 1938–9, when the late Wally Hammond led an MCC party, that all the best players were included. When South African teams could not cope with less-than-full-strength visitors, it is not surprising that they developed the habit of going into games apprehensive and intent on survival by defensive means as the main, if not the only, way to save the game. This was natural enough, for grit in the face of adversity was another basic characteristic handed down from the pioneers.

The single bright thread in this otherwise dull pattern was one historic season in what was once called the Golden Era of South African cricket (which occurred in the period that England also called her Golden Era). In 1905–6, Plum Warner's Englishmen lost the series one match to four against what was literally a South African XI—the same eleven players appeared in all five Test matches. This random and wonderfully-received success pumped confidence into this cadre; many of them were in the team that won the first Test in Australia in 1910–11.

The lessons of enterprise and initiative have been there all along. It was no coincidence that these early few successes stemmed, in part, from South Africa's sudden—and positive—addiction to googly bowling. First, Reggie Schwarz saw, admired and copied the unusual style of leg-break bowling initiated by his county teammate, B. J. T. Bosanquet of Middlesex and England. Schwarz tried out the new technique at nets early in the tour of 1907. The first time he used it in a match, against Oxford, he took 5 for 27.

Suddenly googly bowling was the rage; a great number of bowlers in all cricketing countries took it up. But the historic conversions were those of Schwarz's teammates Aubrey Faulkner, also a star batsman of his time, Ernie Vogler and Gordon White. Despite their triumphs, googly bowling in South Africa proved to be a short-lived craze, like a pop song that holds public fancy fleetingly, then fades into obscurity. So we have the enigma of a deadly weapon that proved its destructiveness only to vanish from the arsenal. In later eras, the potent force was

(Left) Catalyst for success. 'We're as good as the other mob' was Eddie Barlow's optimistic creed that fuelled South Africa to her greatest heights between 1964–70.

(Right) Catalyst for oblivion. When Anglo-South African cricket relations fulminated, the unwitting detonator, Basil D'Oliveira, maintained a stoical dignity. An O.B.E., here admired by son Damian and wife Naomi, was perhaps a small compensation.

off-spin, particularly from the fingers of Buster Nupen, a terror on matting, and Hugh Tayfield, the country's leading wicket-taker (170 wickets in thirty-seven Tests at 25·91 apiece), who excelled in Australia. Among the occasional leg-spinners of note were Xenophon Balaskas, whose short career reached its peak when he played a signal part in South Africa's first-ever victory at Lord's, and the Rhodesian Percy Mansell.

A more sustained line of quality has been a strength that South Africa shares with Kent—the county of Leslie Ames, Godfrey Evans and Alan Knott: exceptional wicketkeepers. Down the years, the masterly displays established by E. A. Halliwell, when wicketkeepers stood up to fast bowlers, were emulated by Percy Sherwell, Tommy Ward, Jock Cameron and Johnny Waite. Like the Kent trio, Cameron and Waite were accomplished batsmen.

English patronage of South African cricket, while invaluable, has had its pronounced credit and debit sides. A steady flow of coaches has been imported for schools and associations. They contributed significantly to the style of play with their emphasis on mastering the correct technique in batsmanship.

It is undeniable that this instilling of sound rudiments did an immense amount of good. Yet, critics have claimed that the gain was offset by a submerging of natural, if sometimes unorthodox, talent and thus tended to prolong the enduring age of caution in South African cricket. There are arguments for both sides of the theory. Herby Taylor, who was South Africa's most accomplished batsman until Barry Richards appeared on the scene, owed his outstanding ability in back play

Herby Taylor, surely the only batsman who ever dented Syd Barnes's composure; he reputedly made the great England bowler stomp off the field in despair and disgust.

to the advice he received from George Cox, the Sussex professional. Dudley Nourse, one of the most aggressive batsmen, was never coached, not even by his father.

Another possible influence was the fact that all matches, for many years, were played on matting wickets. The first Test played on a turf wicket was against Percy Chapman's team in the 1930–1 series. So batsmen developed through learning how to cope with the ball coming through with high bounce and uniform pace. Despite this limitation, the players who did most to achieve South Africa's first-ever victory in England—in 1935—were nurtured on matting.

There were two contrasting differences between the English and Australian influences. From the earliest days—with the notable exception of Don Bradman who missed the 1935–6 tour through illness—Australia always sent its strongest teams on tour here. Invariably they crushed every side that stepped into their path; South Africans had to wait until 1966–7 before the Australians lost a match of any sort; Simpson's men obliged by losing five.

The other difference was technique allied to attitude. There were, so it seemed, no English coaches in Australia. When the South Africans toured Australia in 1931–2, after an interval of twenty-one years, they were startled by the disrespectful slamming the Australians gave their bowlers of repute. If backlifts went towards third slip and many off-side deliveries fetched up on the square-leg boundary, the Australian batsmen were ever ready to attack, often with great success.

The national trait is well expressed in the story the whimsical and distinguished spin bowler Arthur Mailey liked to tell of his experience in a country match. He had been bowling for some time and had been clouted all over the ground when the batsman at his end asked him innocently, 'When's Mailey coming on?' At a higher level, I had an example of Aussie confidence, amply justified, on that 1931–2 tour, when sitting with Bradman in the stand at Melbourne during the third Test.

Bill Woodfull and Bill Ponsford were scoring with such ease that Bradman said, 'If I could get out there, I'd make a century before stumps.' Ponsford's wicket fell and Bradman at the close was 96 not out.

Such bravado was rare among South Africans in their age of shyness. They were inclined to treat with awe the famous players of other countries. Reputations loomed very large. When the 1921 Australians came to South Africa, Charlie Frank batted for eight-and-a-half hours to score 152. While he was lean and debilitated from gas in World War I, much of his timidity came from the names of the opening bowlers on the scoreboard: Jack Gregory and Ted McDonald.

Nasty memories also tended to stay over-vividly in South African minds. At Edgbaston in 1924, South Africa were blasted out for thirty. On the same ground five years later, Bruce Mitchell, in his first Test, scraped together 88 runs in seven hours. Facing Harold Larwood, Maurice Tate and lefthander Jack White, he seemed petrified to lift his bat into any attacking shots.

Strolling around the ground, I met Plum Warner, who exclaimed, 'He'll never be a batsman unless he plays strokes.' In later years, Mitchell did loosen up and rise to play with much distinction, including an innings of 164 not out at Lord's in 1935 that dominated the first Test victory in England. But the malady lingered on. Against Australia in Durban in 1957-8, Jackie McGlew scored what is claimed to be the slowest hundred on record when he batted for nine hours and five minutes, an innings sardonically described by the late Wally Grout as 'a long-playing record'.

But the emphasis has not always been on submission and safety first; one of the truly rich moments in early South African cricket was the result of one player's almost Bradmanesque confidence. During the 1913-14 MCC tour, Taylor had proved himself incomparably the best home batsman through his lone ability to master the great Sydney Barnes.

Taylor and Dave Nourse were playing a memorable partnership for Natal. Nourse, much his partner's senior, called him for a mid-pitch conference and complained, 'I can't get the hang of Barnes. He'll get me.' Taylor replied simply, 'All right, I'll play Barnes.' He farmed the bowling so successfully that, at last, in utter frustration Barnes threw down the ball and cried, 'It's Taylor, Taylor, Taylor all the time!' and left the field. Natal won the only victory against the touring team.

Nourse certainly had ample chances to observe the fruits of positive thinking in cricket. He was at the wicket in a 1905 Test against England at the old Wanderers ground when the last man Sherwell joined him. South Africa needed forty-five to win.

Nourse later related, 'Everyone seemed downhearted and it must have been a terrific strain on Sherwell being skipper. If it were so, then he certainly concealed it well, for he came, as usual, laughing and full of confidence. Sherwell hit his

Only groundsmen had muted admiration for Graeme Pollock—he splintered too many pickets. Crouching John Gleeson wears the face of Australia '70: anguish-ridden.

J. H. Sinclair and G. A. Faulkner going out to bat for South Africans v MCC at Lord's. Sinclair's mighty hits were a menace to cab drivers and goods trains.

first ball for four and with continued aplomb carried the team to their first victory against England.'

In the Melbourne Test of 1952–3, at 191 for four in the fourth innings, South Africa needed 104 to win. The captain, Jack Cheetham, remembering the failure of his side's defensive batting that cost a winning chance at Brisbane, told Roy McLean as he was about to leave the dressing-room in a highly tense situation, 'You must go out there and play strokes.'

'Don't worry, Pop, I'll get them,' McLean said. He was dropped first ball, then launched into a spectacular assault for 76 not out that won the match.

It was such innings that stood out like beacons in the gloom of those lean and defensive years of South African batting. Hidden among its plodders, the country has usually, if not always, possessed individual batsmen of exceptional forcefulness. The first and one of the most famous was Jimmy Sinclair, who played in the early years of the century, and who loved to evict cricket balls rudely from cricket grounds. One of his prodigious hits against Yorkshire at Bramall Lane soared out of the ground and knocked a cab driver off his perch. The cabby later sent him a letter of demand for damages. Another time it was claimed that Sinclair hit a ball from Johannesburg to Cape Town. His six-hit sailed high out of the ground at the old Wanderers; the ball landed in a goods train and was reputedly recovered at the coast a thousand miles away.

In the same mould was sturdy Jock Cameron whose big hits were scientifically judged, never reckless. Cameron joined the immortals the day at Bramall Lane against Yorkshire when he scored 4, 4, 4, 6, 6, 6 off an over from the great left-hander Hedley Verity. This sublime assault triggered one of the most cherished brief dialogues in cricket history.

Yorkshire wicketkeeper Wood: 'Well, Hedley, at least you had him in two minds.'

Verity, much surprised: 'How was that?'

Wood: 'He didn't know whether to hit you for four or six.'

That summer Cameron hit sixes out of many grounds in England. His most valuable innings, 90 not out in the Lord's Test, was fated to be his last; he died tragically after picking up a germ on the way home by sea.

As he left the dressing-room the day of the Lord's Test, he kissed his bat playfully and murmured, 'Are you going to be a pal today?' So quickly did he adjust his sights that he hit the first of several sixes when his score was eleven; at one point he had scored 58 of the 60 runs made in his first half hour at the crease.

Later players such as Roy McLean and Paul Winslow stood out among their colleagues, often being the only attackers in the Test eleven. McLean once came to the wicket in Melbourne when stolid Russell Endean had scored 82 not out. Forty thrilling minutes later wagers were flying above the clink of bottles in the stands that McLean would score his fifty before Endean reached his century.

Youngsters would absorb the facts of earlier stern resolution with disbelief when they considered their country's last Test teams, which contained such a profusion of fierce attackers as Richards, Graeme Pollock, Eddie Barlow, Denis Lindsay, Lee Irvine and Procter.

Bowling also had its docile aspects. As little as a generation ago, South Africans could gaze upon or kindle memories of Larwood, McDonald, Voce, Lindwall, Miller and sigh at the sparseness of such heavy artillery among their ranks. Effective fast bowling had been a rarity, the most prominent of Springbok opening bowlers being J. J. Kotze, G. F. Bissett and R. J. Crisp. Then, in the late 1940s, a tall, flaxen-haired man named Cuan McCarthy arrived and proved the harbinger of a line of speed bowlers that ran through from the country's most successful pair, Neil Adcock and Peter Heine, to the later menace of Peter Pollock and Mike Procter. A fleeting and tormented member of that brotherhood was Geoff Griffin who suffered a cruelty almost too gruesome to reflect upon: a hat trick in the 1960 Lord's Test, then a call against his suspect action and oblivion at the age of twenty. South African observers squirmed uncomfortably at this memory three years later when a series of calls against Australia's Ian Meckiff—bowling at South Africa in a Brisbane Test—hurtled him out of first-class cricket.

Adcock had a spidery build for a fast bowler and had been susceptible to injury. Haunted by the fear of a breakdown, he nevertheless shouldered the double burden after Griffin's departure in 1960. He bowled more Test overs than any other Springbok, took a record-equalling twenty-six wickets and had to leave the field just three times in four and a half gruelling months—each time to have split trousers repaired.

A vital fissure that was to allow South African batting to be prised from its stifling concrete cocoon appeared in 1961, at a time when sections of the Press had been constantly harping about defensive play. That year a seventy-six-year-old enthusiast and benefactor of South African cricket, Mr E. Stanley Murphy, sponsored a twenty-one match tour of England for young players under the dashing Roy McLean.

This team was called Fezelas, the Zulu word for scorpions. Its two-pronged purpose was to instil into a rising generation the tenets of constant attack in batting and to give experience to potential international players. The seed it sowed flowered during the following decade in the deeds of Barlow, Bland, Lindsay, Peter Pollock and the national captain Peter van der Merwe. Yet the selectors still took their time to discard defensive players.

The spark plug that ignited the latent flair was the cocky, thrusting, super-optimistic Barlow. Broad of beam, eyes glinting purposefully behind large spectacles, he was cricket's Billy Bunter, the 'Owl of the Remove' come to restless life. His dressing-room comments would run along these lines: 'We're a damned good team, as good as the other lot; let's get out there and do them.' Master of the cultivated snick, a virtually lethal change bowler, sticky-fingered in the slips, Barlow showed the way through personal performance. He outthought, outfought and outswaggered the Australians. Barlow was a most important catalyst in the dazzling emergence of the teenaged Graeme Pollock. Their slaughter of the Australian bowling in partnership at Adelaide that year must still disturb the sleep of those whose unhappy lot it was to bowl to them.

Just in advance of the more enlightened batting came the uplift in fielding that, in Jack Cheetham's 1952–3 team in Australia, became obsessively brilliant through diligent, seemingly endless practice. They grassed plenty of chances, but one day in Melbourne clung to the most extraordinary sequence of catches ever seen in a single Test match. They were partly the inspiration for Colin Bland, the solitary practice toiler on Rhodesian fields, who carried the art of fielding to previously unseen heights.

This positive and often sparkling play aroused enormous public interest in South African cricket at home. Unaware that isolation was about to drop on them, record crowds watched Lawry's Australians being taken apart in four Tests; the total of 119,000 at the Wanderers ground eclipsed all previous figures.

An even more lasting result of the surge in cricket popularity was its widespread adoption in the Afrikaans' community and schools. The white population is divided roughly into sixty percent whose home language is Afrikaans and forty percent whose mother tongue is English. Throughout its history up to the 1960s players and spectators were mostly of British stock; the reverse proportion to

rugby football. The challenge to manliness implicit in rugby appealed to Afri-
kaaners more than any other sport. There was never any question of their shun-
ning cricket because it was English—rugby was equally anglican; they loved
rugby above all else as a means of demonstrating physical strength through
bodily contact.

Even some with Afrikaans names—and a few took part from the very earliest
days—were anglicized, like Clive van Ryneveld and Peter van der Merwe. But
the advent of Champagne Cricket captivated the whole population; the sport
gained an entire new dimension.

Two of the youngest in this new heroic age, Richards and Procter, are the most
prominent graduates of a system developed to advance cricketers in every stratum
of the game, a system which owes its origin to the generosity of an Englishman.

Cultivation of raw material starts in the schools. A few years before World
War II, Mr C. J. Offord, a veritable worshipper at cricket's shrine, conceived the
idea of holding an annual week of competition between schools in Natal. It was
highly successful and soon copied by other provinces.

In 1939, when MCC were touring South Africa, philanthropist Lord Nuffield
donated £10,000 to be spent to strengthen the country's cricket nationally. The
money went to holding an annual 'Nuffield Week' for teams composed of the
best schoolboys in each province, with the climax a match between a S.A.
Schools XI and the senior side of the host province. From this competition, held
since 1940, apart from the war years, have emerged forty Test cricketers. In 1963,
immediately after the tournament, a team of fifteen schoolboys toured England
for the first time. Its captain was Richards and its vice-captain Procter.

Tapping this success, the national administration launched a 'Universities
Week' and 'Country Districts Week' on similar lines. During summer holidays in
the Transvaal, youngsters down to primary school ages have a chance to join
organized contests in cricket. From these sources and hundreds of league clubs
who play at weekends comes the talent for the Currie Cup tournament.

Until the last decade or so, few non-Whites showed any special interest in
cricket. The indigenous Africans, by far the largest section of the population, are
soccer besotted; they would play all year round.

Four ethnic groups—Coloured, Indian, African and Malays—have cricket
organizations. Except for rare instances some years ago, they did not play against
Whites, until changes in Government policy in the 1970s. Strongest in numbers
and talents are the Coloureds; their cricket has gathered new momentum since
white cricketers funded Basil D'Oliveira to England and a career as a Test player.

White associations and private concerns increasingly contribute funds to and
provide coaches—some of them English professionals—for non-White cricket.
The 1973–4 season had two significant particles in its composition. Two African
players, E. Ntikinca and E. Habane, took part in a double-wicket international

Capetown: April 3, 1971. Brothers Peter (left) and Graeme Pollock, two of the fielding team who walked off after a single ball had been bowled. They were protesting at the absence of non-whites from the chosen team to tour Australia, a tour later cancelled.

tournament and Derrick Robins's touring team, partially plugging the gap of cricket isolation, included in its ranks the Pakistani Younis Ahmed and West Indian John Shepherd. Their presence underlined the sharp change in policy; they played in South Africa less than six years after Prime Minister Vorster cancelled an MCC tour when D'Oliveira had been added to the touring party.

Expulsion from Tests perhaps stimulated the domestic scene. The Currie Cup competition, comprising nine provinces, flourished as never before, especially in the major section consisting of Natal, Transvaal, Western Province, Eastern Province and Rhodesia. Sponsorship, introduced for the first time, gave the game a sharp stimulus. A brewery donated a generous R150,000 extending over five years, with prizes to be won by every province, sums devoted to travelling expenses, accommodation and administration costs and individual rewards for batsmen, bowlers and fielders. Money poured in: a Gillette Cup one-day competition boosted the coffers; a dairy company paid Richards cash for every run he scored.

In 1973-4, his first year as Natal captain, Richards lifted the team from nowhere to win both sections of the Currie Cup and restore the traditional rivalry between the two major cricket centres, Natal and Transvaal. Their final clash in Durban drew a local record three-day attendance of 31,425. Unhappily that season also saw the return of former push and prod methods, slow scoring, growing signs of gamesmanship and displays against umpires' decisions that were far from the euphoria of 1970.

Time had swiftly pricked the bubbles of the champagne team: within a few years Graeme Pollock was suffering from weakened eyesight; Peter Pollock, Goddard, Lindsay, 'Tiger' Lance, Barlow and Bacher had either retired or were on the verge of doing so.

The persisting dearth of top-class leg-spin bowlers showed no signs of improving. There were other shortcomings but outweighing them were encouraging points—the continued triumphs of Richards and Procter, the discovery of the elegant Ken McEwan playing professionally for Essex—that suggested South Africa would have some strength to answer a call back to Test cricket if circumstances did not remain unchanged to prevent or unduly delay that call.

SOUTH AFRICA IN TEST CRICKET
(All statistics up to 30 September 1974)

SUMMARY OF RESULTS

	Played	*Won*	*Lost*	*Drawn*
v England	102	18	46	38
v Australia	53	11	29	13
v New Zealand	17	9	2	6
	172	38	77	57

MOST APPEARANCES

J. H. B. Waite	50
A. D. Nourse, snr.	45
B. Mitchell	42
H. W. Taylor	42
T. L. Goddard	41
R. A. McLean	40

MOST RUNS

	Tests	*Inns.*	*N.O.*	*Runs*	*H.S.*	*Av.*
B. Mitchell	42	80	9	3,471	189*	48·88
A. D. Nourse, jnr.	34	62	7	2,960	231	53·81
H. W. Taylor	42	76	4	2,936	176	40·77
E. J. Barlow	30	57	2	2,516	201	45·74
T. L. Goddard	41	78	5	2,516	112	34·46

MOST RUNS IN A SERIES

			Tests	*Inns.*	*N.O.*	*Runs*	*H.S.*	*Av.*
G. A. Faulkner	v Aust.	1910–11	5	10	0	732	204	73·20
A. D. Nourse, jnr.	v Eng.	1947	5	9	0	621	149	69·00
J. D. Lindsay	v Aust.	1966–7	5	7	0	606	182	86·57
E. J. Barlow	v Aust.	1963–4	5	10	2	603	201	75·37

HIGHEST INDIVIDUAL INNINGS

274	R. G. Pollock	v Australia	Durban	1969–70
255*	D. J. McGlew	v New Zealand	Wellington	1952–3
236	E. A. B. Rowan	v England	Headingley	1951
231	A. D. Nourse, jnr.	v Australia	Johannesburg	1935–6

MOST WICKETS

	Tests	*Runs*	*Wickets*	*Av.*
H. J. Tayfield	37	4,405	170	25·91
T. L. Goddard	41	3,226	123	26·22
P. M. Pollock	28	2,806	116	24·18
N. A. T. Adcock	26	2,195	104	21·10

MOST WICKETS IN A SERIES

			Tests	*Runs*	*Wickets*	*Av.*
H. J. Tayfield	v Eng.	1956–7	5	636	37	17·18
A. E. E. Vogler	v Eng.	1909–10	5	783	36	21·75

BEST BOWLING

9–113	H. J. Tayfield	v England	Johannesburg	1956–7
8–53	G. B. Lawrence	v New Zealand	Johannesburg	1961–2
8–69	H. J. Tayfield	v England	Durban	1956–7
8–70	S. J. Snooke	v England	Johannesburg	1905–06

1,000 RUNS AND 100 WICKETS

	Tests	*Runs*	*Wickets*
T. L. Goddard	41	2,516	123

CAPTAIN IN MOST TESTS

H. W. Taylor 18

* not out.

Other Countries: BILL FRINDALL

Hark at these words that Sir Pelham Warner penned in 1923, 'The game and the love of it have spread far beyond the imagination of our fathers and forefathers, and there is no part of the world where the Union Jack flies that stumps are not pitched.'

The Union Jack no longer flaps in many of those places but, happily, the stumps are still firmly in place. Being of more appealing stuff, cricket has survived the fall of the British Raj; it also flourishes among the peoples in many non-English-speaking countries outside the Commonwealth—notably Denmark, the Netherlands, Argentina and the Greek island of Corfu.

These players can never personally taste the glamour and international acclaim of international cricket, or even savour the excitement of playing before thousands of spectators on a famous cricket arena. No matter, their passion for the game is not diminished by these drawbacks.

Clubmen and taproom pundits often earn themselves an extra tipple by bowling this historical googly into a conversation: which were the first two countries to play international cricket between themselves? Having called out 'England and Australia', the uninitiated are then startled to learn that the countries were Canada and the United States. Also an England team toured the United States two full years before the mother country sent a party to Australia.

Why is it that Canada could not follow through from this precocious beginning; why does it remain the largest British-developed country where first-class cricket is not played? Most likely two factors thwarted the game from becoming a national pastime: overwhelming influences from the non-cricketing Americans and French-Canadians and the relatively short summers in some parts of this vast country.

Mind you, the French-Canadians have not completely shunned the game: as early as 1785—or three years before the first settlement at Botany Bay—they played cricket after Sunday Mass in Montreal. Then came a strange thirty-year void without any written records of Canadian cricket until 1819 when the Duke of Richmond, then Governor-General, played at Kingston, Ontario. A dozen years later, not only were British garrisons and local residents playing, but the game was being taught at leading schools.

In 1844, a decade after Toronto launched inter-club cricket with a match against Guelph in Hamilton, Ontario, Canada began its internationals against

Sadiq Mohammad, last of the four
Test-playing brothers from Pakistan.
He is expected to foster his nephew,
Shoaib, Hanif's son, into the Pakistan
team before he retires.

Thirty-year-old Mushtaq Mohammad, youngest-
blooded of all Test players, hooks Old to the Leeds
boundary in 1974; Mushtaq had then been an international cricketer for half his lifetime.

County rivals, Mike Procter (second from left) and Barry Richards (with bat). Procter knew immediately in 1970 that South Africa's Test days were over; Richards harboured hopes of a return for three years.

National Stadium, Bermuda, the island's first turf wicket and a merry playground for acquisitive MCC batsmen.

the United States; they met for the first time in New York City. This oldest series of internationals lapsed in 1912, was revived in 1963, and has been the subject of an entire book, *The International Series* by John I. Marder (Kaye & Ward, 1968). The spasmodic pattern continued: the first of regular inter-city matches was played in 1846 but league cricket did not come along until after World War I.

In 1859, G. Parr led England's first-ever touring party to Canada and the United States, an odyssey that also spawned the original in that hardy species of literature—the tour book (*The English Cricketers' Trip to Canada and the United States* by Fred Lillywhite, 1860). Canada's first tour of Britain, in 1880, was non-representative and was not, in fact, completed. The Canadians fared better on their fifth tour in 1954 when they were introduced to first-class play in England, including an international against Pakistan at Lord's.

By this time the Canadian Cricket Association was formally five years old—having previously been fifteen years in the blueprint stage. In 1968 it was elected to Associate Membership of the International Cricket Conference and, four years later, F. R. Brown, the first in-office MCC president to visit Canada, attended a seven-day junior cricket development drive that raised $150,000.

By this time Canada had 119 clubs, fielding 166 teams, scattered throughout British Columbia, Alberta, Saskatchewan, Manitoba, Ontario, Quebec and Nova Scotia. A steady flow of immigrants, notably West Indians, has helped to raise their standards since the last war. The Caribbean approach must have inspired

Hong Kong Cricket Club in 1860: Solar topees, knickerbocker trousers, long black socks, paunches, bow ties, pre-Jessop crouching stances, fielders facing away from the striker—Empire-builders rife with eccentricity.

Hong Kong Cricket Club in the 1970s: Batsmen harassed by close-in architecture; six-hits could scatter typing pools in too adjacent skyscrapers. The Club spent £530,000 moving to new premises.

Vancouver player, Roger Cloy, who belted 15 sixes and 19 fours in an innings of 187 not out on a California tour in 1972.

Canada's climate, with its fierce winter cold and high summer temperatures, demands matting wickets. Four out of every five of their pitches have a grass base, the remainder being matting over shale, clay or asphalt. In a season running from early April to the end of September, the Canadians play much Sunday cricket. Worthwhile crowds watch matches in Victoria (on picturesque Vancouver Island), Vancouver, Calgary and Montreal but only a handful attends in Toronto, which is so American in character. Ironically, two of the four best-known Canadian grounds are in the Toronto area: the Toronto Cricket, Skating and Curling Club with eight acres and a magnificent clubhouse and, fifty miles northwest, the recently-opened Inshalla ground where country-house type cricket is played in a woodland setting. The two other noted venues are the shale-wicketed Riley Park in Calgary and Vancouver's enchanting Brockton Point, perched on a promontory beside Stanley National Park and overlooking Vancouver Harbour.

On an Australian tour there in 1932, Don Bradman gazed at the encircling mountains and the Lions Gate Suspension Bridge spanning the harbour and declared this was the most beautifully situated cricket ground in the world. On that tour, The Don left his usual calling card—260 against Western Ontario at Guelph—the highest individual score in Canada.

South of the border in the American colonies, 'Wicket', an early version of cricket, may have been played even earlier than the eighteenth century. In the 1820s, a heavy influx of English mill-workers to New England boosted the game which thrived especially in nearby Philadelphia where it was introduced at Haverford College in 1834. It bloomed for a pitifully short time. Americans took a greater fancy to baseball, which not only needed much less space and time, but also lent itself to commercial backing. Baseball swiftly became the national summer sport and blighted forever the prospect that cricket would ever rise to a first-class game in America.

The peak of American cricket coincided with the sport's Golden Age, 1896–1914. In this brief period, American teams toured Britain, Jamaica, Bermuda and Canada; representative English and Australian teams were received and often beaten; palatial pavilions were built on beautiful grounds with fine pitches; matches were played between schools and universities, and Haverford College five times toured England playing against public schools. Magazines and annuals were published and newspapers even appointed cricket editors. So many English professional coaches were engaged that regular Gentlemen v Players matches were staged.

As England of the Golden Age had Dr W. G. Grace, America had its greatest ever player, John Barton King, who was a world-class allrounder, a fast bowler of savage pace and controlled swing who more than once took all ten wickets in major matches. In 1908, he toured England and headed the national averages with 87 wickets at 11·01 runs apiece. A fine batsman, his 344 not out for Belmont v Merion in 1906 remains the North American record score.

The man who gingered up cricket in southern California more than any other was the perennial commanding officer who repelled revolting tribesmen at the Khyber Pass so nobly on celluloid—Sir C. Aubrey Smith. Dubbed 'Round-the-Corner' Smith for his curved bowling approach, he had captained England in the first Test match against South Africa in 1889. He founded the Hollywood Cricket Club and was the patrician figure of the expatriate English acting colony that included such people as David Niven, George Sanders, Nigel Bruce, Cary Grant, Basil Rathbone, Ronald Colman and Reginald Gardiner and was immortalized by Evelyn Waugh in *The Loved One*. The cricket grounds at Griffith Park in Los Angeles were officially named after him; a gift of a painting of them was the first picture of an American ground to go into the MCC collection.

While cricket has long faded from its halcyon days of Philadelphia, America's formal status has risen; the United States Cricket Association was formed in 1961 and, four years later, it became an Associate Member of the ICC.

And so to Bermuda. Nowadays Britain's oldest surviving colony is a brief jet flight from New York. It was a longer, more arduous journey for her first overseas visitors, the Philadelphia Zingari, whose 1891 tour launched a spate of reciprocal visits. By then British garrison troops had been playing cricket on the island for half a century and the Bermuda Cricket Club was forty-five years old, catering for 'a favorite amusement in Bermuda'.

When Bermuda's first fully representative side played in Philadelphia in 1911 it overcame the problems of unfamiliar wickets and such brilliant opponents as J. B. King, H. V. Hordern and C. C. Morris to win three of its five matches. In one game Gerald Conyers, slow right-arm, took two hat-tricks in successive overs and, against S. E. Gregory's Australians the following year, he had match figures of 11 for 92.

Before the 1933 West Indian team for England was chosen, Bermuda's finest allrounder, Alma (Champ) Hunt played in a trial match. He didn't make the touring party: because Bermuda has never been a geographic part of the West Indies, the authorities did not know whether he was eligible or not. Hunt later came to Britain, developed into an outstanding professional for Aberdeenshire and represented Scotland. His necessary exile pinpoints the main problem for Bermudian cricket. Starved of top-class Philadelphia opposition since 1914, unable to compete in the West Indian Shell Shield, it has to make do with infrequent tours abroad and occasional visits from teams of varying strengths. Not surprisingly, its standards have dropped; recent New Zealand and England touring sides crunched them to innings defeats.

Bermuda's many clubs play in two main leagues with a high proportion of the island's small population taking part. Until recently all cricket was on matting over concrete; a turf wicket laid at National Stadium, Hamilton, drew no complaints in April 1974 from England tourists Geoff Boycott (131) and John Jameson (126). Twelve miles away the small Somerset ground has an amphitheatre look. Hewn out of the coral hillside, it has a sheer rockface marking the boundary on two sides. On MCC's first visit in 1953, Peter May pulled a ball hard to the boundary. When it rebounded off the coral wall, the umpire, unsighted perhaps, allowed him one run. That visit created an immortal for Bermudian cricket: fast bowler Peter Mulder who dismissed MCC captain Len Hutton with the first ball of the tour. Eight years later, Tom Graveney sculpted 205 not out for Stuart Surridge's XI against the Pick of Bermuda, acclaimed as the finest innings ever seen in the colony.

A highlight of the domestic season is the annual cup match between the two leading clubs, Somerset and St George's. First played in 1902, it is the social and sporting event of the year. Two world wars failed to break the sequence of games.

The style is something less than either Sandhurst or Sandham. A royal, if not quite regal, swipe by King Hussein of Jordan batting against British Embassy personnel at Amman.

A public holiday guarantees a large, voluble crowd (15,000 were there in 1964), a carnival atmosphere and some fervent batting.

Much further south, in the Argentine, the exact origins of cricket are somewhat obscure; the strongest theory is that a British expedition interned on the River Plate got it under way. Whatever the beginnings, the game picked up swiftly as an influx of immigrant railway workers and traders created a small corner of England in Buenos Aires. The Spanish-speaking population was intrigued and, before long, many local *boleodors* were trundling the ball towards their opposing *batadors*. These two splendid words, which would add a piquancy to the vocabularies of BBC commentators, were in the glossary of the first Spanish-language cricket instruction book, *La Tranca* by J. W. Williams (Buenos Aires, 1881).

As with cricket in other parts, South American cricket was at its best between the wars; a representative side that toured Britain in 1932 won two of its six matches—a good effort. The game has not advanced uniformly throughout that immense continent. Whereas cricket is still confined to small groups of exiled Britons in Brazil, Chile, Peru and Uruguay, it flourishes in the Argentine. There it is played in English-speaking schools; both Spanish and English newspapers report the Buenos Aires league matches which are played on idyllic grounds. A steady flow of English professionals go there to coach the large British community in the capital.

In the South Sea archipelago of Fiji, cricket is still a very powerful force. Formerly the inhabitants had the attributes that make a good fast bowler: they were hostile and had strong cannibalistic tendencies. Cricket is thought to have been introduced to these two hundred and fifty scattered islands in January 1874, when immigrant enthusiasts formed a club at Levuka, then the capital. Having superb natural agility and brilliantly fast reflexes, the Fijians quickly took to the game with a fierce and simple relish: their creed was that it was a game only for the hardest hitters and fastest bowlers; there have been few Fijian spinners. Before the locals were widely absorbed into the game, European settlers played the earliest matches against passengers of visiting ships on the Sydney to San Francisco run. In 1881 they played a team from *HMS Bacchante* that contained a young midshipman—Prince George, who later became King George V.

In 1895, Attorney-General J. S. Udal, a former Somerset player, led the first Fijian tour to New Zealand. His side, which included six Fijian chiefs, won four of its eight matches. However, such tours were rare. Playing standards failed to improve until 1946 when the Fijian Cricket Association was formed and promoted the game on an interracial basis; previously, European teams had been segregated from those containing Fijians and Indians. In 1948, Philip Snow, a colonial service administrative officer, led a fully representative team to New Zealand. The following year he published his history of their cricket, *Cricket in the Fiji Islands* by Philip A. Snow (Christchurch, Whitcombe & Tombs, 1949).

The Fijian members of Snow's party were marvellous crowd pullers. They looked sensational on the field with their bare feet, bushy haloes of hair and wearing sulus, the traditional calf-length skirts, split up one side to the waist.

One of the most appealing players was an outstanding batsman who mercifully appeared in the scorebook merely as 'I. L. Bula'. His real name, and there are several versions of it, is a cricket record in itself: Ilikena Lasarusa Bulamainavaleniveivakabulaimainavavaoalakebalau, which makes the name of India's fine spinner S. Venkataraghavan (a meticulous commentator's nightmare) seem almost abrupt. Bula's resounding strokeplay and nimble footwork brought him 1,011 runs in 29 innings on the tour; his 246 is also the highest score in Fijian cricket. Good as it is, this record looks mundane beside that of the finest bowling feat there. In 1940, Saisasi Vunisakiki took a wicket with every delivery in an eight-ball over—an achievement that should stay in the record books forever. Fijian grounds are charming but poorly appointed, apart from Albert Park, Suva and Nasau Park, Levuka. Albert Park has a pleasingly diversified setting; it is surrounded by the Grand Pacific Hotel, a line of imposing government buildings, botanical gardens and a palm-hung soapstone cliff.

Less than a century ago, the British Navy was a kind of missionary force for cricket, establishing it among the Pacific Islands. A true man of the cloth encouraged the game firmly in the British Solomon Islands; he was the second Bishop of Melanesia who, as Cecil Wilson, played for Kent. Groundsmen were confronted by local hazards such as Messrs Bert Lock and Bert Flack never had: grounds had somehow to be set out on the steamy side of extinct volcanoes sloping down to the sea; among the spectators who sometimes rushed into the field were scrawny bushdogs and long-eared razor-backed hogs.

The Paw-a Mission School ground on the Island of Ugi has no boundaries at all. In one match a batsman slogged the ball to the top of an unclimbable sago palm tree. The batsmen scampered fifty runs before the tree was chopped down (presumably with an axe on standby for just this purpose) and the ball retrieved.

In Samoa, the fervid natives spent so much time playing cricket that few barges were being toted or bales lifted; to salvage the economy, the game of cricket was outlawed. So they devised their own version of cricket with entire villages playing against each other. One complete village would take the field while opposing batsmen queued across the field anxious to rush to the crease before the bowler could blast down the stumps left unprotected by the last outgoing batsman. In this mêlée, sometimes only one scoring stroke was made in the entire match.

Those ubiquitous garrison troops played off-duty cricket in Singapore as long ago as 1834 yet the game was unknown elsewhere in Malaya until British rule led to the first inter-state match, Perak v Penang fifty years later. British Military Administration Schools helped to spread the game through the major states so well that in 1927 an All-Malaya team of expatriate officials and settlers defeated a strong Australian team. In the thriving cricket scene of the Malaysian Cricket Association League, Europeans and Indians dominate teams that have a sprinkling of Malays and Chinese. Most local grounds have to serve all sports but a few are reserved for cricket, including the Ipoh ground with its unique turf wicket imported from New Zealand.

Malaysia's oldest opponent is Hong Kong where, yet again, armed and civil services introduced the game. The famous Hong Kong Cricket Club, formed in 1851, will shortly lose its charming and skyscraper-encircled ground to property developers, who, in turn, will have interesting thoughts on half the colony's lease reverting to China in 1999. Before long tenants may be sprawled in armchairs watching television above the area where players such as Garry Sobers, Geoff Boycott and Seymour Nurse have struck centuries.

But Hong Kong has already proved resilient enough to recover from the loss of an entire team in a shipwreck and, despite the bare, rocky hillsides, has a number of excellent grounds. These are maintained by Chinese who generally have absorbed cricket only to the extent of betting on it and bowling in the nets.

Among cricket's outposts, Ceylon, now Sri Lanka, has possibly reached the highest standard of local cricket outside the major countries. Certainly, in 1974, they were stiff opponents for the full Indian and Pakistan teams. At the time of writing, Pakistan had announced it would propose full membership of the International Cricket Conference for Sri Lanka at the forthcoming ICC meeting. This would give Sri Lanka full Test status; they will be one of two associate members of the ICC to compete in cricket's first World Cup.

Cricket came to Ceylon along the lines that it was brought to many parts of the old British Empire. A sequence of soldiers, civil administrators, missionaries, businessmen, planters and schoolteachers first spread the game in the main towns—Colombo, Kandy and Galle; later it was played up-country where tea plantations were carved out of the jungle. There were no roads in these remote areas—the domain of elephants, leopards and bears—and cricket grounds had to be hewn out of the mountainsides, then levelled by hand. To reach grounds far from their estates, planters would set out at dawn carrying their kit, tramp up to twenty miles, play their cricket, replay it over planters' punches until the early hours, then march back home again. After the all-powerful Colombo Cricket Club—truly the colony's counterpart of the MCC—was founded in 1863, cricket became popular throughout all sections of the country's population.

Through a sublime accident of geography—it is halfway along the shipping route between Britain and Australia—Ceylon has been an obvious stopping-off port for teams from both countries. So the immortals, ranging downwards from Dr W. G. Grace and Victor Trumper, have trod the turf of the Colombo ground. And, since 1953-4, Ceylon has played a regular series against Madras for the Gopalan Trophy—another boost for its playing standards.

Because cricket is Ceylon's main sport, skill at the game carries much weight as a status symbol in school and adult life. Many Ceylonese players have won Oxford and Cambridge blues; others, such as Clive Inman, Gamini Goonesena, Stanley Jayasinghe and Dan Piachaud, have played county cricket. W. T. Greswell (Repton and Somerset) became a legendary figure in Ceylon's cricket history. Arriving in 1909, he had taken more than a thousand wickets (600-plus clean bowled) by 1923, playing in weekly one-innings matches. He was the earliest exponent of swing bowling on the steamy island and in 1911 his fast inducers earned him 200 wickets at 8·72 runs apiece.

Kenya, Tanzania, Uganda and Zambia (formerly Northern Rhodesia) comprise East Africa, the other associate member of the ICC entered for the 1975 World Cup. Cricket began in these countries as a settler's game during the Golden Age and had a mainly European phase between the wars when it was administered by famous touring clubs (Kenya Kongonis, Uganda Kobs, Tanganyika Twigas). Apart from Uganda, where virtually only the Africans remain, it is now played by Indians, Goans and the few remaining Europeans.

Players have turf pitches only in Zambia and Kenya; in all the other countries they play on pitches of jute matting over concrete or impacted gravel. Entebbe

Filmdom's most persistent pukka sahib and dauntless C.O., C. Aubrey Smith, captain of the Hollywood cricket team, with Vic Richardson (second from right) on Australia's 1932 north American tour.

has one of the few impressive grounds, a large expanse of fine turf bordered by flowering trees with Lake Victoria shimmering beyond neighbouring golf links. Elsewhere amenities are primitive at the Saturday and Sunday league matches: only the hardy can bear to watch for long periods in the unshaded surrounds. One ambitious Zambian club, Lusaka Nondescripts, made history in 1972 when it flew for a short tour to Mauritius, some 1,300 miles from the East African coast in the Indian Ocean. An active cricketing country since 1838, Mauritius has delightful grounds with turf wickets a thousand feet above sea level at Rosehill and Vacoas.

Cricketers who have to endure the searing heat that bounces up from the baked ground at the Mfuwe airstrip in Zambia need more frequent stops for drinks than most. On one occasion, the caterer forgot the soft drinks that players normally gulp during breaks in play and brought only the post-match beer supply. The heat was so fierce that they had to stop every couple of overs and down the beer. By the time the match twitched to a close, the barely-focussing wicketkeeper had to perch on an empty crate as he groped vaguely for some very sloppy deliveries.

There is not a great deal to say about cricket in West Africa, where the game has been played for fifty years much in the shadow of a far greater sporting passion: soccer. Nigeria and Ghana play each other on matting wickets and occasionally tour the East African countries.

On the Continent, British and Commonwealth expatriates play cricket in many cities—Paris, Calais, Brussels, Geneva, Rome, Naples, Madrid and Lisbon in particular. The Standard Athletic Sports Club at Meudon, near Paris, plays on matting over shale in a verdant woodland setting; batsmen and weary bowlers can plop into an open-air swimming pool close to the boundary. This ground also boasts a fine clubhouse, opened by Queen Elizabeth in 1956, that shames many British pavilions. Because few Frenchmen play cricket, and NATO and SHAPE forces have left France, the club now has to rely on visiting teams from England, Holland and Germany for its opposition. Western Germany, which has BAOR units and RAF stations, has an abundance of military cricketers and organizes many unit and inter-service competitions.

The Dutch and Danes have been playing cricket for more than a century— the Dutch Cricket Association, formed in 1883, is the oldest of all surviving national administrative bodies. The game thrives in both countries, where they play on shale-base matting wickets, stage internationals, devour local cricket books and magazines and listen to domestic cricket commentaries. The Dutch usually send a correspondent to cover Test matches in England for their local newspapers. In 1964, their writers had much to celebrate when the Dutch beat the Australian tourists by three wickets in the last possible over.

Around the Mediterranean, British forces play cricket in Malta, Gibraltar and Cyprus; Israel has a national team which visited Britain in the early 1970s. Lord Byron is said to have introduced cricket to Corfu in 1810; the game certainly flourished there during British occupation from 1815 to 1864.

Corfu has two clubs: Gymnastikos C.C., founded in 1893 and, naturally enough, Byron C.C. which dates from 1935. The island has sent touring teams to England and receives a steady flow of privately-organized tours; they staged a cricket festival in 1972. The only pitch, matting over asphalt, is on the Esplanada ground in the old town of Corfu, surrounded by pavement cafés, car parks, balconies and trees. Fieldsmen in the deep can be maddened by the clink of glasses, weakened by car fumes and distracted by noisy barracking from crowds that delight in their complete ignorance of the game. Through the cacophony boom such words as: *bombarda* (from the Italian for 'bomb') and meaning a full toss; *tsinto*, a 'box' or protector; and *palla*, meaning bat.

So willow plunks against leather in some most unlikely parts of the world. And that most pleasing sound may spread to even more locales through the ICC's 'spheres of assistance' scheme to aid non-Test-playing countries with tours and coaching.

Viva los boleadors y batadors!!

Part Two: Arts and Crafts

Leg-break Bowling:

RICHIE BENAUD

Much of the enduring delight I derived from cricket came from my principal trade in the game, leg-break bowling. There was also frustration, anger, failure and weariness to balance the pleasure but generally the scales were tilted the right way. Captaincy provided the thrill of walking a tightrope, batting the enjoyment of a physical battle, fielding the gamble of reflex action, but leg-spinning was an excitement, a stimulation apart.

Nowadays, in England, I feel sorry for the young first-class cricketer because he is not encouraged to take up over-the-wrist bowling; indeed, it would be near madness for him to do so. The types who make the selectors' eyes narrow with interest, if not sparkle with delight, are the seam bowler and the medium-pacer, both able to dig the ball in short of a driving length and, therefore, restrict scoring in the one-day events.

Even Australian selectors, for decades basing their bowling attack for England tours on leg-spinners, sent a team there in 1972 without an orthodox leg-spinner. I've heard this called progress. So be it. From my vantage point, I'm happy that my own career coincided with a time when leg-spinners were popular and a strong thread in the fabric of international cricket.

However, the art still flourishes in Australia, the West Indies, India and Pakistan, where the harder pitches allow some bounce and where not quite so high a premium is placed on run-saving compared with wicket-taking. In Australia, well into the 1970s, there were half a dozen leg-spinners on the first-class scene, three of them fighting for a place in the Test team.

Around this time, India twice beat England with four spin bowlers in her squad; Intikhab and Mushtaq have long been key bowlers for Pakistan, and the West Indian islands produce tweakers at the drop of a coconut.

All spinners who have reached the top share a basic knowledge drawn from experience: it is a long, hard apprenticeship. Some bowlers, the few and lucky ones, have the ability to force their way into a Test team, are effective straight away and then hold a place for many years. Many spinners, though, need several years' experience before they can get it all to hang together: perfect line and length, flight, the ability to 'read' a batsman.

I started in first-class cricket in 1948, but it wasn't until 1957 that I was near my peak. Those nine years represented a lot of hard work, practice and, as I mentioned before, frustration. This long application is one of the things that dis-

Up, up and away: Alan Davidson hooks Wes Hall to the fence at the MCG. The dual strain of batting and fast bowling has cost even great allrounders (and spectators) the joy of many runs.

suades some youngsters from turning to the art of over-the-wrist bowling; they prefer the easier task of medium pace or off spin. I hasten to add that there is just as much skill needed by the good bowlers in those departments, but a young player can make his way in the cricket world as a batsman who can bowl a few overs of medium pace or trundle a bit of off spin before the new ball is due. This part-time, more casual approach never seems to work out with leg spin: you either go at it with everything you have or you don't bother at all. The averages of occasional leg-break bowlers in Tests and other areas of first-class cricket bear out this point.

Perhaps the most important single thing that started me on a career of leg-break bowling was a small paragraph in a book by Clarrie Grimmett, the name of which I cannot even recall these days.

Grimmett stressed that from the time the bowler turns to run in to bowl the eyes must be firmly fixed on the spot on the pitch where he wants the ball to land. I have found that, no matter how much I stress this to a young bowler, there is still a tendency for him to look at the batsman's feet, the base of the stumps or even the top of the pads.

It is a logical thought that if you are fielding, gathering in the ball and then throwing it to the top of the stumps, then your eyes should be fixed on the top of the stumps. Equally, it is logical that, in the technique of bowling, which requires the ball to land on the pitch, the attention should be focused on the exact spot where it is to drop and not on some extraneous object.

I was lucky in my early days that my father, Lou Benaud, was himself a good leg-break bowler just below Sheffield Shield standard. He was able to guide me carefully along the correct path, especially through the hazardous area of over-coaching. For example, I wasn't encouraged to bowl leg-breaks until I was around eleven or twelve years old because of the extra strain this unorthodox delivery puts on the fingers compared with, say, the off-spin or medium-pace ball. In fact I bowled off-spin at school in the Fourth XI and then had a season in junior cricket where I took the new ball. During the period I was bowling these styles on the field, I would practise leg-breaks on a carefully marked strip in our garden ensuring, under a watchful eye, that I was getting myself side-on to where the batsman would stand.

This was the second formative fundamental brought into my coaching: that bowling is a completely side-on art. There may be good bowlers who have shown all their shirt buttons to the batsman on delivery but thirty years ago my coach insisted that I have my left shoulder facing the batsman and my left arm pointing up to the sky so that I looked over my front shoulder rather than inside the line of it. For simplicity I think bowling fundamentals can be broken down into three parts that I would recommend to any aspiring leg-break bowler:

watch the spot where the ball is to land from the time you turn to run in;
look over your front shoulder;
have your front arm extended and pointing to the sky.

The finest hour: Benaud's neckline plunges; so does England towards defeat on August 1, 1961. Dexter departs, caught behind, after scoring 76 of the most lordly runs ever seen at Old Trafford.

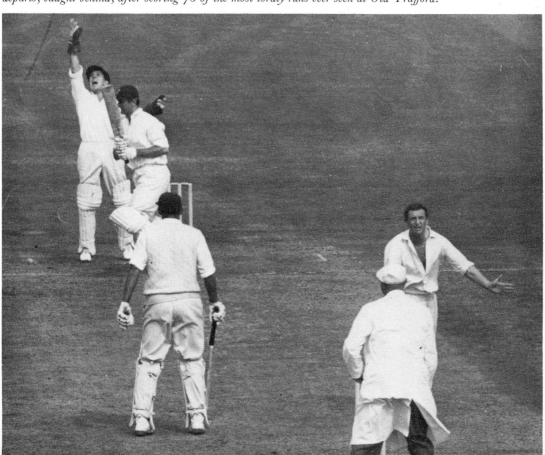

I am a great believer in orthodoxy in bowling. . . . I suppose for every classical action I can produce someone can name me a good bowler who defies a fundamental, but my firm conviction is that, if you start with a classic action, you have the basis for your bowling that will sustain you through the bad periods which inevitably come along.

Returning to personal history, it didn't take long for my father's coaching to pay off. Perhaps it was too successful, for I displaced him from the Cumberland side for which we both played in Sydney grade cricket. Our selectors said there wasn't room for two leg spinners; I was in the side primarily as a batsman so the Benaud working partnership in that team was relatively short. Two years later, it was my batting that gained me a place in the New South Wales team, although the scores in my first game hardly sustain that fact.

I had moved into the NSW Second XI, then advanced into the State side with another bowler who had been a schooldays' rival—Alan Davidson. In those adolescent years, Davidson had played in the Northern High Schools when I was in the City High Schools. Then he was a kind of mirror image to myself: an unorthodox over-the-wrist left-hand spinner, and clearly he was already a cricketer of above-average ability.

Opportunity and responsibility have a great deal to do with the emergence of any young cricketer and in this sense my career and Davidson's also ran along parallel lines. We both had to be patient, toiling away for several years until we became Australia's front-line performers in our different styles of bowling. On our first tour of England in 1953, Davidson was in the formidable shadows of Miller, Lindwall and Bill Johnston; I was second string to Doug Ring and Jack Hill. In 1954–5 and 1956, Miller and Lindwall were still there, although Davidson was learning quickly. On my second England tour, I was picking up some wickets but still—after four years as a Test player—as an apprentice to Australian skipper, Ian Johnson.

Then opportunity was thrust at us immediately after that tour; a long list of players—Miller, Lindwall (temporarily), Langley, Rutherford, Maddocks, Crawford and Wilson—disappeared from international cricket and Ron Archer broke down in such tragic circumstances in a Test against Pakistan on the way home to Australia.

Thankfully, in 1956, I had begun the long process of adding a new delivery to my armoury: the flipper, which Clarrie Grimmett had devised and which he experimented with for twelve years before he used it in a first-class game. That year, Bruce Dooland, that splendid Australian leg-break bowler, took me to the nets at Trent Bridge and showed me how to bowl the flipper that Grimmett had taught him. It seemed a weird delivery; I was fascinated to learn that, to incorporate it into his repertoire, Dooland had completely changed his run to the crease and bowling action so that his two hands were holding the ball at face level in the instant before the arm described the circle of delivery. It had taken him years to perfect and he bowled it magnificently.

I set out during that England tour to try to perfect it in the same way and, in later seasons, it was to prove a tremendous wicket-taker for me. The flipper needed hour after hour of practice, first of all to strengthen the ligaments and tendons on the hand because it was flipped from underneath the wrist rather than over the top and came from a slightly different arm action.

It is no good a young bowler anticipating he can work up any type of delivery without constant practice; it took four years before I was completely proficient in bowling the flipper.

So it was very much in the experimental stage when Ian Craig took a new-look team to South Africa in 1957–8. He had a completely reconstituted bowling attack of Davidson, Benaud, Meckiff, Kline and Drennan, with little choice other than to use a fast bowler, Davidson, and a slow bowler, Benaud, as his spearhead. That South African tour was the making of Davidson and myself. To underline my earlier mention of hard practice, it is worth recounting that, in the fortnight leading up to that tour, I spent every day in the nets in Johannesburg bowling an equivalent of twenty-five eight-ball overs.

At the official net practice in the mornings, I would follow the usual Australian method of bowling in one net to a number of different batsmen. Then, in the afternoon, I would return on my own to bowl at a handkerchief placed on the pitch where a good length delivery would land.

No amount of practice, however, can save the bowler from the inevitable, despairing moments that come when, after all those hours of sweat and toil, the bowler learns that the opposing batsman has him all worked out and deals him a terrible thrashing. The assault happens often to the best and it is the bowler with temperament who is able to fight back, perhaps not that day but the next: to do his job: to claim his share of the wickets for the team. Batsmen like Graeme Pollock, Garry Sobers, Rohan Kanhai, Neil Harvey and Peter May were so good there were times I would despair even of finding the edge of the bat, let alone getting past it or taking a wicket.

Oddly enough, my greatest despair and highest moments of my entire bowling career both came in a single day; for most players these points are usually widely spaced. My special day was August 1, 1961—the final day of the fourth Test when Australia retained the Ashes by taking a two-one lead in the series against England. The low point was at a time in the early afternoon: England were in full flow in their second innings; I had not taken a single wicket in the match. It seemed certain that England, through Dexter's brilliance, would walk away with the match with time to spare. The high point arrived a few hours later after the England side had collapsed and I had moved my wicket tally from none to six, including Dexter, May (first ball) and Subba Row. If ever there was a case to be made for youngsters never to give up, the Australian side made it that day with a combination of out-cricket brilliance and courage difficult to better.

This match proved emphatically how much influence that luck can have on a sportsman's career. Had we been beaten that day, my own career would have been shortened by a couple of years in the light of performances on that tour and injury, plus pressure from the various media for which I now work.

Davidson once more featured large in that day's play; he scored a vital 77 not out in the morning and clean bowled Statham to end England's innings and the match. I have often wondered how much better an allrounder he would have been had not such great physical demands been made of him. It was never easy to prise the ball away from him but, like Miller and Lindwall, he faced a much more arduous task than a slow-bowling allrounder such as myself.

How many times can you recall Miller or Davidson batting brilliantly in the middle of the order—perhaps to the end of the innings—then having to go out and open the bowling and be expected to break through the top half of the opposition batting? At least I knew that probably a dozen overs would be bowled before I had to begin flexing my fingers—time to recover from the rigours of batting. And the physical effort of sending down an over was nowhere near as great.

I have always regarded Davidson as one of the really great allrounders in cricket history but, if pressed to choose only one, I would be inclined to nominate Keith Miller as *the* greatest allrounder in my time in the game. Some regard it as a sterile, others an impossible, task to nominate a number one: *the* greatest batsman, *the* greatest bowler the world has seen. With the extraordinary Sobers to

Motion that has inspired poetry. The lonely, dedicated hours were starting to pay off; a balletic, sinuously-grooved action; batsmen discovering yesterday's bland summer punch had become a cyanide cocktail.

consider, placing the allrounder's laurel wreath veers towards the impossible.

There is always likely, in these cases, to be a leaning towards someone with whom you have played your cricket and whom you have seen win matches. Miller turned so many matches Australia's way in the time I watched him play that his qualifications for the crown are, I think, unbeatable.

Sobers came along as a lad in 1953–4 and was only starting to mature when I went to the West Indies in 1955. He was perhaps not at his peak when he came to Australia in 1960–1, a judgment I cling to although he made so many runs against Pakistan two years previously, including the world record Test score of 365 not out.

Sobers has possibly been the most remarkable cricketer I have seen and certainly a thorough credit to the game. When he came back to Australia to play Sheffield Shield for South Australia, he had an astonishing influence on our cricket—an influence that was always good.

I know of no sport better than cricket to mould or mirror character; I know of no aspect of cricket better than bowling to emphasize character.

When confronted by master batsmen on the rampage, a bowler feels much like a long-distance runner, racked with pain and knowing he still has to complete another dozen laps before he reaches the tape. Skin reddens, chafes, then lifts from the bowler's fingers; his shoulder and bowling hand are so tired he starts to despise the sight of a cricket ball; his feet silently scream out for release, to be rested on the dressing-room table or a soothing bath. But solace is still far away. At the other end of the pitch May, Sobers or Pollock is still belting hell out of you and forty thousand applauding and enthralled people are all too aware that on this day the batsman has been the master.

All this sounds hard. For me it was hard. Yet it remains the most rewarding part I have known in any sport.

Off-spin Bowling: JIM LAKER

In 1959, my last full season in first-class cricket, eleven spin bowlers passed the coveted figure of 100 wickets. In 1973, only Bishan Bedi, playing for Northamptonshire, reached the three-figure mark. That season, in fact, the only English-born spin bowler able to collect his wickets at less than twenty runs apiece was Hampshire veteran Peter Sainsbury. Peter was then thirty-nine years old, so he had learned his craft over the previous twenty years. Spin bowlers have been gradually disappearing from the landscape. There has to be a logical explanation, a copper-bottomed reason which compelled the England selectors to send Fred Titmus, fine bowler that he is, to spend his forty-second birthday on tour in Australia.

Without a doubt the answer lies in the reduction of our County Championship cricket to embrace the money-spinning limited-overs game. Other Test-playing countries, without our domestic financial problems, could afford to look with disdain upon one-day cricket, as we have come to know it. As a result, these countries continue to discover talented and promising spinners. Had they been born Englishmen, Mallett and O'Keeffe of Australia and Barrett and Padmore of West Indies could well have been lost to cricket. Would Northamptonshire have persevered with a young, inexperienced Bedi? It's a moot point. And many times Intikhab Alam, Pakistan's captain, who has taken over 100 Test wickets with his wrist-spin, has been placed in the Surrey side for his batting alone.

How, then, are we going to reverse this downward slide of the spinner? Can we learn a pointer or two by whirling the clock-hands back thirty years to reflect on how my contemporaries and myself set about carving out successful careers as slow bowlers?

I was always extremely pleased, and relieved, that I was never considered a schoolboy prodigy; and, on reflection, thankful that I never bowled a threatening off break until I was twenty years old. Thus, I began to spin a cricket ball when my hands were fully developed and my fingers possibly at their fittest and strongest. So I have fought shy of ever explaining to teenagers the various grips I used and the methods I practised. Unless a boy is unusually big for his age, it is physically impossible for him to wedge a $5\frac{1}{2}$ oz cricket ball firmly between his first two fingers and propel it with spin, length and control, no matter how much he may practise. He will, in the end, adjust the grip to establish control and develop, most likely, into the mundane, run-of-the-mill slow bowler.

Therefore, if I quest around to discover a top-class off-spinner, I should, ideally, be seeking a youth eighteen to nineteen years of age, about 5 ft 10 in in height, with long, strong fingers, suppleness of wrist, a good basic action and the patience to serve a five-year apprenticeship. Most importantly, I would make sure he was not involved in any form of limited-overs cricket until he was ready for it. All these details could be taken from my own personal file. The war years robbed me of first-class playing experience until I was in my twenties. This meant I was hurtled into big cricket: on tour with MCC in the West Indies in 1947–8, then tossed in rudely at the deep end against Don Bradman's 1948 Australians with only some thirty first-class matches behind me. In those early years I had two main virtues: sufficient accuracy to bowl a reasonable length and line, plus the ability to spin the ball more than most players.

At this stage I was totally unaware of the intricacies of flight, pace variations and so on, nor did I know at all how to bowl on differing pitches and how to control the amount of spin. Thus on a hard, true wicket in Barbados or Nottingham, I must have looked a very ordinary performer. But, as soon as the pitch offered any assistance, from rain in particular, I knew I could be a match-winner. Take, for example, my first Test match in Barbados. At the end of the first day, West Indies had scored 244 for three; my figures were one for 78. Overnight rain seeped through the covers on a good length. This gave enough bite for me to bowl out an immensely strong West Indies batting side for 296, finishing with seven for 103.

Unfortunately such helpful conditions never prevailed during the 1948 series. My considerable inexperience counted heavily against me. I not only took several heavy batterings from Bradman & Co. but was abruptly discarded from international cricket. It really was a case of back to the drawing board: hour upon hour of hard toil, split fingers and aching bones over a period of four years before I became a true Test match spinner. I was naturally disappointed in being left out of Freddie Brown's 1950–51 MCC party to Australia after taking 150 wickets at 17 apiece the previous season. Yet the omission proved a blessing of sorts. I had the consolation of a short tour to India with a Commonwealth team. And it was during an unofficial Test in Bombay that I began to feel the pieces of the jigsaw starting to fall into place.

I had what seemed an endless spell of bowling in the sultry, humid atmosphere of Brabourne Stadium on the easiest of pitches. My second innings figures were 65 overs, 34 maidens, 88 runs and five wickets. Polly Umrigar and Vijay Hazare both made centuries against an attack which also included Bruce Dooland, George Tribe and Frank Worrell.

Statistically, of course, my own figures did not compare with the 19 wicket collection at Old Trafford in 1956, but I still believe my marathon effort at Bombay remains my best performance in first-class cricket. More important than that, it gave me an enormous amount of confidence; I finally knew that I had the ability to bowl against top-class batsmen on good wickets.

Into the records book forever. Ian Craig, one of Laker's nine victims in Australia's first innings at Old Trafford, 1956—and nineteen in the match. Miller (left) ponders happier times.

The intricacies of true off-spin are many and varied and the mastery of them adds so much more enjoyment to a long spell with the ball. For instance, the wicket at Bombay, like many in West Indies and Australia, was hard and had some bounce, as opposed to the slow, easy-paced pitches in England. Experience had taught me to reduce my pace, give the ball more air to develop more bounce from the pitch. I used three different grips to vary the amount of spin. On a good pitch that allows you little or no spin, the ball given a real 'tweak' will hurry off the surface far more quickly than the gently-spun ball. As you develop, you learn use of the crease for a continual change in the angle of flight and even off a six-yard run, batsmen can still be deceived by variations in the speed of the run-up. But all these subtleties count for nothing without length and accuracy; lacking them you are just a Santa Claus for Test batsmen. For young readers, who may be bursting with the impatience of youth, may I emphasize that it takes time to combine all these facets.

At the age of eighteen, Pat Pocock of Surrey was an off-spin bowler with more potential than any other I can remember. Full of ambition, he wanted to master all the arts and also become a Test match cricketer in his first season. As a result there was usually one bad ball per over and a long period of frustration. This period was perhaps longer than it should have been because Pat listened to advice but very rarely acted upon it.

Ironically, he was beginning to put things together when Ray Illingworth took over the England captaincy so successfully that Pat's chances of playing again for England diminished. As I write, he is twenty-eight years old and a very experienced cricketer. With his competitors gradually disappearing, I see no reason why he should not return as England's No. 1 off-break bowler. I am convinced Pat Pocock will be a far better bowler in his thirties than he ever was in his twenties.

Scan a list of the best off-spin bowlers since the last war and you will find that most paid physically for their mastery; they suffered from split and lacerated spinning fingers and enlarged joints. Tom Goddard, Lance Gibbs, Ray Illingworth, Ashley Mallett, Jim McConnon and now Pocock are just a few examples. There is no way to avoid these injuries and disabilities if you want to impart real spin on a cricket ball.

After all, spinning a cricket ball thousands upon thousands of times is an unnatural practice; the process of evolution was not geared to accommodate off-spin bowlers. My own career came to a pretty abrupt end because of arthritic conditions affecting the joints of my forefinger. When a sparking plug is worn out, a new one can replace it. Unhappily, the only answer to a worn-out spinning finger is retirement from the game. Off-spinners are durable performers but they suffer for their rewards.

Pat Pocock of Surrey and England. The author believes latent talents will surface when he does more than listen to advice.

The apprentice Laker of 1948 felt more goose than fox when bowling to Bradman & Co. Eight years on, the protruding tongue had moved inside the cheek.

People who have not played cricket at the highest level are eternally curious about it; they bombard you with questions. One constant query is: how does a batsman go about combatting top-class off-spin bowling. The answer to that one I'll leave to coaches and the batting manuals. Another question, for which I have an instant reply, is this: which batsman of your time did you fear the most? Without any doubt, Denis Compton was the supremo on all types of wickets.

At his peak, around 1947, on a good wicket, it was impossible to contain him or set a field to him. On a spinners' pitch, he took longer to score his runs and, being human, Denis had his occasional failures. Basically he came forward whenever he could. People tend to remember most the delights of his sweep, square cover drive and late cut, but his forward defensive shot against the turning ball was also played to perfection. The action was complete and classical: bat close to the pad, never in front of it, and angled at forty-five degrees as he played the ball with the spin towards the on side. Two other fine exponents of this method were Arthur Fagg of Kent and George Emmett of Gloucester. Surprisingly, there always seemed to me to be a chink in the defensive play of the great Len Hutton and, for this reason, I bowled with more enthusiasm, and indeed more success at him than at any of the other great players.

And Bradman? It would be difficult to argue that Sir Donald Bradman, who made a century every third time he went out to bat, is not the greatest batsman who ever lived. He certainly was the only man who gave me an inferiority complex, and for fairly obvious reasons. There was a period in 1948 when I felt he could tell each time I bowled just what kind of delivery to expect, where it was likely to pitch and exactly how many runs he would score from it. I think it is only fair to say that, at that time, I bowled purely from instinct on wickets overloaded in favour of the batsmen. If one could visualize Bradman—at the same age—playing on the pitches that Ian Johnson & Co. encountered in the middle fifties, I am absolutely certain that the great man's Test match batting average would have been substantially lowered. If Malcolm Hilton could reduce him towards normality at Old Trafford, then I am positive that Laker and Lock would have repeated the performance more than once.

For many years it was claimed that ordinary off-spinners were meat and drink to Australian batsmen, and indeed average spinners took repeated thrashings

(Opposite top left) The vanishing breed. Seamers proliferate. Leg-spinners, such as Pakistan's captain, Intikhab Alam, fade from the game; the strummed harp replaced by a stick beating a tin dish.

(Opposite top right) By 1973, when he captained Australia in West Indies, Ian Chappell had attuned himself to leading the side. Here's four of his 97 at Port of Spain in the Third Test.

(Opposite bottom left) Barry Richards's left hand has done most of the work; his timing is faultless; cover point can only guess that a supersonic projectile has passed by him.

(Opposite bottom right) Off-spinners pay for their mastery with enlarged joints, chafed and lacerated fingers. Ray Illingworth, perhaps unwisely, protected his fingers through underbowling himself when England skipper.

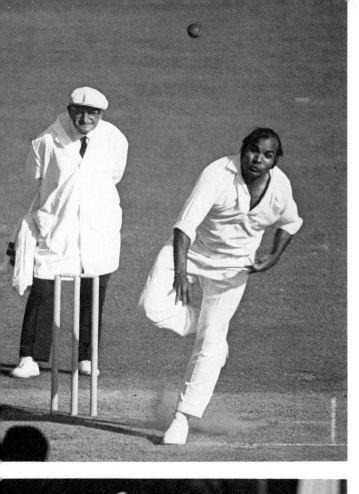

The 'harsh run-up and gather' of Hampshire and West Indies fast bowler Andy Roberts puts a question-mark about his durability in John Snow's mind.

Greig—too tall for express pace. Oh, Maurice Tate, thou shouldst be living at this hour to witness a Sussex medium pacer bowling in Bertie Wooster plimsolls.

Laker has much praise for Australia's Ashley Mallett (right), here sitting out the rain at Lord's with his 1968 tour skipper Lawry. Lawry's preference for Mallett as drink waiter hardly advanced Mallett's career.

from them. But, when England began to produce a much higher class of spinner, it became apparent that the Australian method was vulnerable; England bowlers —Bob Appleyard, Fred Titmus, David Allen and myself—enjoyed Australia and met with a fair measure of success. So, of course, did Ray Illingworth in more recent years. Apart from Colin McDonald, a tough, gritty competitor, the three Australians who played my type of bowling supremely well were all left-handers: Neil Harvey, Arthur Morris and Alan Davidson. This is not surprising as the Australians have always played the ball leaving the bat better than the one spinning into it. No great mystery surrounds the Australians' persistent bother with good off spin: they see so little of it at home they cannot build up experience and confidence against it. My memory can offer up only two off-spinners really worth their salt in the last thirty years: Ian Johnson, who bowled them with great success in Australia and more recently, Ashley Mallett. I have a very high regard for Mallett, who has shown constant improvement since he came into big cricket.

Australian pitches make life bleak for off-spinners. Young players trying to extract something from those pitches must have been discouraged and tempted to concentrate their efforts on some other aspect of the game. By contrast, the young wrist-spinners do find enough turn and bounce to encourage them to carry on; most metropolitan club sides in Australia seem to include at least one leg-spin bowler. As I mentioned before, there are rewards down there for the off-spinner, but only after he has really learned his craft.

Memories of great moments in a player's career are not likely to fade. They not only stay sharp in the mind through their own strength, but people will never allow you to forget them. More than eighteen years have passed since I left the Old Trafford ground in a complete trance, trying to convince myself that I had really taken nineteen wickets in a Test match and that it was not a schoolboy's dream that had belatedly caught up with me. I would be foolish to say that the passing years have dimmed my memory; I can still vividly recall each of the dismissals; they are etched there very deeply. More surprisingly, I am far from being alone in this respect. Seldom a week goes by without my being reminded of it all by two, three or more strangers. The weirdest aspect is that most of them appear to have been at Old Trafford on that memorable day. If that is true, there must have been a great discrepancy in the reported attendance figures! Even Melbourne Cricket Ground, filled to the very rafters of the stands, could scarcely have contained this unending, and ever-growing number of eyewitnesses.

Others, who could not really say with a straight face that they were at Old Trafford, have written or told me personally in great detail exactly where they were and what they were doing on 31 July, 1956. Among hundreds, I quote the whereabouts of just a few informants:

aboard a freighter in the China seas;

listening to a radio in a café on the Champs Elysée—the waiters must have been baffled by their excitement!

cutting cane in a Barbados field;

camping out in the Malaysian jungle.

I know that so many of the stories I have been told are true, and I treasure to this day three hundred cablegrams which arrived from all corners of the world.

Inevitably, that performance has made me a kind of father-confessor figure. Down the years I have been approached by a succession of pub raconteurs who have much the same amazing story to tell. On the very day that I took all those Australian wickets (my informant usually says it was at Leeds or Lord's) he too had his greatest bowling triumph as an off-spinner. Would I believe that he took ten for 21 against Nether Down—all clean bowled?

'Ee, Jim, now there's a coincidence!' Indeed it is.

If I swallow hard and believe this astonishing story, which usually contains all the wrappings, I know that my unsung hero did not have as great an asset as I had—a bowler of the calibre of Tony Lock bowling sixty-nine overs from the opposite end. If it has taken me all these years to keep on absorbing the truth that my success really did happen, I shall go to my grave totally disbelieving that Tony Lock, one of the greatest destroyers of all time on a turning wicket, could finish with figures of one for 106. Still I suppose this is what cricket is all about.

Captaincy: IAN CHAPPELL

'The buck stops here.'

That description of his job as President of the United States is possibly the best-remembered phrase of the late Harry Truman.

It is also an apt motto for any cricket captain.

A sensible captain will never close his ears to tactical advice from teammates or those people whose opinions he respects. In the field the captain may absorb and digest suggestions on such things as field placements and bowling changes; in the dressing room he'll listen to counsel about declarations and switching the batting order. But, like the President, he is the person who must make the ultimate decision alone. Because of this, the cricket captain has one of the toughest jobs in sport.

Compare his task to that of captains in other sports such as baseball, soccer or any of the football codes. The playing captain there can be largely a figurehead. A coach or manager controls the tactical flow of the game from the sidelines; he is the man who plots the strategy. But, unlike football, no messenger rushes on to the ground at Lord's or the Adelaide Oval to instruct the captain to bring on a spinner or switch his opening bowlers to opposite ends. (Thank Heavens.)

Also in cricket, the leader must cope with continuous mental pressures that are more prolonged than in any other sport. For every moment of a full day in the field—and that can be up to seven hundred deliveries over six hours—he has to be responding to an ever-changing situation, while staying alert to do his job as a fielder. When you first take over a Test team, this double job is no picnic.

There is no doubt that both my fielding and batting suffered during my first half dozen matches as the Australian Test captain. In the field, I found I could cope from the first match when the fast bowlers were on. As the bowler was walking back to his mark, I had time to look around, assess the field and ponder on my next bowling change. But I had a real problem fielding in the slips to spinners. This agitation was a new experience; I had always enjoyed fielding there, and best of all when the spinners were at work.

But I found that I was putting down catches that my young daughter Amanda could have taken one-handed. Part of my mind, and therefore my concentration, was intent on the job of captaincy and the slow bowlers were getting through their overs too quickly for me to keep abreast of the game; I didn't have time to sort things out in my mind.

Doug Walters at Worcester 1972, before his Test rot set in. Ian Chappell believes he helped to win that year's Oval Test, in which he did not play.

Aussie skippers Bobby Simpson (1964–8) and Bill Lawry (1968–71), a fecund yet still-underrated opening pair. Ian Chappell assimilated their captaincy traits he liked, ignored those he did not.

The real crunch came in the fifth international match against the Rest of the World at Adelaide early in 1972. After Australia had made only a moderate score, our spinners Kerry O'Keeffe and Ashley Mallett were bowling us back into the game. Graeme Pollock had just passed his hundred and I felt that, if we got rid of him soon, we could hold our opponents to a small lead. Mallett flighted a ball higher, Pollock checked his drive and the ball dollied off his bat straight at me. At that very moment I was engrossed in deciding on a possible move at the other end.

When the ball came to me suddenly, I snatched at it as if I was waking from a dream; the ball went straight to the ground. Right then and there I said to myself: 'I've got to get out of the slips to the spinners.'

So, when we toured England in 1972, I fielded there only for the fast bowlers. I went to mid-off or mid-on for the spinners.

This was a sacrifice; I prefer fielding in the slips to any other position and I believe I'm of best value to the team there. It was also unsettling because I wasn't as happy captaining the team from mid-on; I felt I didn't read the angles of field placing as well out there. But I stuck it out for the five Tests. When we returned to Australia for the series against Pakistan, I had eleven matches as Australia's captain behind me, and felt I could do both jobs. I put myself back in the slips. In 1973-4 season I had one of my best series, taking something like sixteen or seventeen catches in the slips.

With batting, I had similar upsets, but not to the same extent. At the crease, I had more time, while the bowler was walking back, to chew over the state of the game in my mind. But, at odd times, I would play a ball, then find that thoughts about other things—a declaration or calculation of the run-rate—would intrude into my mind. When this happened, the bowler would sometimes actually be delivering the ball to me before my concentration was fully back to my batting. Naturally, I could only do my best job for the team thinking at all times purely as a batsman. When these lapses hit me, I had to talk firmly to myself to pull my concentration together again. Even now, I find that I still suffer from a touch of mental drift, but very seldom.

Once I had eased these worries out of my system, my apprenticeship was over and I knew that captaincy was making me more responsible as a batsman; I was tempering my game through responsibility. You sense, as captain, that the state of a game can be more serious than you do as a player. When you are in charge of the team, you have to set the example, so you become more watchful in stroke-play.

In many ways I feel that the captain dictates the pattern of his team's innings. The rest of the specialist batsmen can often take confidence or uneasiness from the way he plays. If he gets going and plays a few strong shots, and the scoring rate seems to be moving well, the rest of the team can pick up the tempo. Also, if the ball is moving off the seam and swinging through the air, and he has to battle it out, this tension can be relayed to the lower list batsmen.

When a player has fifty or sixty runs up, the instinctive thought may be to feed on this confidence; in going for shots, he can get out through doing something rash or silly. But, as captain, I have to see those runs primarily as part of the total my team must score and concentrate on adding as much as possible to that total. While this may restrict my stroke-play, I'm less likely to play the wrong shot. Of course, part of this responsibility must be that I'm older and more experienced, but obviously having this tough job has contributed a great deal. I'm sure it was a strong factor in my battling through to a century at The Oval in 1972, when I had a big partnership with my brother Greg.

While captaincy is diverse and demanding, I believe the aim—as in batting— should be to simplify and not to fog up your mind with too many theories. In keep- ing the game simple, you should observe the obvious: be quick to plug the gaps in the field, consult with your bowlers and fieldsmen, and know when to apply pressure on the batsmen and when to ease it off. I thought Ray Illingworth was a master at building pressure, then cutting it back when the situation warranted it. I learned a lot from watching Ray, especially in my first Test as captain when his fine tactical control played such a large part in beating Australia.

You must exercise your own personality rather than try to adopt those of a captain who has been successful; you should never be afraid to try the tactics that are natural, that make sense to you. Of the things I noted about my two Test captains, Bobby Simpson and Bill Lawry, I discarded those I didn't care for and remembered those I liked so that I can bring them into play at the right time. I feel I'm lucky in that my basic instinct for the game was developed under Les Favell, who was my captain in South Australia for eight years. Les instilled a positive approach in me; he preferred to accept a challenge. This has now become a natural instinct to me. We have so many close finishes in South Australia that I think I could have a heart attack before I'm thirty-five.

The simple and positive approach was one of the two pieces of advice that my grandfather, Victor Richardson, gave me. When I was very young, he told me I must look like a cricketer at all times. When I had just gone into the Test side, he told me that, if I ever captained a first-class team, I must remember that it's still only a game of cricket and had to be played in the right spirit. I took this to mean that the game should be entertaining and good to watch.

The most important thing I like to get across as captain is that the leader can only be as good as the other ten men around him. Ray Illingworth coaxed as much as he possibly could from his England teams, but no captain can expect to take a hopeless side and convert it into a champion side; inspiration has its firm limits. You can't go it alone; I'm a great believer in the saying that eleven heads are better than one.

This touches on my earlier point that you must be ready to accept advice, as well as give it. So I'll always listen to suggestions and act on those that make sense to me. In one Test match in England in 1972, Rodney Marsh told me he thought Dennis Lillee might do better bowling a different line to one of the batsmen at the crease. Because Rodney keeps wicket to Dennis in Western Australia's Sheffield Shield games, and knows his talents better than I do, I told him to speak to Dennis about it. The direction does not have to come every time from the captain.

In the Oval Test on that tour, Lillee had just taken a wicket. Ray Illingworth came in and I was looking around asking myself how I could put pressure on him. I was swiftly running through some alternatives and wasn't happy about any of them. Keith Stackpole, the vice-captain, said to me: 'What about a third slip for him?' I brought a fieldsman into that position, Illy snicked the first ball to him and was gone. If I hadn't had that advice from 'Stacky', the catch would not have been taken. It's amazing, and very satisfying, to think back on the number of successful ideas that came out of the constant chats that I had in many Tests with Rodney and 'Stacky'.

Off the field, I have learned an enormous amount from discussing cricket tactics with Richie Benaud, who is at most of our Test matches. Many times we sit down in the evenings and just talk over a drink, not specifically about captaincy. I don't have master-and-pupil lessons and we certainly don't get together for the sole purpose of my picking his brain for advice. We have general chats, and from these I have got some impression of his ideas on the game. As an old friend, he knows my style, how I think, so it's easy for us to discuss cricket in tactical terms.

When I have something on my mind, he will mention situations similar perhaps to those I'm facing and say how he went about handling them. This information from his experience is there for me to consider while I sort out the problem for myself. Richie and Les Favell are the only two former first-class captains that I've ever discussed the business of captaincy with at length. But, as I stated at the very beginning of this article, basically you have to work out all your solutions for yourself. On the field you have dozens of decisions to make a day, many of them covering situations that, grouped together, are unique. You could seek advice from many former captains but a dozen men can give you a dozen different answers and you would find yourself going around in circles. It's interesting, and I suppose inevitable, that many people outside South Australia believe that Sir Donald Bradman still controls cricket there at the top levels. Certainly this opinion bobs up a lot in conversations. By coincidence, my first match as the Australian Test captain was Sir Donald's last as a selector. While I have been captain, he has never offered me any advice and I have not sought any from him.

There has been a strong mood of every player in the Australian teams of the 1970s helping everyone else—which is a help to a captain. Players in form receive encouraging words from their teammates; and some advice is given to out-of-form players at the nets. This comes from the senior players and there isn't much of it because people of Test standard don't do many things wrong. In this we seem to vary from players of earlier days who apparently made a firm point of never offering unsought advice. We find also that the younger players get together among themselves to help each other. The attitude nowadays is not to regard the newcomer to a Sheffield Shield or Test team to any large degree as a competitor for your place. I personally look at it from the viewpoint that I have to keep up my performances so that I'm not ousted from the team, but I will tell the young player enough to help his performance for the team. All young players are going to have to sort out much of the business for themselves, but guidance is going to help the team in the long run. The newcomer must be made as sound and know-ledgeable as possible to keep Australian cricket up to a high level. We don't want retirement of senior players to drop the team's standards into a valley, as hap-pened in the mid-1950s and late-1960s. On our New Zealand tour early in 1974, I told Ray Bright, a young spin bowler making his first trip, to have a dinner one evening with Ashley Mallett and, over a few beers, ask him some questions about spin bowling. Then I told 'Rowdy' Mallett that Bright would be approaching him and to give him what help he could.

Cooperation of this kind is part of moulding the team, or touring party, into a unit; it promotes harmony among the players, something I put high on my list of priorities from the outset as captain. Team spirit can lift a medium-calibre side above itself; perhaps the team can outperform its true talent. The social side counts: I think I'm lucky that I like a beer and generally have one or two at the end of the day with the team. This helps the captain to get to know his entire team and understand them better. In a sense you are living with your teammates; you must know their personalities and be able to respond to them, coaxing this one, handling that one a little more firmly, to get the best from them.

Before each Test match on tour we have an informal team dinner which is a great help for morale. We don't have them in Australia because we don't want to drag away from their families those players living in the city where the match is being played. Occasionally, on tour, we will have an informal meeting on the bus or train heading to the ground, if I think there is something wrong with our play that warrants a discussion. The business side of these team dinners usually lasts about half an hour; we deliberately don't get too theoretical because finely de-tailed plans can quickly become unstuck. On the last couple of tours we sang at these dinners, and on the buses, songs with lyrics adapted to describe various members of the team. At the right moment, the bloke in question would leap up and sing about himself and the rest would join in the chorus. This kind of nonsense helps to keep team spirit high and keeps the team laughing.

I remember one sad and awkward moment at the team dinner before the Oval Test in 1972, a moment that, I feel, actually spurred us towards winning that match. Doug Walters had reached a slump in that series; it looked as if he wouldn't be likely to make runs in the final Test, so we had to drop him. This was the biggest setback in Doug's career; he had been an automatic choice for Australia since he came into Test cricket seven years before. I felt bad about this because Doug is a tremendous personality as well as a fine player. In dropping him, we had, I believe, chosen the first-ever Australian side without a New South Wales member.

Doug works very hard and keenly at his cricket at official team practices—he applies himself as hard as any other player—but isn't terribly keen at handling a bat outside team practices. When I had finished reading out that Oval team, everybody was very still. Doug was sitting a short way down the table from me. He obviously felt worse about his omission than anybody else.

Yet, in typical Walters fashion, he wiped his brow in an exaggerated way and said: 'Well, that's a relief. I won't have to get up early and go down for practice in the morning.' This remark broke up the place. Our manager, Ray Steele, turned to me and commented: 'He is an incredible character. This must be the worst

Garry Sobers, useful as batsman or bowler, enjoying an interlude away from his golf course, where he and the author sought and achieved therapy from the strains of Test captaincy.

Denness tosses with Kanhai, for a one-day match, his first as England skipper. Chappell says a player should have twenty Tests behind him before being captain; Denness had nine.

moment of his career and he can still come up with a remark that takes a lot of the sadness out of it for us.'

Everybody who has ever played with Doug likes him and I really think that single statement gave us the extra bit of resolve to go out and win what proved to be a very exciting, but very nerve-wracking, Test match. More than anything else I've known, it showed what morale can do for a cricket team.

A Test captain must gain the respect of every member of his team; he has to have shown there is no doubt that his playing talents have earned him the right to be in that team. Ideally he should have advance warning that he is in line for the captaincy. When I was appointed vice-captain of Australia for our India-Pakistan and South African tours in 1969–70, I knew I had a chance one day of leading my country. Immediately my outlook changed; I began to study more intently the tactics on both sides; the pace of my cricket education stepped up. This mental gearing was an enormous asset when I suddenly found myself Australian captain for the final Test of the 1970–1 series against a very tough opponent.

It's hazardous to state that a player should have a specific number of Tests behind him before he is appointed Test captain. In Australia, for instance, a player can come into Test cricket in his teens and have more than twenty Tests up by the time he is twenty-two. He is an experienced player but, I believe, still hasn't matured personally to a point where he could take over the team; he still has a lot to learn about life and himself before being ready to lead a team at that level.

It has been proved you can give a man the captaincy too young and put too much pressure on him. Richie Benaud, Bobby Simpson and myself all took over around the same age—twenty-seven or twenty-eight—when we were ready, as players and personalities, to do justice to the job. I certainly would not have liked to have started any earlier as captain.

It is best for the captain to have played a lot of Test cricket in as many countries and under the widest range of differing conditions as possible. This means he should have at least twenty to twenty-five Tests under his belt. The touring captain needs first-hand playing knowledge of the country—whether it's England, India or wherever—so that he is qualified to give sound advice to young players who seek it. This is very important because the newcomer will very likely have strong doubts—as I did—whether he is up to playing Test cricket; he needs all the counsel and reassurance he can get.

I must admit that I prefer the Australian style of selection where the selectors pick their twelve players for a Test, then nominate a captain and vice-captain. This list goes to the Board of Control for approval. And for touring parties, the Board receives the names of captain, vice-captain and third selector. Through this system—which is broadly the way a number of other countries also choose their leaders—the man in charge will be established in the side and has the vital respect of his teammates, who are assured of his right to be there as a player. I think this is much better than the English procedure of appointing a captain, then picking a team or touring party around him. It avoids awkward complications.

Tony Lewis, of Glamorgan, had not played in a Test match before he was chosen to lead an MCC party to India and Pakistan. I would hate to have been put in this position of having to face the very demanding job of needing to control and inspire proven Test players without personal experience of Test matches. The captain has enough pressure on him from the complex demands of that job alone without the extra—and needless—burden of having to justify himself as a player. It is asking a lot of team members who are forced to go through the process of telling themselves that they must accept the man chosen to lead them even if they have quiet doubts about his right to be in the Test team as a performer. This state of affairs must make for apprehension for proven players confronted by a new captain without the confidence that he can pull his weight not once, but repeatedly, in Test matches. If you like him as a person, you will hope for his sake, and for the team, that he can do his stuff, but it is a difficulty that should not be introduced. Morale and potential performance are both exposed to extra strains.

I'll conclude by briefly summing up what I think are the things that a good captain needs. He must have:

Proven playing ability, experience and a flair for captaincy that all give him confidence to do his job in a natural and effective way.

Common sense to keep the job simple in the fundamentals of field placings, bowling changes and accepting challenges rationally.

Ray Bright, a young Australian spinning prospect. Over a steak and a beer, some advice from 'Rowdy' Mallett.

Flexibility in keeping an open ear for advice and quickly knowing what to heed or discard; never being above using the collective brains and experience of his men.

Social ease to mingle readily with players off the field so that he knows their personalities and can advise, coax and instruct them in a way to draw the best from them.

The ability to relax and not allow the job to get on top of him. As soon as he is walking through the gate at the end of the day, he will be unwinding, easing the tensions from his mind and system. He must not allow a stream of 'if-only-I-had-done-this-or-that' thoughts to churn through his mind. Reflection and talk on the day's play with the team must be constructive, steering away from harping on things that went wrong, but learning from errors. Like Garry Sobers, I discount the theory that golf is bad for cricketers. We have both found it a marvellous aid to relaxing away from the cricket field: I'm convinced that golf has helped me a great deal as both captain and player. Also, I don't carry a mass of thoughts about the match we are playing, or have just finished, around with me. When my head hits the pillow at night, I'm straight off to sleep to refresh myself for the next day or the next match. Heaven help the uptight, fretting captain.

A first-class manager who can effectively handle everything about a tour that doesn't relate to what takes place on the field. I count myself lucky, a very lucky man to have had such a superb manager as Ray Steele on our England tour of 1972.

The knowledge, and I share this with Richie Benaud, that the successful captain needs luck at the right time.

Small postscript: A captain must also stay serene, avoiding extraneous sources of potential bother and irritation. Before coming to England in 1972—the most important tour of all and my first ever as captain—I resolved not to read cricket stories of any kind in the newspapers. I'm willing to oblige newspapermen whenever I can—I realize and appreciate their importance to the game of cricket—but I felt I could learn very little from reading their articles and match reports. So I didn't read a single one in four months. With respect to the correspondents, I am sure it helped me.

(*Editor's Note:* Ian Chappell wrote this story before Mike Denness became MCC's 1974–75 tour captain to Australia. His original article contained these words: 'Obviously the captain should not be a man whose talents make him a marginal member of the Test team. Otherwise, if he does little in a couple of Tests, everybody, including his teammates, wonder if he warrants his place!' In the first three Tests Denness scored 6, 27, 2, 20, 8 and 2—av. 10·83. Graciously, inevitably Denness dropped himself from the team; oblivion faced him; flak burst all around the English selection system, but in the 6th Test Denness did score 188—highest ever Test score by an England captain in Australia.)

Attacking Batting:

BARRY RICHARDS

Setting down a definition of attacking batsmanship is not easy. Attack is relative: it means different things in the context of separate matches or even at different phases of the same match. It can mean a batsman scoring at a run a minute—the storybook hero. Or, if a team needs to average, say, two runs an over to win a match, two batsmen scoring at a rate slightly above this would be attacking—they are moving their side towards victory.

Let's suppose that, in the broadest sense, attacking batting means the ambition to play positive strokes that allow a batsman to amass runs at a rate that gives him and his side the initiative. This scoring rate will harass the opposing bowlers and force the fielding captain into defence: he will be agitated into changing his bowlers and his fielders' positions to try to cope with it. On this basis, my natural instinct as a batsman is to attack.

This is marvellous . . . as an isolated theory. The realities of modern cricket—especially as the county game is played in England—mean that attack as a regular policy is beyond the scope of even the most talented batsmen. Too many factors are at work eroding the intentions and performances of the so-called cavalier batsmen. I'll spell out these points later on.

By tradition the major attacking roles belong primarily to the number three and four batsmen. Whether he goes in at 0 for one or 150 for one, the number three should have the most impact on the shape and character of his side's innings. Don Bradman is cited as the ideal number three, but his play and influence were unique. Often the number three will have to pull the side together with tenacious play to recover from a poor start. Because of this, the tactical hindrances on a number four are often fewer. So the array of batsmen who played there contains some of the most exciting players of all time: my boyhood hero Roy McLean, Dudley Nourse, Wally Hammond, Ted Dexter, Norman O'Neill, Peter May and so on.

I feel I would have fitted comfortably into this slot. But, because of my intensive coaching in the fundamentals of batting as a lad, I was said to have been a correct player and batted at number three at school. I started with Natal in that position. This suited my plans because I scored a lot of runs there in 1966–7 when Bobby Simpson's Australian side were in South Africa. I knew that if I was going to break into the Test team that year it had to be in that position: we had a good opening pair in Eddie Barlow and Trevor Goddard. As it happened, I didn't get a Test cap in that series. Then, through lack of recognized openers in Natal, I was ordered to go in first. In my first season there I scored four centuries in six games. By the time our next Test series came along—against Australia in 1970—I was established as an opening batsman with Natal and Hampshire. In between, I'd had another very brief spell at number three; this was my place in my first two matches when I joined Hampshire in 1968. Then the captain, Roy Marshall, asked me to open. I scored a hundred in each innings against Northamptonshire; that settled my place in the line-up.

My technique has allowed me to do well either as opener or first drop. But technique is relative to temperament. Greg Chappell is possibly the finest of contemporary Australian batsmen because he is the soundest and plays the straightest—his two seasons of county cricket were a wonderful investment of time for him. Ideally he should bat at number three for Australia, where he can either pursue runs or offer the most perpendicular of Australian bats to the shiny ball. Greg doesn't like that position, so his brother Ian fills it most capably. If a player is apprehensive about batting in a certain slot, it has a psychological effect that can reduce his performances. It is better to have a player of slightly looser technique, and perhaps lesser talent, going in where he enjoys it than having the sounder player going in where he doesn't feel as comfortable.

Part of the cruelty of cricket—and its fascination—is that success or failure is measured in inches. This is why correct style is imperative for the consistent run-getter in all conditions and especially for the attacking player who likes to hit hard through the line of the ball. Yet, no matter how solid your technique, it can only prevail regularly if your tactics are right. People brought up on good wickets tend to play more off the back foot. In South Africa, I was essentially a back-foot player, which proved to be a problem when I came to play in England. In my first match with Hampshire, I was lbw playing back to a ball that nipped into me off the seam. Roy Marshall told me he had had the same trouble when he came to England from fast West Indies pitches in the early 1950s. To succeed in England, he said, you have to play off the front foot; the slower wickets allowed this. I changed my style straight away. The fact that I scored more than 2,000 runs in my first county year was due in large part to Roy's advice at the very start of the season.

The orthodoxy that was drilled relentlessly into me as a youngster (practising until darkness drove us from the nets) was a vital component in my settling readily into county cricket and to play as an essentially enterprising batsman for my first three seasons in England. You won't find many unorthodox batsmen who really come off in county cricket. Batsmen vary in their stances, their grips, their footwork, but to succeed they must have one vital requirement: they all play straight.

Doug Walters, a brilliantly talented batsman, would have struggled to have been a success in county cricket; there is no way he could have consistently made

Lassitude settled on the great Graeme Pollock after South Africa was sacked from Test cricket. Rest of the World matches rekindled interest: a century's worth at The Oval, 1970.

a lot of runs; he simply doesn't play straight enough. Had he joined a county, Doug's considerable ability and common sense would have enabled him to have adjusted; his tendency to play across the line would have been eliminated from his play.

A crucial thing to remember about cricket is that the batsman is so reliant on the surface on which he is playing. A player can be very accomplished, his instincts will urge him to go for his shots, but a poor playing surface will virtually cancel out his talents; he simply can't perform to any reasonable degree at all. English wickets, which have become progressively slower and slower, are not as suited to my style of play as they were when I first came to England as a professional in 1968. In those days they were decidedly quicker and more comfortable to play on. Then, I could hit through the line of the ball and get it through the ring of fieldsmen without strain. Nowadays, they can reach the ball and cut it off more often. It takes more effort to get the ball away; the task of putting together a long innings is more strenuous, more physically exhausting than before.

With the ball creeping up more slowly from the pitch, and seaming persistently for long periods from it, attack has become a greater gamble in English cricket; the two inches that separate the middle of the bat from the edge have become more significant. The fine player who is prepared to play his shots can begin to swing through the line, only to discover the ball has not come through as he thought. So he is forced to check the stroke and perhaps push the ball to mid-on or cover, an important switch of intention not apparent to a great number of deckchair occupants beyond the boundary. After a while, the batsman may be frustrated into a stroke that is not really on and that finishes him. So dull wickets reduce good attacking batsmen to a lower level, and the game itself suffers. By comparison, the man prepared to plod endlessly off the front foot can graft and graft his way to a faceless hundred. On poor wickets, where the natural difference in standards between great and ordinary players shrinks towards its minimum, the great player is compelled to adapt and grind out more of his runs. These torpid pitches, and there are far too many of them, have helped to put the elegant strokemaker out of context in English county cricket. If they were starting their careers in the mid-1970s, touch players such as Tom Graveney and Colin Cowdrey would find it harder to compile big scores; their reputations would have been that much more difficult to establish. In Australia and South Africa, on faster and truer wickets, the batsman who plays forward in the accustomed style to a Procter or a Lillee would be likely to get his head taken off. Relying more on timing than strength, I prefer the ball coming through to me. So playing in the hot weather, hard wicket countries is a much greater pleasure; there the pitches deliver more of the two basic needs—pace and bounce. Pitches with a modicum of life seem a memory in England; I believe that I caught the tailend of an era for stroke players that lasted until around 1970.

Naturally attack is more hazardous on nondescript pitches and, as I said, the county player encounters many of these during a Championship season. Pitches somehow seem to produce the qualities that suit home teams; this coincidence occurs time and again. Clubs with three or four spinners offer visiting teams dead-stop pitches that bring best results for slow bowlers. The arrival of the very fast Antiguan bowler Andy Roberts for his first full season with Hampshire in 1974 made the job of batting outside our home county more tedious than ever. Roberts began that season sensationally. In an early match, he tore through Kent's batting line-up—one of the best in cricket—and felled Colin Cowdrey along the way as he destroyed them twice inside two days. The news on Roberts was out before he led us from the field at the end of that match. From then on, Hampshire played away matches on many pitches that were noticeably slower than they were the year before. The host teams were prepared to sacrifice some of their own capability to score runs to neutralize, or much diminish, Roberts's pace and threat.

This illuminates an aspect of modern cricket that has sharpened the dangers for the attacker. Professionals have always played the game hard. We can't argue with this; after all, the game is their living. So, down the years, they have developed a whole catalogue of ploys, the tricks of their trade ranging from the acute to the snide. I have felt that gamesmanship has grown significantly since I became a professional cricketer. Each year, more fingernails stray into the seam of the ball; more feet walk absentmindedly across the pitch when the opposition is batting fourth; appeals fly up for everything, no matter how grotesque. Money has smothered the old Corinthian code. Players battling for the much richer rewards that come with the flock of one-day competitions have stronger reason for being more 'professional' in their attitudes.

Slower pitches and, to some degree, one-day cricket, have brought about an evolution in cricket in the seventies. The elegant batsman, so much dependant on timing, has waned; too many factors have choked off his natural and flowing stroke play. The strong and muscular batsman, who I call the 'power player', has come more to the foreground and should become even more dominant in years to come. As people like Rohan Kanhai and I have sweated harder for our runs, conditions have swung the emphasis to brutal strikers such as Mike Procter of South Africa and Gloucestershire, Clive Lloyd of West Indies and Lancashire, Brian Davison of Rhodesia and Leicestershire, John Jameson of England and Warwickshire, and my Hampshire colleague, Gordon Greenidge, who also plays for Barbados and is an outstanding prospect for the West Indies. All are muscular, immensely powerful and give the ball a fearful thump.

Gordon Greenidge of Hampshire, Barbados and West Indies. Barry Richards believes the future in English county cricket belongs to power hitters like him.

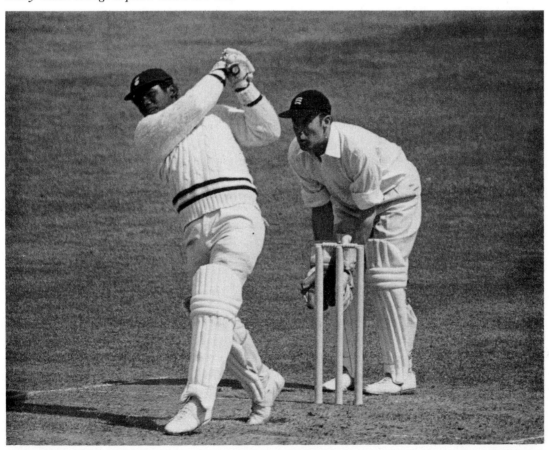

Gordon Greenidge has devastating power. He proved this by hitting thirteen sixes in an innings of 273 not out for D. H. Robins' XI in 1974, one of the most astoundingly complete innings I have ever seen. When you see Gordon shirtless in the dressing room, you can see he is magnificently built. Everything about him is lithe and strong; his forearms are immense. Unlike me, a lean type, he has the muscle and weight to fling into his strokes to back up his primary talents of eye-sight, timing and coordination. Someone like him, Procter or the others I've listed above, will always hit more sixes than I will. They have the confidence to go for them, knowing their fiercely-swung bats have a chance of carting the ball out of the park. When they play along the ground, again this weight and strength allow them to belt their strokes past the fieldsmen with greater ease. Such strong players naturally have an advantage in one-day cricket, now such an important part (financially and therefore for survival) of the English scene. With batting against the clock and restrictive fields, the essence of limited-overs cricket, it is not surprising that their teams have fared so well in these competitions. Unless the trend of morbid pitches is reversed, the future must belong to the power men.

Will the growing rôle of such players compensate for the decline of the elegant batsman? If they succeed in scoring runs consistently, winning matches with hefty blows, they compensate the most important people—their employers. Nothing succeeds like success and now everything revolves around finance.

When muscle replaces grace, the game must lose something as a spectacle for the true connoisseur. But where are the connoisseurs now? The ranks are dwindling of those people who can distinguish the class shot from the merely effective one. In England, people go mostly to cricket grounds to watch one-day matches, which have stultified the silken touch just as much as dead pitches. With defensive fields set, players ringing the boundary, a fine cover-drive will be worth merely a single—and draw no applause. The subtleties of footwork, wristwork and timing do not register deeply in the eye of people whose simple creed is action. In the scramble of one-day cricket, judgment from the other side of the fence is pared down to this: any ball that goes for four is a good shot irrespective of how it gets to the boundary. The hoick, the scythe slash, even the French cut, are rapturously received. Debased in this way, the game registers much more differently with contemporary youngsters than those of my generation. When I went to cricket grounds as a boy, we would watch in awe as a famous player strode out to bat and would say: 'Good luck, sir [always sir]. We hope you get a century today.' Now the call has become: 'Hey, Barry, let's have a few sixes.' What the flowing stroke-maker attempts and achieves out there means less to them; when finesse retreats towards the background, the grandeur of the game is diminished.

I said earlier that I felt the spirit of attack that had been nurtured in me survived for my first three seasons in county cricket. A number of things made me a different alloy: more iron, less silver. One was my status in the game. Until a player is twenty-four or twenty-five, he is striving to establish himself, even if he has been a Test player for several years. Less is expected of him; the phrase 'impetuous youth' is still valid enough. So he can attempt the daring stroke and respond forcefully to containment. After three years with Hampshire, I had built a reputation there, proved myself in Test cricket and become a more senior member of the side. I had greater responsibilities; more was expected of me. So I had to change my approach to the business of scoring runs. I was paid money to score runs steadily at the right time, so consistency became uppermost in my mind. To achieve this, I had to take fewer risks. For the benefit of my team throughout a season, I had to aim for the regular, and more inhibited scores, rather than the brilliant, thrilling knock.

This easing back, fitting a governor to the batting motor, happens to everyone who makes a full-time career of wielding a bat. I have seen many fine batsmen who don't seem to play as excitingly, or as well, after five or six seasons as they did in their first two or three. Majid Khan was a magnificently punishing batsman when he first started with Glamorgan; some of his innings were as breathtaking as you could wish to see. After several seasons, he did not look the same player much of the time; the blood may have been as hot, but the mind was much cooler.

(Left) Richards exercises his natural attacking bent for Hampshire against Lancashire while Engineer, a man of similar instincts, uncoils, open-mouthed in admiration.

(Right) Majid Khan, one of the world's greatest attacking batsmen, agitating fieldsman David Lloyd in a Lord's Test. Playing for Pakistan, Majid sheds his bonds of Glamorgan responsibility.

First, dreary wickets were taking their toll on him. Secondly, as Majid Khan, Glamorgan captain and county batsman, he was expected to score a certain number of runs each season; he had to rein back his exuberance to improve his chances of getting them. He could still cut loose and pummel an attack into a sickly paste, but this was more likely to happen outside his regular bondage. Two of his wonderful innings as a seasoned player—98 in an Oval Test and 109 in a one-day international in 1974—were as a member of a touring team when he was mentally receptive to flaying bowlers he would have played more circumspectly in the different demands of a county match.

Like me, Majid plays with experience and all that this means in its positive and negative senses. We know better now than to try to hit ourselves out of a lean patch. If we struggle, we stay patient for a while, knowing that we will eventually get a full toss or long hop that we can put away for four. It's percentage cricket: the English game inevitably makes the people who play it English in outlook. A young batsman named Vivian Richards came over from Antigua in 1973 to qualify for Somerset. He played with the wonderful freedom of a batsman who wants to succeed but who is prepared to go for his shots. This was exhilarating. I wanted to see him after five years, when he had settled into the work of being a county cricketer, and more was expected of him. If he follows the pattern of Kanhai, Majid and myself, he will produce the odd innings of brilliance but not as consistently as he did in his first relatively carefree year with the county.

Above all, what bleeds attack out of batsmen is the sheer volume of cricket they have to play in a county season. When cricket is a seven-days-a-week job, your appetite for the game is dulled. Apart from the other factors that close up your play, you are less inclined to put into it the enormous effort that sustained attacking play demands. You feel like a tradesman, so you play like one. I don't envy those players who have never known any other type of cricket.

I have the contrast of the much shorter South African season, just nine matches. Over there you can build yourself up mentally for a game, develop a sense of excitement and competition. Then you go out and give of your absolute best, apply yourself non-stop for three days, instead of doling out a certain measure of what you have to offer. Afterwards, you can relax, flop down and let it all drain out of you until you are ready to key yourself up for the next game. Yet, even in South Africa, where pitches, light, the pattern of the seasons suit me so much more, I never entirely discard the defensive style that has become part of me as a Hampshire cricketer.

An element of this has to be the emptiness of lacking Test cricket, the finest stimulus of all. For three years after South Africa was pushed out of Test cricket, I kept alive hopes that we would return in my playing lifetime. But, after that time, I realized that too many things would have to change for this to come about—so my Test days were over. This realization sent a lot of wonderful South African players into early retirement or eroded their general performances. Graeme Pollock, for instance, seemed much more lethargic about the game. Playing the South African season I don't practise anywhere near as hard as I used to do. Those five-mile runs I made daily through the noonday sun to keep fit for Tests have become a faint memory.

The unfettered desire to attack as a batsman belongs to wide-eyed youth when everything is possible, when you are carving, not sustaining, your reputation and can focus on the brighter, carefree side of the game. Realities must change your outlook. I could never recapture in full that zest for attack because I am a different player and a different person. But I could regain much of it if I could play the majority of my cricket in England on quicker and more reliable wickets and if— given twelve months' notice to become fully fit and mentally attuned to it—I had a chance of playing once more for South Africa.

Opening the Innings:

DENNIS AMISS

A reader has to turn to the pages of the New Testament to encounter as triumphant a return from the wilderness as that made by the England batsman, Dennis Amiss. For almost seven years, between 1966 and 1973, this amiable, pipe-smoking Warwickshire player had ricocheted in and out of England teams. The figures against his name on the scoreboard too often had a chilling, symmetrical roundness about them. Even as late as 1972, when he was twenty-nine, his name seemed to be lightly pencilled into the Warwickshire list, rather than typed there in bold and reassuring print. A candid friend—yes, a friend—in a rival county said: 'Down here, we all liked Dennis but regarded him as an easy roll-over; we knew how to get him out cheaply.' At this low point, Amiss as a Test player seemed to have feebler career prospects than a gondolier in Marrakesh.

Then, suddenly, in March 1973, almost thirteen years after his first-class debut, Amiss became a scintillating overnight success. It happened in Pakistan, on the second leg of MCC's tour of India and Pakistan. In India, it had looked, after shaky performances against Chandra & Co. as if he was once more—in Tom Lehrer's immortal phrase—sliding down the razor-blade of life. In three Tests against Pakistan, Amiss scored 406 runs, including two centuries and a 99, for a series average of 81·20. The talent and resolution packed inside his sturdy frame were finally expressing themselves in the only officially acceptable way. After many fruitless visits to the telephone booth, Clark Kent had, at last, emerged as Superman. To the delight of many (including the player quoted above) Amiss had side-stepped the grisly epitaph of Hemingway's writer hero in The Snows of Kilimanjaro: *'It was always what he could do, never what he had done.' Just what he could do, Amiss proved with his match-saving 262 not out in the second Test against West Indies at Kingston in 1974. As an exhibition of application, stamina and grace under pressure (thank you again, Mr Hemingway), this was one of the heroic innings in Test history.*

Dennis Amiss had proved himself as an opening batsman, the pathfinder of the innings. In the following chapter, he offers little instructional advice on how to be a successful opener; this he has reserved for a later book. Instead, he asks the reader to climb aboard the open car, to grip the safety bar tightly and to plunge and soar with him along the switchback railway that has been his life in cricket. It may be wiser for those who suffer from vertigo to retreat straight away to the Tavern.

The year 1972 was a crucial turning point for me—just one of many in my cricket career. Perhaps this was the most important of them all, because it was the year I changed from middle-order to an opening batsman. I was out of the Warwickshire side, which was stiff with batting talent. The year before, our openers John Jameson and John Whitehouse had both enjoyed good seasons; they seemed to have established themselves. At number three we had a great player in Rohan Kanhai. M. J. K. Smith was at number four and Alvin Kallicharran batted at five, fresh from having scored centuries in his first two Test innings against New Zealand. Then came the wicketkeeper Deryck Murray—a Test player capable of scoring centuries—and the bowlers. There was no room for me. I was playing for the Second XI.

In 1972, luckily for my plans and future, both Jameson and Whitehouse were out of the runs. I thought to myself: 'I haven't opened for Warwickshire since 1966, but my only way of getting back into this team is as an opener.'

I went down to see our skipper Alan Smith and told him: 'I'm an experienced player and I want to play in the first team.' Alan said, very reasonably: 'I can understand that, but where can we put you?' 'I want to open the batting.'

Alan must have been startled but did not show it. He looked at me for what seemed a long time, then said slowly: 'You want to open the batting? But we have two good openers.'

'That's so,' I said. 'They are friends of mine, I respect them both but they aren't scoring runs at the moment. I'm in good form with the Seconds, scoring plenty of runs and want a chance to open.'

'All right,' Alan said. 'You can give it a try. You can open in the next match against Middlesex.'

When I walked away from his office, I wondered what I had done. Until twenty-four hours before, I had never given serious thought to being an opening bat, had never turned over in my mind the enormous difficulties there are in succeeding at that job. As a middle-order batsman in a powerful team, I usually went out to tackle spinners or seamers using an old ball. Now I had volunteered to face the fast boys who were fresh and eager and had a hard, shiny new ball to hurl towards me. If my bid was to succeed, I needed intensive practice against the fast stuff. So, the next time we went for indoor nets at Edgbaston, I asked David Brown, Bob Willis, Steve Rouse and the other quickies to work away at me.

'Don't be gentle. Bounce some down at me and give me plenty to think about. Let me know when I'm shuffling my feet as the bowler comes in, or any other mistakes I'm making.' The boys responded readily to all this, especially the part about not being gentle.

These strenuous sessions must have sharpened my game a lot. The Middlesex match was a triumph: I scored around 150. My confidence moved up a notch. Having taken runs from bowlers like Fred Titmus and John Price, I began to feel like an opening batsman. But I was aware that one tall score was not proof enough that I could handle the job; a blob in the next innings could put me back where I started. So I returned to the onslaught at the nets, with the fast bowlers sometimes

using new balls that had the extra pace and bounce to give me a more authentic work-out.

The decision to seek an opening berth had been mine alone and my main reason for trying it was the most basic of all—survival in the game. That season, I scored five centuries, finished second in the county averages and was chosen to play in a one-day international against Australia—about which more later. I reflected afterwards that, if I had not asked to open, if Alan Smith had not agreed (with little evidence to back his gamble), if I had not played that international, my revival as a cricketer might never have happened.

This had not been my first personal crisis with Warwickshire since I had joined the staff as an under-sized fifteen-year-old in 1958. After reaching the county team in 1960, I bobbed around in the batting order between numbers four and six for the next few seasons. Usually I would come into the first team when Mike Smith and Bob Barber were away on Test duty. At the end of 1964 season I was despondent. Warwickshire always had a good batting side which was hard to crack. I wondered if I should move to another county to get more regular first-team cricket. This would have been an enormous upheaval for both playing and family reasons. I had grown up in Birmingham. Warwickshire was the only team I had ever really wanted to play for.

Luck kept me where I felt I belonged. During the 1964–5 winter I heard that two of our stalwarts, Horner and Hitchcock, were retiring. Their departure would mean vacant batting slots; the chance was there for me to prove myself and take a grip on a regular place. I could delay thoughts of having to move elsewhere for at least one season. As it turned out, in 1965 the county gave me six games on the trot; I scored reasonably well; that problem was suppressed until it rose again in 1972.

Between these two county troughs, I had my first couple of Test careers. In 1966, after I had scored 166 for Warwickshire against West Indies at Edgbaston (the first and only time I had opened for the county), I was one of six changes in England's team for the Third Test at The Oval. Despite that hundred against the tourists, I had no expectations of making the England team then. While I had daydreamed as a boy about playing for my country, I secretly thought it could be beyond my talents. I felt some confidence about scoring runs, but in the dressing room I was overawed. Around me were Tom Graveney, Colin Cowdrey, John Murray and other famous players whose autographs I had been chasing not that long before. It took me years to overcome this feeling; it was part of the difficult process of adjusting myself to all the demands of playing at international level.

I scored seventeen in that first Test, hardly a dazzling debut. But I was included to tour Pakistan with an England Under-25 party the following winter. I

Intikhab pulled for four at The Oval. Amiss on his much-interrupted way to 183, his fifth Test century in 1974.

had started my years of shuttling in and out of the Test team. The revolving door never worked faster or more frighteningly than in 1968. My resurrection lasted one match, the first Test against Australia at Old Trafford, which was the nadir of my cricket career—in fact, of my entire life. I scored a pair of blobs. McKenzie had me caught off a swinging ball at third slip in the first innings. In the second, I optimistically tried to punch Cowper through a gap in the inevitable cluster of close fieldsmen, played all around the ball and was bowled. It has been said before but it is true: after the second duck, the walk back to the pavilion seemed endless. In the dressing room, I was more or less in tears; I thought that, without doubt, I was finished forever as an England cricketer. All my teammates tried to cheer me up ('Now you're a real cricketer' and sympathetic nonsense like that). But, of course, the Aussies didn't want to know—they had done their job. I had to wait more than six-and-a-half years after shaping to take my first ball against Australia before actually scoring a Test run from them. It was as sweet a run as I ever scored.

I did take runs in a different context off the Aussies in one of the most vital innings I have ever played. This was in the first one-day international of 1972, that I mentioned earlier on.

During most of that revival season, I was a tiny speck hardly visible to the naked eye at Lord's; I could not have been on even the broadest selection list for any of the five Tests. I was not stunned, but was very surprised when I was invited to Manchester to be considered for the one-day match at Old Trafford. Very gratifying, I thought, but Barry Wood had just scored 90 as an opener in his first Test and this was his home ground. Drink waiter was the best I could envisage. But in our car going to the ground, captain Brian Close (filling in for injured Ray Illingworth) said: 'You're playing, Dennis.' A man of few but pleasant words.

When we batted, the first ball from Bob Massie leapt up and missed my glove by a fraction of an inch. My future as a Test batsman could be measured by the distance between that ball and my glove. (If cricketers don't become philosophers, it's not for lack of material to think about.) I scored a century, built up confidence for the second one-day game and was selected in the touring party for India, Sri Lanka and Pakistan. I think a vital factor in my finally coming good was an unspoken sense of obligation I had developed towards the England selectors. They had kept on picking me. Somehow they rated me, they had faith in what they thought I could achieve. Some of that faith seeped into me. After what the selectors had done for me, and kept on doing, I had the obligation to them and a growing belief in myself. If people who know their cricket and cricketers placed me in the highest company, then perhaps I belonged in that company after all.

However I was not yet out of the forest. The five-match series against India proved a playing misery for me, as it did for most of the England batsmen; we lost 2-1; Chandra took thirty-five wickets in the series. Yet I flew out of India, bound for Sri Lanka, then Ceylon, excited and elated. I felt I might well have worked out how to apply myself successfully to building consistently high Test scores. How this came about is a fascinating story that I never tire of telling.

On pitches that suited them perfectly India's spinners—Chandra, Venkat, Bedi and Prasanna—seemingly killed another of my Test careers (I think this was the third one). I had used unsuccessful tactics against them, trying to get down the wicket to hit them; instead of messing them about, I kept getting out. I was dropped after three Tests. In England's first innings of the fifth Test at Bombay, Fletcher and Greig put on 254, a record fifth-wicket partnership for England in all Tests. I noted that they played carefully and patiently, waiting for the loose ball and then for the bowlers to flag before laying into them. While India were batting, I could not get a net with any of our players. I mentioned to a group of Indian players—Prasanna, Venkat, and Abid Ali—how much I wanted to have some practice. They told me they would put one up after the day's play had finished and would bowl to me. They would not have done this early in the series, but this was the final Test and they might have thought they had seen the last of me as an England player. Even so, it was very decent of them.

So, after stumps, they came out and put up the net. The group of bowlers included Bedi, Venkat, Solkar and Abid Ali. Chandra was there but was injured and didn't bowl. The pitch was terrible, with the ball bouncing high and screwing off it at awkward angles. I said to the bowlers: 'Right, we will do this under Test conditions. Imagine you've got five men around the bat. When I get a bat and pad that would do me, or an lbw, let me know. I want to find out just how well or badly I'm really playing you.'

Amiss has just been declared 'Man of the Series' after two one-day internationals against Australia in 1972. Australian tour manager, Ray Steele, congratulates him.

They bowled to me, and me alone, for an hour. It was one of the most generous gestures I've ever known from opposing players. I couldn't imagine any others doing it, even for a batsman they had no cause to fear. Of all the turning points, pivots, call-them-what-you-will that have tugged my career this way and that, this particular net was perhaps the most important. After many years in England and right at the very end of our four months in India I sensed that I had just absorbed a momentous lesson in batting. Something told me that I finally knew more than the rudiments on how to set about putting big scores together. I had sorted out the method of approach that suited me: I had a firmer foundation to my play such that I could, with a fair measure of confidence, adapt to whatever conditions I met. Opening the batting had rescued me and, as far as I cared to look ahead, I did not want to be anything but an opening batsman. I am grateful to those Indian bowlers, and will remain grateful to them. I only hope that the runs I scored off them in the 1974 series in England did not make them regret their generosity.

If that tour had been to India alone, the trapdoor could have opened under me once more. As it was, we went to Sri Lanka, where I played reasonably well, then to Pakistan for me to launch my fourth Test career (I'm guessing the number; it really has been hard to keep track of them). This particular career has differed from the others: so far it has been a success. In Pakistan the wickets were faster and firmer. I went into the first Test with a good ration of confidence and scored 112 in the first innings. This seemed to confirm my feeling of assurance; I felt that I could be passing from the critical—and so protracted—stage of clinging to the outer edge of the Test team; that I was by rights an England player with an England future. Having scored that first hundred—in my twenty-eighth Test innings—I told myself I should begin thinking of myself as one of the main batsmen in the team. I was building up a new picture of myself altogether.

Possibly more than in any other sport, succeeding at cricket revolves around frame of mind. It's because I like to build an innings without irritating or unnatural pressures that I was happier almost as soon as I switched to opening the innings. I had hated batting at number five, which I did for Warwickshire for a couple of seasons. With such fine players above me in the line-up, plus the scramble that batting for bonus points often brought to an innings, I would many times go in on a good wicket for the last few overs. There was little chance of playing myself in steadily and responsibly. It was almost a beer-match situation: take guard, then start whacking the ball straight away. I wasn't getting enough match practice against the new ball and so lost confidence when playing the quickies. This is why I had needed so much net practice against David Brown and the others before I had sorted out how to handle them properly.

After becoming an opener, I had to restructure my game to some degree. I would go to the nets and try something new: standing a little more upright, picking up my bat a little earlier, adjusting my stance and so on. I had talks with Geoffrey Boycott about opening and watched John Jameson more closely to see what I could learn from him. (John is a most dangerous man to study since his instinct is to go in and belt the ball from the word go; he is also much physically stronger than I am.) I tried one or two things that they were doing, but found they did not suit me and quickly discarded them. But through experiments of this kind I was learning more about my capabilities and fashioning the technique that worked best for me.

Some players—and very successful ones, too—are happy to go on indefinitely without trying to take an attack apart. I find that, once I am in on an easy wicket and have a good score up, I want to try to take control. It's my style to want to play myself in, master the fast bowlers, then raise the tempo of my innings until I can dominate, really belt the bowling around. Obviously I'm keen to get a century, then make it a double, but, at the same time, there is nothing better than a good assault on the bowlers.

Ideally you want to accelerate as your innings progresses. At times the circumstances of a match just won't allow you to do this. My 262 not out against West Indies at Kingston was such an innings. I had no alternative but to play defensively all the way through. Saving the game was the objective there. The need to achieve this kept me going. I could have become physically shattered batting on hour after hour but the enjoyment of scoring runs and saving the team prevented that.

This was the second Test of the series. I was buoyed up by having scored a century in the first at Port of Spain. The Kingston pitch was so superb for batting I knew the ball would do nothing unpredictable. So I kept saying to myself: 'Just stay there. Just play it, play it, play it. The runs will come.' I'd been involved in two runouts with Frank Hayes and Alan Knott and fretted a little at the thought that I was partly responsible for these setbacks. Unless I stayed in, I would really have let the side down. And, while I told myself over and over that I must not get out—we were running out of wickets—I somehow felt that I wouldn't; the pitch was so good. Backed into such a tight corner, I couldn't afford to go for the runs but they kept on ticking up. Kanhai had set attacking fields which inevitably left many gaps. The outfield was so glassy smooth that strokes that were little more than defensive pushes were skimming through those gaps for four; in England these prods would have brought tight, even daring, singles.

At the end of the Indian tour of 1972–3 I had played fifteen Tests for a batting average no higher than some of the bowlers had managed. Less than eighteen months later I had scored eight Test centuries and batting records were looming. Other people's faith and a whole string of improbabilities had kept the small, feeble flame of my Test career alight. Now there are so many things I want to do in many areas of cricket: score many runs for a winning side against Australia;

So hard to forget: Amiss dabs at McKenzie, Cowper snaffles at third slip. One lens in Amiss's traumatic 'pair' against Australia at Old Trafford, 1968.

score another double century and a triple in Tests; get a century in both innings for Warwickshire and England; be a leading player for the county when it wins the Championship and several of the one-day competitions.

Players with much more ability than myself have somehow missed out along the line. I don't want to be one of that group. There is still so much to learn and so much that I want to accomplish. I want Warwickshire and England to prosper and do my part towards their successes.

The Allrounder: MIKE PROCTER

To succeed at cricket, the player must have a deep love for the game. Without it, he won't be inspired to apply himself constantly to the serious pleasures of scoring runs, taking wickets or staying alert in the field. When a player is expected to do all of these things, as an allrounder, he must have an enormous genuine appetite for the game. He has to maintain a sustained eagerness—something more than mere professional application—to accept willingly the multitude of exertions that are his job. For the allrounder there are no short cuts: he must be prepared to drip a lot of sweat both bowling long stints and spending long hours at the crease. Sometimes these tasks will come so close together that they seem to fuse into a blur of exhaustion. But fresh obligation has to be confronted straight away; it can't be slid into a pending tray until your aches subside and you are fully refreshed. In terms of the physical and mental efforts you need to pour into it, being a cricket allrounder—especially one who is a fast bowler and not a spinner—is a tough and exhausting way to make a living.

Luckily I relish the workload: I want one hundred per cent involvement in every match I play; any less and I feel out of the game. I have a compulsion to be active, a central figure in the pattern of things, rather than merely standing in slips or at mid-on and then moving from one position to another at change of over. I get much more tired than specialist batsmen who never take the ball, but I don't envy them their passive rôle.

Having been an allrounder right through my first-class career, my mind is geared to think of cricket as strenuous effort with occasional passages of repose. When I'm denied the chance to express all my talents on the cricket field, my game suffers. During the 1974 county season, strained ribs kept me out of the Gloucestershire side for several weeks, then prevented me from bowling for a number of matches on my return. Not being able to bowl, I felt completely out of the game. So, during this phase, I did not bat very well; feeling a partial cricketer, I batted like one. My mental approach had slipped from that state of fine adjustment that you need to score runs consistently.

While I was easing my way back, I had the frustration and education of watching John Jameson and Rohan Kanhai of Warwickshire score an undefeated 465 (a world second-wicket partnership) against Gloucestershire at Edgbaston. I had to endure standing on the field for the entire 100 overs of their fine stand without a chance of bowling a single ball at either of them. An experience like this tempers

your patience, but I would have been seething if my disablement had been anything but temporary.

Because of the way I now regard myself as a cricketer, I'll have to keep that
sense of participation as an organic part of my cricket. When the time comes, for
whatever reason, to accept that I'm no longer a fast bowler, I won't give up bowling altogether. I'll become a seamer, or allow the wheel to complete the circle by
bowling off-breaks, as I did in my senior years at Hilton College in South Africa.

Fast bowling was the final arrow I put into my quiver—it got me into Test
cricket—but it was forced upon me. I had opened the bowling during my last two
years at senior school only because we had nobody else to do it. I wasn't really
effective; at that time I could have laid no claims to being an allrounder. Most of
my school career, I was essentially a batsman. At junior school, I kept wicket, then
opened the bowling in my final year; at senior school I was again a wicketkeeper,
and had my period as an off-spinner before getting my hands on a new ball once
more.

My batting had been laid on very secure foundations. I first held a cricket bat
when I was five or six years old; then my father coached me in the garden of our
home in Durban. When I was at junior school, between the ages of ten and thirteen, a splendid coach named John Saunders guided my batting. I had a good
eye for the ball but, up to then, played mostly 'hoick' shots. John took hold of me

*Mike Procter cuts M. Buss of
Sussex for four during his
match-winning innings of 94 in
the Gillette Cup final at Lord's in
1973. Success is vital for
motivation, he says.*

and made me play straighter; he even went as far as to take films of me playing shots—a considerable help.

When I finally turned to quick bowling at school, my idiosyncratic action was so ingrained that the coaches could not change it. Mercifully they didn't insist rigorously on trying to mould my movements into a classic action. One fundamental of good coaching is to appreciate that every player has an individual way of doing things; technique in whatever you do—batting, bowling, catching, throwing—should be kept as natural as possible. I had been lucky at junior school in that my coaches didn't regard me as any kind of bowling prospect, so they hardly felt it worth their while persevering to make me change. In fact, I can hardly remember anything about my bowling coaching.

By the time I entered first-class cricket, the action was there to stay; I was too old to change it. Many people still regard me as a wrong-foot bowler, but I am not wrong-footed as such. Normally, a right-arm bowler brings his left foot down to brace the effort of swinging his body into the delivery; then he releases the ball. My speed comes entirely from arm action, so my arm must whirl through as hard as I can rotate it. This arm action is so quick that I release the ball fractionally before my left foot comes down. Because I rely completely on my arm the equation becomes very simple: the faster I run, the faster I bowl. People like John Snow, Dennis Lillee and Andy Roberts all use their bodies in delivery and don't have to rush pellmell up to the wicket; they can vary their pace through controlling their run-up. My way makes the act of bowling very hard work and it cast strong doubts in my early days as to how long I could survive. Sceptics gave me three years of fast bowling at the most before I broke down irreparably. They reasoned that some part, or parts, of me would have to give way—my arm, shoulder, back or legs—the laws of anatomy and physics would do me in. However, certain physical laws were in fact my allies: the process of so much bowling down the years developed my strength and endurance.

Certainly I couldn't succeed or keep on bowling unless I stay absolutely fit. I always have the fitness but, even so, I become very tired after a long spell of bowling. Doing almost all of the work, my arm gets heavy; when I can't move it fast enough, I lose my pace. In my fledgling years I had the best incentive of all to become and stay perfectly fit: my main chance of breaking into the South African team in 1966 was as a bowler. So, in the evenings after work, I would go for long runs and do work sprints for half an hour or an hour. And I needed long practice sessions of bowling itself. The act of bowling a cricket ball at speed employs your muscles in unique combinations. Sheer physical fitness is not enough. There have been times when my physical condition has been supreme but I have become winded while running in to bowl.

During the crowded English season I need nothing more than match bowling. But the sparser fixture list for Currie Cup matches in South Africa makes it

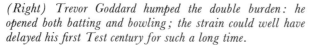

(Above) At least six champion cricketers are involved in this handshake in 1969 as Sobers presents Procter with the Reg Hayter Trophy as the man who did most for his county that season.

(Right) Trevor Goddard humped the double burden: he opened both batting and bowling; the strain could well have delayed his first Test century for such a long time.

imperative for me to keep up my training runs. My all-year-round schedule, while bringing regular fatigue and a jaded feeling now and then, does at least eliminate the conditioning period at the start of each new season; I'm always bowling fit.

While I confounded those pessimists who predicted that I would fall apart by the age of twenty-three, I began to develop slight injuries around 1972, when I turned twenty-six. Each season since then, I have felt a little less powerful, a little less resilient. In part, I've compensated through doing what everyone has to do: developing professional savvy. It's slightly embarrassing to recall a match in one of my early seasons with Natal when I bowled on a very flat wicket in punishing heat. As the spearhead of the side, I bowled about 36 or 37 overs, charging in as hard as I could from a full run for every ball. The harder the batsmen hit me, the harder I wanted to bowl; this was youth applying itself zealously but not very rationally. I finished completely spent with none for well over 140. Nowadays, when the pitch has nothing for me—and plenty of slow English pitches are like that—I use the shorter run and work at line and length, the obvious and inevitable thing to do. This way I find I can still test batsmen's reflexes.

Experience has other benefits, especially for an allrounder who must put a lot of effort into his cricket. Once you have built up some experience, and tasted some success along the way, you regard yourself less as an individual performer and more as a unit of the team. It is your team successes that hold the warmest pleasures, because they mean the most. Without them, your motivation is much reduced and lack of motivation can turn cricket from a delight into something else.

Without the spur of a strong run in the Championship or staying alive in at least one of the limited-overs competitions, the English programme can seem oppressively long and arduous. Lack of incentive puts weights on your arms and legs; having to drain yourself bowling twenty overs or batting for three hours in a meaningless match reduces your livelihood into a grind; in this the allrounder gets a double dose of dissatisfaction. This is why Gloucestershire's winning the Gillette Cup competition in 1973 was an important revitalizer for both club and players.

As a flesh and blood creature, an allrounder can resent being regarded as a perpetual motion machine (Garry Sobers expressed himself sourly on this point more than once). Talent, fitness, the acquired knack of taking wickets or scoring runs at the telling moment all bring fulfilment, but can have their debit side as well. Success in one sphere can shrink your effectiveness in another; there is a danger in being too proficient and too versatile and no allrounder is proof against it. It is said that the considerable demands that were made on him as a bowler cut back Keith Miller's ability to harness his brilliant batting talents, although he was capable of playing historic Test innings to the end of his career—his allround performance won the Lord's Test of 1956 at the age of thirty-six. The rigours of opening the bowling must have deprived teams and spectators of potential batting triumphs from such gifted batsmen as Alan Davidson, Ray Lindwall and Trevor Goddard, who humped the massive double burden of opening both batting and bowling.

I know that other demands have affected my own batting capacity. It is debilitating to come off the field after a long innings, barely have time to unbuckle your pads and wipe your brow before you are back on the field with a shiny new ball in your hand and another heavy job to do.

I think I felt this most when we played a semi-final of the Gillette Cup against Worcestershire in 1973. We batted first and I scored a hundred. Near the end of these limited-overs matches you really have to struggle to hit boundaries because the fielding captain has posted his fieldsmen around the fence. So you have to run a great number of twos and threes. That particular day was hot enough to wilt even a South African like myself. At the end of our innings I was shattered, really exhausted mentally and physically. But immediately I was in action again, knowing that, as a main Gloucestershire bowler, I had to bowl as well and tight as possible. I managed to get three wickets but felt much older than twenty-six as we came off after winning by five runs.

While this sequence of batting, then bowling, drains you, it is easier than the other way round. A long stint of bowling can leave you in no mood to face the prospect of needing to put together a long innings. After a heavy day in the field your feet are tired and perhaps your shoulders and bowling arm ache. All you want to do is have a shower, then relax for the rest of the day. When you bat four or five, as I do, you have to put the pads on straight away. If a couple of wickets fall quickly, you are out in the middle again and perhaps not attuned to settling down for a long innings. To stay there you have to concentrate to your utmost for every ball. And this is your vulnerable point: the effort of what you have done not so long ago in the field dulls your concentration. I've been out many times, often feeling that I've virtually tossed my wicket away, because fatigue, or slowness to adjust to this new task of batting, have undermined my concentration. And sometimes I've taken a good haul of wickets, thought that I was at least earning my bread as a bowler, and allowed my batting to slump. There are times when I ponder what I might have achieved with the bat if I had never been a fast bowler, had never put so much effort into that.

Knowing the strains, the tensions, the demands on limbs and mind of producing allround performances, I can only marvel at the durability and sustained brilliance of Garry Sobers. For twenty years of almost unceasing play around the world—sometimes playing ten Test matches a year—he was four cricketers in one. He played more than a hundred internationals and had the responsibility of captaincy in almost half of them. When he retired I looked at his career figures; they really are almost unbelievable. I usually don't bother about statistics, which can be so shallow and misleading, but for once they convey the quality and unique abilities of this man. In each area he was an unqualified champion: the highest number of Test runs; second greatest number of catches; among the top six of all-time wicket takers—each section a magical career in itself.

Whenever he was on the field, something extraordinary, some savagely taxing feat, was expected of him, without his seizing up or showing signs of wear or staleness. Garry was sometimes criticized for batting at number six, which was lower than his talents. Yet, as one who knows what all that effort can do to you, I understand his wanting some respite from responsibility and physical exertion. A single player pulls his weight when he does one eleventh of the work; why ask him to do four fifths of the chores? It's no wonder that golf, which through its own piercing demands could wash the cares of cricket from his mind, became such a solace and therapy for him.

Garry had two qualities that, I believe, enabled him, the ultimate allrounder, to remain so great for so long. First of all, there was his suppleness: he had the body and movements of a superb natural athlete. Garry looked fluent at whatever he did on the cricket field; he had a marvellous action for all his different types of bowling, especially loose and economical for his fast stuff.

The action Procter's coaches could not change: all arm-powered, open-chested but definitely not wrong-footed. The author wonders how long he will be able to keep on doing this.

Bowling as I do, I could never hope to last two thirds as long as **Garry** did. Some mornings, the day after I have bowled twenty overs off my long run, I wake up very stiff, feeling soreness in my knees and twinges here and there. If this keeps up, obviously I'll have to ease back. Also, whenever it sagged, Garry's interest in the game was regularly revitalized with Test matches, a stimulus I believe I shall never know again. As soon as the guillotine dropped on South Africa, I sensed we were in the wilderness for keeps.

The second of Garry's assets was his magnificent attitude: I don't think he worried about anything particularly, except getting peevish during those periods of staleness that afflict all of us from time to time. Almost always, I'm sure, he would just stroll onto the field and play and delight in what he was doing. This may be the essence of his durability: his deep and uncomplicated love for the game of cricket.

I'm a different type of individual: I worry when my form is poor; I worry when Gloucestershire or Rhodesia are not doing well: I feel the weight of responsibility as captain of Rhodesia. Leading a team in the fiercely-competitive Currie Cup—where every run is vital and rivalry is cut-throat in many senses— I have pressures that deny me rest, and I must respond to all of them. When players are so keen and captains are much more tactically sound than they were previously, you must be on your mettle. With my strong sense of competition, I'm prepared to drive myself hard doing at least three jobs in playing each game to the utmost.

As I said, figures don't register strongly with me. Satisfaction is not necessarily the glamour of scoring a century or taking a swag of wickets; it certainly is not the dull and sterile business of batting for not outs that is so important to some players. Fulfilment is shaped in the context of a match; it is what you can achieve when it counts and runs don't mean more than wickets, or vice versa. Getting a breakthrough, wiping out two or three tailenders at the vital moment registers far more with me than six or seven wickets for ninety when it doesn't matter. You need the incentive of going for something definite. I would much prefer to score the timely thirty or forty runs to win key matches than hit the best hundred of the year in a match that is already dead or insignificant. The ultimate is for you to play well and to have done your share towards earning a win for your side. In cricket, success for the team is what counts. So the allrounder, or any player for that matter, can feel the greatest pride in contributing in steady and relevant doses rather than racking up blazing triumphs that are good for nothing else than his ego and that source of mischief and selfishness—his averages.

'Reliable when needed' is a good enough epitaph for anyone. I'm prepared to keep on oozing a lot of sweat trying to earn it.

Fast Bowling: JOHN SNOW

Fast bowlers really are the people who win Test matches and series. This had been proved time and again. They are most likely to get the breakthrough, the needed wicket when it counts, or bowl a side out either on good wickets or bad. Apart from providing the most exciting sight in cricket (what else can compare with Dennis Lillee, Wes Hall or Lindwall careering in to bowl?), they bring the feeling of urgency. With their straightforward aim—bowl 'em out—they want to slice a batting side open and watch it bleed before the shine goes from the ball or the pitch dies on them.

The fast bowler's job is also the hardest in cricket. A batsman playing a long innings needs great physical and mental stamina, concentrating at the crease for hours, running quick singles, or twos or threes. But the most lashing stroke or most reckless single doesn't inflict as much strenuous movement as bowling a single really fast ball. In its entirety, fast bowling is a science that takes years to learn.

Fast bowling makes immense and curious demands on your body. Unless you are freakishly strong or have an astonishing action (which will either legally or physically put you out of cricket in a hurry) you will run in fifteen to twenty paces along a line that curves very slightly. This curve sharpens in the last few strides so that you can fall away correctly off the pitch when you have released the ball. Well before delivery, you have to line yourself up properly. Despite the vigour of your run-up, your head must be locked steady, so that you gaze only at the spot where you want the ball to pitch. With every pace you are assimilating your speed of approach; a brisk tail wind can float you along to overstep your chosen point of delivery. On the run-up, you are also intent on the placing of your feet, the coordination of head, torso and legs. To avoid bowling a no-ball, your feet have to be planted in precisely the right place.

To achieve your selected line, the movement of both balancing and bowling arms and twist of body on delivery must be exactly judged and carried out. Intelligent fast bowling is not just a raw, tearaway, thick-muscles and thick-headed thing. Watching a professional and experienced fast bowler in action, the spectators are seeing a body and mind computerized in fine detail. With every ball, the bowler must be aware of each item of feedback and get it right. If he does not, the machinery can go haywire. People who have never done it should try to keep all these points in mind as they watch a fast bowler while perched on a grandstand bench or in a deckchair or overstuffed armchair inside the pavilion.

It stands to reason that a fast bowler must have a strong, well-balanced physical frame. A great many of the best fast bowlers have been reckoned to stand between 5 ft 10 in and 6 ft 2 in at the most. In modern times the select fast bowlers have usually fallen within these size limits: Lindwall, Miller, Statham, Trueman, Tyson, Procter, Peter Pollock. Notable exceptions who were an inch or so taller were the South Africans Adcock and Heine, Lillee and Wes Hall. But a man above 6 ft 4 in in height, could never be a truly fast, effective or durable fast bowler; he is just too large for the job; he cannot coordinate his limbs and body in the right way. David Larter of Northamptonshire, who was very tall, did achieve the smooth movement to some degree but he was haphazard and in-accurate. There is no way that extremely tall men such as Norman Graham of Kent and Tony Greig of Sussex—who are both 6 ft $7\frac{1}{2}$ in—could sort out their movements to bowl as fast as the others listed above. There seems to be some-thing about height and the ratio of length of arms and legs and the coordina-tion of a well-knit frame that dooms the 'giraffes' to hit an upper limit of fast-medium.

To some extent height will determine the style of fast bowler you become. If very short, like Harold Larwood, or slightly taller than average, like Dennis Lillee, there is a fair chance you will be a run-up-and-jump type. If you are about average height, either powerfully-built or wiry with very flexible joints, your style may well be slide-up and slide-through, such as Trueman, Lindwall, Statham and myself.

Obviously a fast bowler needs strength in his legs to keep going and strength in his back because that is where the effort will hit him most, as Miller and Lillee found out. Along with carefully developed muscle structure, he needs a sound pair of feet to endure flat-out breakthrough efforts and donkey work which together, in a county season, can add up to six or seven hundred overs. Body building has to begin in the formative years. Tradition and necessity can take care of this: Lar-wood, Voce and Trueman down the mines. I chopped a lot of wood as a teenager. My father very probably had me wielding an axe for this purpose; it both broad-ened my shoulders and gave them a loose and easy swing. To keep them supple and to protect my back from strain, I do a lot of bending and stretching exercises and play a great deal of squash. However, fast bowling imposes such peculiar demands on the body that the only way to be fully fit for it is plenty of pre-season exercise. Only bowling makes you bowling fit. Every sport has its special definition of fitness. You will find footballers in perfect condition become quickly puffed and worn out running around a cricket field in a social match.

From their facial expressions and demeanour on the field, some bowlers seemed to have hated the batsmen. Perhaps some did. More likely the bowler looked vexed and hostile because he hated giving away runs—a very different matter. Still, a successful fast bowler must be aggressive. You are there to do an aggressive job and you either become aggressive or you quietly drop out of the game before the game drops you.

There are times when you have to bowl on wickets without an ounce of kindness in them for you. You have to rush up and down and keep whacking the ball into slow pitches—and in England you can encounter a string of them in succession—and it can be an absolute bastard. There is nothing you can do except keep working away. On pitches good or bad, when you are belted for four, you have to come back with something from somewhere inside you; this is where the aggression really counts—in trying to establish mental authority over the batsman. This aggression does not include beamers but the bowler must wipe as much compassion for the batsman as he can from his mind. The bat in the opponent's hand is a potent weapon. He hasn't come to the crease bearing soft and gentle thoughts about you; he is there to give you as much stick as he can; to blast you out of the game if he can manage it. So, while you are bowling, there is a hatred not for the batsman as a person or an individual, but of what he can do in his general rôle, how he can overcome you. 'Jolly-good-show' politeness must be

(Left) The run-up-and-jump school. Peter Pollock of South Africa while inflicting five for 39's worth of distress on a hapless Australia at Johannesburg in 1970.

(Right) The slide-up-and-slide-through school of fast bowling as shown by an outstanding exponent. Ray Lindwall of Australia.

sparing. You are there to confound the player physically and mentally; you want him coming in full of apprehension, then becoming more agitated and uneasy about scoring runs or even surviving. Handsome gestures are fine in theory but they can ease the tension and dilute your impact on the batsman. In return, you don't need the batsman, when he gets one in the rib cage or past his nose, to rush down and say how impressed he is with your performance; the movement of his bat, feet and body will tell you all you want to know. I think I brought a high measure of what I call aggression with me into the game, and experience has only served to intensify it.

The rules of cricket firmly control the use of the bouncer, and rightly so. But, for the fast bowler, the bouncer is very important, technically and tactically. It is a short and emphatic examination paper that you put to the batsman. You sort out somebody's technique with it; you test his mettle as well as his strokes. When a new batsman comes along and you know little about him, the bouncer is as effective a probe as you have; better and easier to bowl than, say, a swinging yorker. Does the batsman try to counter it with a hook? If so, you learn how well he hooks, and whether up or down. Or does he try to get out of the way? And in what fashion: does he merely sway back coolly from the hips, take a smooth and quick step away or does he scuttle off to some urgent business he has just discovered in another part of the crease? And, as you run up to bowl the next ball, are his feet jittering a little, ready for prompt evacuation should this ball rear towards his breastbone or eyebrows? You have to know these things. They are vital pieces of data to drop into the mental files you carry on every player you have encountered. He is doing exactly the same to you, working out your pace, line and other things.

The laws confining the use of bumpers are reasonable. There is a limit to the number that should be bowled, not only on the basis of intimidation; it is stupid to keep on banging the ball in short. Persistence is a waste of time. It is far better to bowl two or three, then pitch a fast ball well up to undermine the batsman who has darted onto the back foot expecting another short one.

Strictly speaking, it is hard to define a bouncer. Is it a short ball that darts up to rib height or one that bounces and flies towards the batsman's head? Technically, the ball going towards the head is not the really dangerous one for a batsman of reasonable talents. The quickness of his eye and his disciplined footwork should enable him to sum it up and deal with it as he sees fit: a swift, harsh stroke or evasion. The ball to damage his composure is the one that leaps up to thump the rib cage. This is more likely to bustle him into the wrong position for succeeding balls. You may then slip him a ball that bounces even higher. If a man is het up by a bouncer, and is aware that this shows, he may think another will soon follow. Then you are doing your job: tipping him slightly off balance, making him uncertain which way to go, worrying him about the risk of playing onto the front foot. When this happens, he is less complete; you have a chink to work on. You are softening him, too, for bowlers at the other end.

Before moving on from the subject of bumpers, I'll make one or two remarks about the so-called 'Fast Bowlers' Union'. There is no pact as such among fast bowlers not to heave short-pitched balls at each other. You quickly recognize among fast bowlers those who don't bat very well. Since you are not setting out to do anybody harm, you leave them alone. You are liable to hit them rather than get them out. If a fast bowler can bat with a certain competence, he must expect some ginger. Similarly, one who is not a good bat but cannot be classified as an absolute rabbit, must expect life to get a little harder if he hangs around in the crease for a while. No player who can put a few runs together, or who is perhaps freakishly doing it for the first time in his life, should expect to be able to play forward forever to a fast bowler with complete impunity. The name of the game for a fast bowler is to bowl out the other side. He does this in two major ways: breakthroughs against established batsmen to rip an innings apart or efficient mopping up of the tail. Your dues go to the team, not to a fanciful 'Union'.

There is a story of Fred Trueman and a young Essex batsman who hooked at his short stuff on a slow wicket at Bradford and got away with it. However the boy's father went around shouting about Fred's brutality. Fred said: 'He can try the hook at Bradford, but he would be wise not to try it when we play at Leyton.' Well, the batsman *did* keep on trying to hook Fred at Leyton and finished up spitting out his teeth. This was most regrettable but the batsman should have worked out all the factors: his hooking ability against Fred's pace from a good wicket. Commonsense prevents accidents.

The most discussed incident of my playing career—striking Terry Jenner on the back of the head in the final Test at Sydney in 1971—was the simplest of batting accidents. At the time, I was distracted; I was thinking more about umpire Lou Rowan than about Jenner. I bowled a bad, not an intimidatory ball. Jenner ducked into it; it was one of those things. If he had not turned and squatted— hardly the wisest response to a short ball—the ball would not have struck him in such a dangerous place. Also, on that tour, when a ball struck Graham McKenzie in the face, it was sheer bad luck for him. The ball was not that short; the pace of the wicket made it leap up so high. Incidentally, I received only a few abusive letters after the Jenner episode. There are always a few nutters around ready to write offensive letters, even when nothing unfortunate has happened. I received many more letters of sympathy after damaging my finger from running full tilt into the fence in the same Test than the nasty kind. People were also sympathetic after the drunk grabbed hold of me when I was fielding near the fence in that match—it really was an eventful few days. For me, the point about Australian crowds is not whether most of them appreciate the tactical depths of the game, but that their strong involvement and commitment allow them to enjoy watching the

(Left) A batsman can sway, duck or scuttle from the path of a bouncer. Ian Redpath has the nerve and experience to choose the swaying method.

(Right) Final Test at Sydney 1971. A Hill barracker with over-quenched thirst uses old-fashioned debating tactics on Snow, who rightly contends that Australians have a strong sense of involvement in their cricket.

game so much. I respond more eagerly and think I play better when a large crowd is there bringing a lot of emotion and tension to the game. So the atmosphere of Test matches has revved me up to do my work as well as I can irrespective of whether the match was in Leeds, Melbourne or Auckland.

I don't think it is wise for any young bowler to try to model himself assiduously on another, no matter how fine the older man's action or career record. No two bowlers can be the same; the good bowler must do his own thing. My action is more like Brian Statham's than anyone else's. I picked up a few pointers from watching him. These were not so much physical but the way he applied himself, the line he chose to work, how he fell away after delivery etc. As a fledgling, and certainly in his early county years, a fast bowler must analyse his bowling in minute detail. He must learn to tear himself apart in his mind's eye, to break down all the component parts of his action (placing of the feet during run-up, holding the head steady, movement of both arms on delivery, splitting his effort, falling away and follow through) and know they are all linking together into an effective whole. Without this analysis, you cannot achieve smoothness and the finest co-ordination; to save every possible particle of energy without losing speed and thrust. Otherwise fast bowling is reduced to a brute physical thing; the bowler is wearing himself out for little effect. To shape a career you just cannot avoid this process, which boils down to professional application. As you rise, from junior to seconds to senior team, the demands change, the margin for error must be reduced. So you must be continually re-thinking what you are doing.

I think of a newcomer to professional cricket as having to play on a three-year basis before he finds his level. The first year you can bowl a lot and achieve some success because you are strong and eager and partly because nobody has seen what you can do. The second year will almost certainly be harder: batsmen will have some information to use in countering you; and perhaps you will have a physical reaction from the hard work of bowling. The third year, if you are any good, you are going to settle into it; you assimilate what you have learned and find out if you have the physical capabilities for the job.

By this time any shortcomings in your style will be taking their toll. Andy Roberts of Hampshire had a wonderful first season, more than 100 wickets and top of the county averages. But, while he is young (born in 1951), he projects a sense of strain when he bowls. There is a harshness in his run-up and his actual gather, just before the moment of release, is rough. I hope I am wrong, but I am sceptical about how durable he may be because of this strain. Perhaps the important thing about Roberts's bowling is that it works; he gets results. There is something to be said for refraining from trying to bring about major adjustments to an effective style through striving for a classical action. Nonetheless it will be interesting to see how my three-year basis works out with Roberts.

Fast bowling has become much tougher work, both in England and elsewhere. In recent years preparation of wickets has changed; the fizz has gone from them. MCC started it off one year with a directive to produce spinning wickets. Dead grass was left on pitches; they were not properly prepared. In addition, clubs suffer because it is difficult to get and retain ground staffs. But the one factor that has worsened wickets more than anything else is Surrey loam. Groundsmen have sprayed it around as if it was Dr Johnson's cure-all. To get any response on these doped wickets, fast bowlers really have to whack the ball in hard. Sometimes it's a hopeless task. Batsmen also find it harder to play their shots with the ball not coming through to them. So we are just not getting good cricket wickets where the ball bounces evenly or adequately. Bowling sides out is the bowler's job but, on the whole, we are denied the chance to do this while providing lively cricket.

In Australia most of the Test wickets seem little faster than the county ones in England, although their overall preparation is much better. If you are lucky, the Sydney pitch might do a bit, but Melbourne and Adelaide are dead. Since a fast bowler will defeat batsmen from bounce rather than movement off the seam,

Perth is the best, the most satisfying. It is fast and its hardness promotes bounce, although the ball does not seam as markedly as at Sydney. I like Perth as well as any Test pitch. English Test pitches are a very mixed lot. Leeds usually gives movement off the seam; Trent Bridge is just blisters and backache; Old Trafford is variable, sometimes offering a little, sometimes nothing; Lord's used to be consistently the best but has not offered a great deal in recent years; The Oval for the final Test against Pakistan in 1974 was, for those who bowled on it, the slowest, weariest and most unfair pitch of the generation.

Despite slower wickets, fast bowling is still a good trade for a strong and thinking young cricketer who wants to make a career of cricket. He'll have to work hard, putting more muscle and patience into it than luckier bowlers of some earlier eras. But if he does work hard and achieve some success it is very satisfying. The major satisfaction comes from mastering the many things he must control to become an intelligent fast bowler. He will have built the most stimulating and complicated piece of sophisticated equipment in cricket: himself—a purposeful and, hopefully, enduring fast bowler.

(*Editor's Note:* During the 1974–75 Test series in Australia, the words 'bouncer' and 'bumper' sprawled across massive headlines more often than the more universally pertinent words 'unemployment', 'recession' and 'bankruptcies'. On January 10, 1975, the *Daily Mirror* shrieked: BUMPER WAR GOES ON. On January 8 the *Daily Telegraph* expostulated: TIME TO CALL NO BALL TO INTIMIDATORS.

The causes of all this nostril-dilating and neck-purpling were two hirsute Australian fast bowlers Dennis Lillee and Jeff Thomson, who had pummelled and fragmented a somewhat threadbare England to its worst series defeat in seventeen years. Thomson, completely unheralded, was so fast he had the ball bruising breastbones from a fairly full length. Little direct criticism of deliberately bouncing was levelled at him. On the other hand, Lillee—thirty-one wicket hero of the 1972 series—seemed, from the tricky vantage point 12,000 miles distant, to have turned into a cricketing werewolf: reportedly flinging down bumper after bumper, snarling at opposing players, livid at Tony Greig for replying with his mosquito-bite bouncers. Lillee's churlish and unwise confession of bowling to hurt batsmen, made in an over-ripe book on the eve of the series, set him up for demolition in print. Meanwhile, John Snow, the major figure in the few bumper dust-ups four years earlier had only his eyeballs involved this time. He sat in the broadcasting box at Test grounds cool and serene in his madras cotton shirts and snug slacks, earphones emerging from his froth of curly hair. Reports that Snow kept pulling pats of unmelted butter from his mouth while watching the Australian pair crunching his compatriots were interesting but unconfirmed.)

Wicketkeeping: ALAN KNOTT

For many years wicketkeepers have been compared to soccer goalkeepers. The comparison was not so valid in earlier times when wicketkeepers were almost always vertical; their strengths were standing up to quick bowlers and plenty of stumpings from wrist- and finger-spinners. Nowadays it's a different job. To me the similarity between the two rôles has increased in the last decade. When you are standing back—as we are a considerable amount of the time now—every ball bowled towards you is like a penalty kick. You think: is it going to deflect? And which way—left or right? You must be ready to get yourself airborne in either direction. The contemporary wicketkeeper must be largely gauged on the number of diving catches he can reach and hold. Leg-side stumpings remain as spectacular and skilful as any of the 'keeper's other arts. But, like the spinners, who provide most of the stumping chances, they are being phased out of the game.

I'm not mad about statistics but they can sometimes make their point. When Leslie Ames of Kent set a wicketkeeper's record of 127 victims in 1929, well over a third of them (48) were stumpings. So far, my biggest haul, in 1967, is 98. Of these, only eight were stumpings. These days, if a dozen stumping chances come your way in a full Test and county season, it's miraculous.

The bulk of the bowling in any county side is done by quicker bowlers, ranging from fast to slow-medium. Conditions—heavy atmosphere and the ball usually doing something off the seam—favour seamers, so they are most often in action. And the place to take the most wicketkeeping catches from them is standing back.

A lot of the time there can be little value in crouching over the stumps to medium pace bowlers. English wickets have become so slow that batsmen can comfortably watch the ball off the pitch before moving into their stroke; they can easily play off the back foot. So very few of them seem to play out of their ground. When I first came into the Kent side in the mid-sixties, I stood up for Alan Dixon, a medium-pacer slightly faster than Derek Underwood. In three seasons I had two stumping chances from him. In that time, there were an enormous number of catches that I put down or had no chance of getting near, especially when batsmen flicked the ball down the leg side. Catches went down to fine leg for four or flew to the offside past my shoulder instead of ending up in my gloves.

When I stood back to Dixon I began to take many more diving catches. The team benefited so there was no argument about where I was better placed. Some bowlers do prefer to have the 'keeper right up at the wicket. Basil D'Oliveira is one. When we first played together for England I had problems because Basil can swing the ball prodigious distances. Until I was used to taking him, I would often move well to the leg side only to have to leap back the other way as the ball curved away to the off. In one-day cricket it sometimes pays to stand up because you are playing against batsmen trying to force the pace. Now and then, in their quest for quick runs, they charge down the pitch. In these matches I stand up quite a bit to Bob Woolmer, a medium-pacer. He feels that he bowls better when he knows the batsman is going to play him all the time from the crease.

On slower wickets, which have become the norm in England, even Derek Underwood bowls less than he did when we first played for Kent. So, during the hundred overs of an opposing side's innings under present regulations, I am likely to be right up at the stumps for perhaps only twenty overs. This lack of close-up work can definitely blunt your neatness and effectiveness at the wicket; taking can be a little less sure and maybe you will fluff a stumping chance that you would take if you were over the stumps at least half of the time. On tour I do spend more time close up. Batsmen, especially Australians such as the Chappell brothers, Doug Walters, Ian Redpath, are more inclined to get down the pitch. Keeping abroad in better light, to the pick of England's bowlers operating on harder, faster pitches, you have more chance for your all-round game to come to a peak and stay there. Certainly I have never kept better than on my first Australian tour in 1970–1.

Cricket must have changed considerably since the between-wars years and the immediate post-World War II era. No matter what their speciality, all players have had to adapt their styles and attitudes to these distinct changes. I have talked with Leslie Ames and Godfrey Evans about wicketkeepers spending most of their time well back from the wicket and the inevitable massive decrease in stumpings. Leslie's era was the twenties and thirties; Godfrey's the forties and fifties. They say that batsmen played differently then than today. On faster English wickets, the regular style was to play forward; many batsmen would topple forward out of their ground swivelling after the ball on the leg side; hence the higher incidence of stumpings. Notably in Leslie's time wicketkeepers were proud of their ability to stand up to all but the most ferociously quick bowlers. For the spectator this was dramatic. But, looking back, I cannot really see the point of it. Anything but a thin nick from the bat on either side was a terribly hard catch to gather. 'Keepers of those times must have dropped so many awkward catches or simply did not get anywhere near them.

It is said that Alec Bedser always wanted his wicketkeeper right up at the stumps; he was wonderfully served by Godfrey for England and Arthur McIntyre for Surrey and England. Alec Bedser came into big cricket just before World War II. So he obviously inherited the outlook that the 'keeper stood up to a bowler of his pace. If he had started playing thirty years after he did, and had therefore had

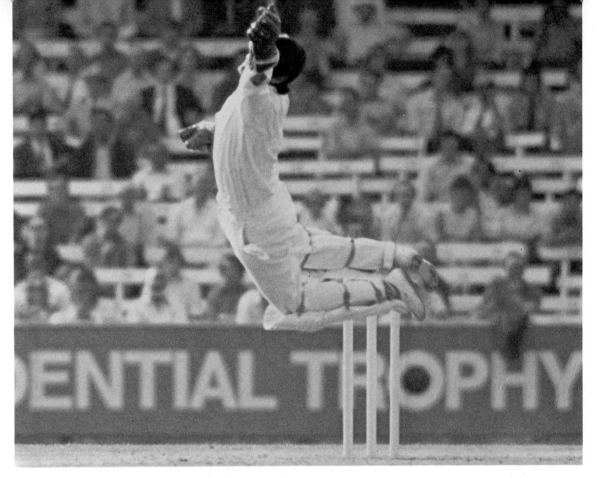

Alan Knott in his element—airborne—above Kennington turf. Such dives, Knott says, knock the stuffing out of a wicketkeeper who, in modern times, must be super-fit.

The old-style vertical 'keeper, Alfred Lyttleton (1857–1913) of Oxford, Middlesex and England, who also took four wickets for 19 with his lob bowling at The Oval in 1884.

(Overleaf) The Don at the nets at the start of his final tour in 1948. Fingleton had the impression sometimes that playing under Bradman meant playing for Bradman.

Lethal on a turner, Underwood brings anxiety on any pitch not certified as dead. A ball from his customary full length has leapt up at The Oval to discomfort Greg Chappell.

no first-hand experience of pre-war play, I think he might have told himself: 'I bowl big in-swingers at a fair pace. I am going to get most of my off-the-bat wickets caught down the leg side, so I need a 'keeper back where he can dive for deflections.' In his day, without restrictions on leg-side fielders, he could have a leg slip and two more in leg-trap positions. But today the bowler is confined to a leg slip and a fine leg, and a Bedser-style in-swing bowler has a more compelling reason to have his 'keeper back to take the place of one of these leg-trap fieldsmen.

To hold his place, an efficient wicketkeeper must be good at both stumping and catching. But it is best to be of the highest class at the thing you are going to do the most. These days, this means diving catches. Maybe forty or fifty years ago the accolade was to be a brilliant leg-side stumper and to take thunderbolts over the stumps without flinching. You hear that 'keepers of those times did not dive so much. When the ball flew from the bat down the leg side, I have been told, they often watched it go past, even when standing back. In today's very different cricket, this just won't do. If you were the best in history at taking the ball smoothly at the stumps but the ball bounced from your gloves most of the times you dived for it, then you would find it difficult to keep your place now—even in a county side. Perhaps because of the overall higher calibre of bowlers and batsmen in Test cricket you don't have to fling yourself about so often for wide deflections in Tests. However the ability to take these in Tests is still a more important ingredient in a modern 'keeper's make-up than before.

Spending so much of his time lunging horizontally, the wicketkeeper has to be much more supple than of yore; he must be supremely fit and agile. Apart from countering my liability of being naturally stiff-muscled, my bending and stretching exercises on the field keep me loose and keyed up for instant take-off. You have to be as fit as a footballer; three or four dives knock the energy out of you. Limited-overs county matches are really exhausting. Seamers bowl most of the overs. With run-saving fields set back, the wicketkeeper is isolated; he often has no slips or leg slip for company. So he has to do three men's work: retrieving the ball when it comes off the batsman's pads to the off side (slips or silly point would normally collect these); diving for catches that fly towards leg slip's vacant position, plus his regular chores. On top of this, he has to run twelve to fifteen yards to the wicket for almost every ball. This is no restful life. But it has its dividends. With so much work to do, so many half-chances to plunge after, I have been taking more and harder full-length catches since the number of limited-overs matches proliferated in the early 1970s.

In Tests I am also busier. In Australia in 1970–1, I hesitated a couple of times about diving for catches going towards slips; the slip fielders put both of them down. So the skipper, Ray Illingworth, said to me: 'From now on, Alan, you go for everything.' He moved the slips wider; they looked more like Australian slips who have always spread themselves wider than we used to do. The new pattern worked. We have retained it in England sides. This suits me because I believe the wicketkeeper has to go for everything that is snicked. It is nonsense to caution a wicketkeeper to hurl himself only for those chances that are not likely to reach the slips. By the time you have done your on-the-spot surveying, the ball has gone. When slips and 'keeper are not set diving distances apart, they are all wasting ability and territory; they reduce the odds of taking catches, which is what they are there for.

The different and more rigorous demands on the wicketkeeper's physical resources must take their toll. I believe they could shorten the active playing careers of wicketkeepers. Success depends on agility, on the thrust and elasticity of your legs to launch yourself soon enough and far enough to gather in the wide catches. Once that springiness declines, when you fly too late or your outstretched glove lands a foot short of the ball, you will almost certainly be on your way out. If you look right back into cricket archives, you'll note that wicketkeepers have been among the most durable of cricketers. Bert Oldfield and Wally Grout for Australia, Godfrey Evans for England, were still playing Test cricket capably when they were almost forty years of age. As I have said, the greater athleticism is not as vital in Tests, but will 'keepers playing seven days a week for their counties survive until forty? And if you are not in a county side, how can you be chosen for Test matches?

I doubt that many wicketkeepers in the future will last that long. Like the

Evans stood up to Alec Bedser even here, playing for an Old England XI v Lord's Taverners, long after both had retired. Knott queries these tactics. Taverner is Stuart Surridge in stone-walling mood.

footballer or tennis player, when their legs start to lose their zip, the strains of trying to do their work effectively in such crowded schedules may prove too much. So thirty-five, or even thirty-two, will become more significant and worrying ages for 'keepers in England; overseas they could still keep going until their late thirties as Wally Grout did. In a home season, the top English players can be involved in five competitions: Tests, Championship matches and three limited-overs competitions. They are all tough. A wicketkeeper will need to be made of granite, and have a lot of luck, to survive well into his thirties with the accumulation of so much mental and physical pressure, plus the strains of travelling and possible tours overseas most winters. It would be horrible to start struggling to cope; it is not a fate you would wish on yourself or anybody else. I hope I realize immediately I am slowing down and retire before my performances become embarrassing to myself and my side.

For some time I have felt that I should be keeping most effectively in my early thirties, around 1978–9. It would be foolish to think that this means my performances will steadily improve in a straight and unbroken line rising ever upward. I can't truly say that I am a better wicketkeeper after more than sixty Tests than I was when I played my first in 1967. What I want is the rippling line of my performances—rising from good in one series, then dropping to so-so in the next—to level out at a higher peak. While I had a marvellous time with the gloves in Australia in 1970–1, I did not keep all that well in West Indies in 1973–4. I don't know why form fluctuates the way it does, but I do look forward to perhaps an extended stretch where everything goes really well in my prime job of keeping wicket.

I don't expect a prolonged spell of absolutely top form with both gloves and bat. When I was a very young player with Kent, Leslie Ames—the most successful of all wicketkeeper-batsmen—told me it was always a problem to be simultaneously in form with both or to hold that form once you strike it. He warned me not to be surprised if I was 'keeping like a demon but getting few runs. Certainly I have discovered that this happens. On that West Indian tour I mentioned, I was below par with the gloves but had one of my best series as a batsman. A reverse of this was my keeping adequately but scratching for runs against the Indian spinners on tour in 1972–3. It has become terribly difficult for me to strike batting form for home Test series. Kent bats so deep that I go in at number eight or nine. Innings close after 100 overs. Thus my chances for long and careful innings are limited. Whereas on tour the captain sometimes puts me in at number three or four in State or Island games, giving me the opportunity to hit form and build confidence for Test innings. Along with the faster wickets and clearer light, this is one of the things that make overseas tours so appealing.

A few words about Derek Underwood. When we first began playing for Kent in 1964, his medium-pace cutters were too quick for me. More often than not, balls that passed the bat and stumps bounced from my gloves instead of sticking in the palms. I learned how to cope, but have since discovered that the biggest problem Derek often sets for me stems from one unexpected source: he is just too good a bowler for comfort. He is amazingly accurate—rarely a long hop or full toss—and his line is seldom off target. So there can be long and barren periods, especially in Test matches, without a single ball coming through to me. This makes sustained concentration very hard; to stay alert I have to tell myself over and over that the next ball will definitely reach me. It is sometimes a relief and great fun, for me if for no-one else, when he bowls on a dusty wicket or a turner. I know that a few deliveries at least will work past baffled batsmen for me to take. I seldom expect stumping chances from him. Derek is so quick and so on the spot that batsmen rarely attempt to leave the crease. On all types of wickets catches are always a prospect: when he does bowl the odd wide ball on the off, batsmen are often tempted to cut him—perhaps out of relief.

It is his accuracy and flat path of the ball through the air to pitch just where he wants that make him such a deadly bowler on a turning pitch. Deprived of looping flight, the batsman just cannot get down the pitch safely to him. Derek drags his fingers down so hard across the ball on delivery that he achieves a lot of turn from the pitch when it is there. It is fascinating to see batting sides sometimes go into a mental tailspin when they face Derek on a wet or turning pitch, or one they expect holds something for him. I have seen sides practically give up against him, with the failure of one batsman feeding potential failure for the next. Or if they don't give up, they worry themselves into dismissal, condemning themselves sometimes on evidence that is not present. Take, for instance, the great success he

Every ball is now like a penalty kick, says Knott. Mankad perishes to Arnold at Edgbaston as Knott follows a former skipper's advice : dive for everything.

had against Australia at The Oval in 1968. On this pitch the ball did not turn; it just lifted. Not one ball beat the bat to reach me. The Australians were looking for the ball to turn. It didn't, so they kept getting inside edges to be plucked up in the well-packed leg-trap. I found it puzzling that the Australian batsmen did not notice how easily John Inverarity was playing to the ball; he had twigged that it was not turning and played accordingly.

In the 1974 Lord's Test against Pakistan, the side collapsed quite astonishingly against Derek. I always judge how bad a wicket is by the number of balls coming through to me. In the first innings of this Test, just two did; in the second innings, only one. Rain had seeped through the covers overnight (raising a terrific furore); there was a small damp patch on the wicket and Derek was bowling for it. As soon as the Pakistanis saw the ball was turning, knowing that nobody bowls as well as Derek on this kind of pitch, they became nervous and maybe lost a little heart. Certainly I don't think they batted as intelligently as they might have done; there was a touch of panic. And when you are not functioning at one hundred per cent capacity in Test matches you will not survive.

To hit that damp patch, Derek had to bowl over the wicket where his chances of lbw decisions were almost non-existent. When he bowled around the wicket, the ball was landing on a part of the pitch as good as it was the day before. Yet the

Leslie Ames told Knott he must expect his batting to suffer badly at times. Boyce rams the lesson home at the Oval in 1973; Knott is lbw five.

Two examples of increasingly-rare positions in first-class cricket: the wicketkeeper, Knott, up at the stumps and the batsman, Ian Chappell, well down the wicket.

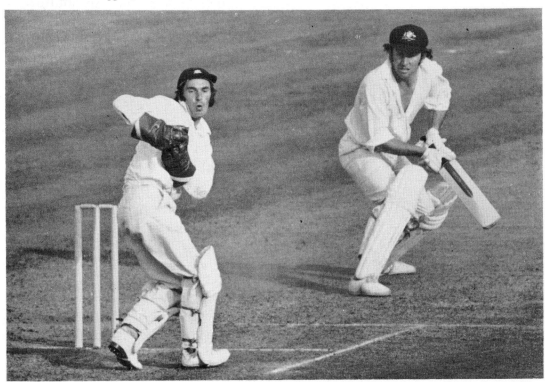

only batsman who played him with tactical sense was Wasim Bari, the wicket-keeper, who came in towards the tail. While he did not last long, he showed the senior batsmen what they should have done. With Derek bowling over the wicket and pitching outside the leg stump, an lbw was not on; Wasim just kept padding him away. He made Derek go around the wicket where he could not turn the ball.

Another aspect of the wicketkeeper's art can be his closeness to the captain. My four Test skippers—Brian Close, Colin Cowdrey, Ray Illingworth and Mike Denness—have all sought advice from me. Colin needed the least: from first slip he could see clearly the kind of things captains want to know: the line of the ball, where bowlers are pitching, how fidgety the batsman were, how he was angling his bat to work the ball away, and so on. Ray and Mike had a good overall view of things when fielding at mid-on or mid-off. But Ray Illingworth and Brian Close conferred with me most when they fielded at bat-pad (close-in positions) where they lost the line of the ball and its behaviour from the pitch. A novice wicketkeeper, being more worried about his job, finds these details do not register so well with him. But á more experienced wicketkeeper is particularly valuable to a captain in conveying batsmen's strengths and weaknesses and the more minute details on how the bowlers are performing. As with so many of the arts and crafts of cricket, wicketkeeping can be a matter of mind as well as physical ability.

Fielding: An Interview with M. J. K. SMITH

Close-in fieldsmen can be among the kindliest and staunchest of citizens. Yet to the uninitiated ear they sound an unsavoury lot. They crowd the batsman; they harass and confine him. They loiter with intent. They crouch near the batsman 'close enough to pick his pocket'—indeed, one of the best of the breed, Sid Barnes, the Australian, was featured in a memorable profile entitled 'The Artful Dodger'.

Commentators seem to impugn their motives and behaviour. When fieldsmen are moved into close positions 'the vultures gather', 'the sharks close in', or 'Bodger, at silly leg, is breathing down Rasseltyne's neck'. Bodger, who seems sorely in need of some form of corrective treatment, may then 'dive on a bat-and-pad chance like a starving seagull'. Clearly, using these phrases for his judgment, no responsible father would permit his daughter to go out with a man of such unhygienic and violent ways.

But, such action verbs, similes and metaphors are unjust to Bodger and Co. While their aim is sinister—they are abroad to claim victims—they are men of courage and high skills; they are entitled to more noble comparisons than sharks and vultures. Consider two splendid close leg fieldsmen—Fred Trueman and Colin Milburn. They had the bulk, yet the speed and nimbleness of Muira bulls; their lunging movements to gather catches could have an almost fastidious grace and neatness. And, if a commentator knew the gentleman was listening, he would speak of 'cougar' or 'jaguar' rather than 'grey nurse' to describe Brian Close as a near-the-bat fieldsman.

In this chapter, former England skipper, M. J. K. Smith, tells of these predatory men, and offers thoughts on other aspects of fielding. He has been a distinguished member of the close-in clan. He ranks among the most successful of contemporary fielders, having taken almost 600 catches in first-class cricket. The majority (including his Warwickshire record of 52 catches in 1961) were taken in short-leg positions before he retreated to spend more of his fielding time in the quieter sanctuary of gully. However in 1974, when forty-one years of age, he would still crouch a few paces from batsmen's hips at short leg to county spinners Hemmings and Jameson, possibly willing them to advance some day to the comforting precision of his old Test colleagues Titmus, David Allen, and Underwood. M. J. K. Smith's lithe durability there might astonish and bemuse Australia's Ian Redpath, who considered in his late twenties that a man of thirty-three would be pressing his luck as a close-in fielder.

Q: Were you a close fielder when you first came into top cricket?
SMITH: No. When I was at school, the accolade was for cover fielders, which was very definitely a carry over from the glamour of Hobbs and Bradman—two of the

finest in that area—and then Neil Harvey. In the old days, the Press wrote up the spectacular cover fielders and outfielders. Today the emphasis has swung towards greater efficiency and this finally means taking a higher percentage of chances. Thus, the first need is for fielders in positions where the chances are going, starting with the wicketkeeper.

Q: When did this begin to blossom? Was it in the Surrey days of Bedser and Laker?

SMITH: It's hard for me to pinpoint, not having much experience of the first-class game before 1954. I would have thought that, around the early fifties, one significant move was the re-positioning of older players who couldn't run about so well and hadn't a good arm. Up to this time, they had been rested at slip, provided they could take their fair share of catches. Teams then decided to put in the slips people who were going to catch the most chances—and make do and mend with the rest.

One assumes that, pre-war, your close catchers basically were slip fielders; there was not half so much leg-side fielding up close. In any era there will always be exceptions and, of course, plenty of short-leg fielders were available for 'body-line'. The first I can remember of short-leg fielding was Alec Bedser having Bradman caught by Hutton at backward short leg in 1948. Getting the great Don out there must have given the position a lot of impetus. Then, as you say, we had the great Surrey side of the fifties, with Lock, Laker and Bedser. Among the catchers, Lock was the central figure, although Micky Stewart, an exceptionally good short leg, appeared about that time.

With their successes, we really started going to town on close catchers. Like Stewart, some of the younger players coming into the game then were immediately pushed in close if they were good enough. It still goes on. Certainly, at Warwickshire, we are always looking for them, and I am sure it is the same for any other county.

Q: How do you guide them along? What kind of coaching do you give youngsters, say, in their mid-to-late teens when you single them out as having an aptitude for this kind of close-in work?

SMITH: First of all, when a lad comes to the club, you ask him where he fields: he will say in or out or that he does not really care where he goes. The usual pattern is that a young player will come into your team as a batsman or bowler and, after a while, you find out if he can catch or not—and where. Of course, your close catchers will be those who can seize the chances best. This means they can take them in the outfield as well. Tony Lock is a good example. He specialized at backward short leg, particularly to Alec Bedser and Jim Laker; he was a magnificent catcher. While I didn't see him field much elsewhere, he was also a very fine outfielder.

Mike Smith does more damage to The Oval pitch than to South African Tiger Lance's innings. Having hurtled and rolled from forward short leg, Smith spilt the chance.

Fine close fielders don't need Nureyev silhouettes. Colin Milburn's eighteen-stone bulk lunges to pluck up Inverarity off Snow at The Oval in 1968.

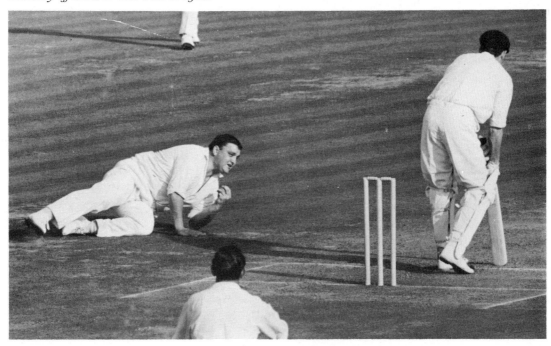

Your recruit may not fancy going in close, but most of them seem to, even at an early age. I think young players realize the advantages of being a valuable fielder to establish a place in the side.

Q: What about instinct and reflexes? They are obviously very important because many catches can come in a split second, often without a good line of sight.
SMITH: There seems to be a definite division between players who prefer either leg side or off side. I have spent a lot of my time close on the leg side (now that I am a bit older, I spend a lot of time in the gully). While I caught my fair share on the leg side, I never really fancied going into slip; when I have gone there I have dropped too many. There seems to be a difference and I am not quite certain why it should be. You have to find out the preferences.

Q: Where do the close fielders look when the bowler is running in and delivering?
SMITH: In general, I think the majority of close catchers watch the bat, but some first slips, who are a law unto themselves, will watch the ball. Other than first slip, most players watch the bat. Now, in saying that, I understand that Garry Sobers, who has been a great short-leg fieldsman, and got in exceptionally close to Lance Gibbs at backward short-leg, watches the ball. This gives him an idea of the shot to be played and from that how the catch will come to him—if one does come.

Most close catchers crouch down as it is easier to 'get up' for a catch than to 'get down' for one. It is difficult to work into the habit of staying down until the shot is completed. A close catcher must expect every ball to come to him—e.g., the on-drive which comes off the outside edge to slip or gully. If the fielder anticipates from the batsman's movements that the shot and the ball will go to the on side, he is obviously at a disadvantage when it comes to him, and so it may well go down. The catcher must train himself to expect every ball. After a while, he will learn how a catch is likely to come to him from any particular shot and, if he is expecting the catch, then he has every chance of pouching it.

Q: Would you describe the advent and decline of forward short-leg position?
SMITH: In the late 1950s, the authorities for county cricket limited the number of fielders behind square on the leg side to two. Previously many bowlers, inswingers like Cliff Gladwin of Derbyshire and Alec Bedser of Surrey—and, when it was turning, offspinners such as Laker and Tom Goddard—had bowled with two backward short legs, and one man deep behind square. The inswingers in particular bowled a lot of balls missing leg stump, so the batsmen were pretty limited.

After the change in regulations, they often still wanted the extra catcher, and so put him in front of square. Immediately the position started to claim a lot of catches, either direct from the bat or from bat and pad. Thus every county put a man there. He had to be a really good catcher and very agile since the catches

Solkar of India shows why he is one of the greatest forward short leg fielders by disposing of D'Oliveira off Chandrasekhar at Lord's in 1971.

were coming at him from every angle. I think the best were Micky Stewart of Surrey and Peter Walker of Glamorgan, who were taking as many as sixty or seventy catches a season. Dick Richardson of Worcester also took a lot of catches.

Q: If forward short leg was so productive, why did it fall from favour?

SMITH: The position is very specialized since it was obvious the fielder could get hurt and badly. The ball can be hit with tremendous force at that man, and however good the bowler, he can't really stop the batsman from swinging in that direction. The bowler can give greater protection for the similar position on the offside by good control of his line. Sidney Barnes was a bit straighter than square when he was hit by Dick Pollard in 1948, but the same principles applied.

Roger Davis of Glamorgan was hit badly while playing against Warwickshire; the hit was made from a perfectly good length straight ball. Thus the fielder has to be prepared to take evasive action, to cover up or turn his back. I think they all gear themselves for an early indication of the shot he is going to play by watching the batsman's feet. The most dangerous ball is the half volley on leg stump, which the batsman can flick away extremely powerfully without moving his feet; and this was the ball that all these fielders were apprehensive about.

Q: Is there any position to compare with short leg for danger?

SMITH: Only forward short leg is really dangerous. You are all right behind the wicket. The problem with forward short leg is that the ball can be hit there from anywhere, from outside the off stump, from straight, you name it. The ball can be hit exceptionally hard but, behind the wicket, batsmen can't produce the same power in their shots.

Q: Did you ever collect a bad blow fielding there?

SMITH: I broke a wrist once. A seam bowler was on and he bowled one that swung away; it was, in fact, knocking middle stump out. The batsman went to have a swing down the leg side, thinking the ball was going down there. Finally he hit it in the middle of the bat, and that was that. I just had time to get my hands up in front of my face and the ball hit me on the wrist. As often as not, these shots miss you, but you hear them whistling by, which doesn't help. Finally, instead of going forward as the batsman plays a defensive shot—rather on the same principle as in the covers you are moving forward so you can leap either way—you find yourself going sideways. Ultimately you finish up moving backwards. So you are losing that split second to get in on the bat and pad chance that is dropping slightly short.

A good forward short-leg fielder was always coming in on the defensive shot ready to dive in any direction for the catch. However, after being hit or having many near misses, human nature being what it is, he wasn't so keen to keep risking his neck; he was keener on getting out of the way. Once this state of mind was established, then he started catching fewer chances, and this, I think, happened to everyone who fielded there for any length of time.

Q: So the enormous amount of trust you needed to field there in the first place diminished?

SMITH: Even though you are fielding close in front of the wicket to a bowler you know is accurate, you have to accept that he is going to stray on occasions, and also that the batsman may deliberately try to shift you. If you are upsetting him there you probably have to stay anyway, even though you may be hit, since your presence may influence his dismissal.

Q: Did you feel very safe fielding there to a bowler like Lance Gibbs when he was with Warwickshire, knowing he had fine control?

SMITH: Lance was swept an awful lot when he came into English county cricket, because his line was very much off stump and outside. Whereas somebody like Freddie Titmus bowled from much closer to the wickets; you were certainly safer with Titmus than Gibbs.

Q: Did any particular batsman take it on himself to belt forward short leg out of the game, somewhat like the way Hammond used to slaughter up-and-coming spinners abroad?

SMITH: I don't think so. So many catches were taken there that obviously the thing to do was to move us out of there. It wasn't that difficult, just a matter of laying very heavily into a ball occasionally. Batsmen did start sweeping more than before to clear us away. Bowlers understood the value of having a man there: it was an aggressive position which put a fair number of batsmen off. If it did not work straight away, they appreciated the batsman was going to get apprehensive and very tired over a period because of the concentration involved. Very often, a catch would finally be popped up to that position. But, for the reasons I have mentioned, the position did become less effective. Now you don't see so much of it, except that the 1974 touring Pakistani team used it quite a lot to the leg spinners, Intikhab and Mushtaq.

Q: Could it be that forward short leg has crossed over the pitch to the off side? We have seen Tony Greig, in particular, in recent years extracting a lot of nuisance value from standing in very close on the off side.

SMITH: You see a man there to the offspinner particularly, although Derek Underwood uses it a lot as a standard position to his bowling. Underwood is unique; it is very difficult to categorize him as a slow left-arm bowler because he is just a little below medium pace. He is very accurate, cutting the ball, and beating the batsman on either side.

Prior to the forward short leg, batsmen tended to push right out to the ball. If it turned or swung, then often it would hit the edge, then the pad and go up in the air. When the crowding fieldsmen came along, the batsmen developed the bat and pad technique, pushing way out with the pad in front of the bat, which was in line of ball and wicket. If the ball then moved in, it tended to hit the pad first. Any off-side edge off the bat was shielded from going out into the leg-trap by the pads. A number of edges then went from bat and pad into the off side, hence the development of the short square off-side position that Tony Greig favours.

Q: So this is a more worrying position for the batsman than forward short leg?

SMITH: The position on the off side to the offspinner is very dangerous from the batsman's point of view. If there is a bit of turn from the pitch, the really class offspinner, such as Titmus and Illingworth, find a fielder there very valuable indeed; he is a counter to the batsman playing behind his pad to the turning ball. It is a position where the accurate bowler can look after you; you shouldn't feel apprehensive that you are going to get hurt fielding there.

Be gone you bounder! Pakistan's Zaheer Abbas instructs Greig in the perils of silly-point fielding while striking four of his 240 runs at The Oval in 1974.

Q: Does this new position seem to be the end of the line for close-catching positions?

SMITH: It's very difficult to know just where a player could go to create a new position within ten yards of the bat. We seem to have covered them all; progress has come full circle.

Q: A couple of more general questions to finish. Australians use the baseball-style throw which is more effective than the variety of throws one sees in England. After seeing, and praising, it for so many years, why haven't English players more widely adopted the Australian-type throw?

SMITH: England has produced very few powerful throwers, and I've got no idea why. Over here, you see fellows winding up and trying to throw underarm, side-arm and all sorts. There is no standard method and we have very few good, strong throwers, people with a fine, accurate return from fifty yards out. The majority of the Australians who come to England are powerful throwers. Children in Australia definitely have better models to watch; they can look at players as good as Sheahan and O'Neill and study the way they pick up and release the ball. So youngsters naturally copy them. Baseball in their winter months has, I feel, made

Australians good outfielders; they use the method of catching baseball-style, which is most safe and effective. Few English cricketers do it because that is not the way we are brought up to catch.

Q: Can bad fielding be infectious in Test cricket, where you expect players to be above that sort of thing? During one pre-lunch session of the third Test against Australia at Trent Bridge in 1972, one player fumbled badly several times and the English outcricket seemed to fall to pieces.

SMITH: It should not do, but it can happen; you have cited an example. Of course, you get depressed at somebody else's bad fielding. You ask yourself: 'What the hell is he fielding like that for?' And this irritation takes some of your concentration away from your own job in the field. Similarly, it works more obviously the other way around. When a player makes one or two brilliant stops, it encourages the others; the team can take on a snap and purpose.

Part Three: Miscellany

Portrait of The Don:

JACK FINGLETON

Mr Fingleton, the shrewdest observer of cricket extant, waited a full twenty years after Don Bradman's retirement from cricket to write the following profile of his extraordinary compatriot. Apart from the author's authority and power with words, another prime factor has contributed to making the piece a classic: its long period of gestation. In a sense it was not a mere twenty, but forty years in the making. This was the time span over which Bradman—as unsurpassed player and all-powerful administrator—had unavoidably kept darting to the foreground of Mr Fingleton's line of vision and thoughts. The Australian teams that Mr Fingleton played in and later watched and wrote about (as he mentions in his early paragraphs) had Bradman writ large upon them. So, down four decades of playing, watching, analysing, digesting, debating, cogitating on Australian cricket, the author would inevitably collide with Sir Donald's influence. Pervasive is the word. Small wonder that all the data, the vivid recollections were there to transfer from brain to paper so graphically and succinctly forty years on.

The Bradman-Fingleton sixth wicket partnership of 346 still rests snug and secure in the record books. The imagination flickers brightly with fantasies of the record they would have pursued had Fate cast them together at the Oval in 1938 with more than two sound legs between them. In that match, seared forever into many Australian minds, Fingleton injured a leg muscle and Bradman chipped an ankle bone: they could not bat. So a partnership of 346, in pursuit of 903, would have been a fragment of overture, a mere clearing of the batting throats. Futile but intriguing conjecture.

Humble toilers in cricket's writing vineyards—and some slightly less humble than pharaohs—willingly concede Mr Fingleton's pre-eminence among them. So Fingleton on Bradman is a fusion of masters, the rare occasion when writer matches subject. If you are lucky enough to read a better cricket profile than the following, the odds are short that Mr Fingleton wrote it.

I recently wrote to Sir Donald Bradman, seeking, for the purpose of this article, an opinion from him on the merits of modern cricketers. He surprised me with the depth and generosity of his reply—ranging over Tilden, Lindrum, swimming, athletics, golf ('what about the implements used? Nicklaus would have been in great trouble trying to drive today's distances with a gutta-percha ball and a wooden shaft') and so on, down to cricket.

It was a fascinating letter, which recalled his batting. His letter was precise and deep-thinking. He brought to bear the same analytical approach with which he first dissected all bowlers of his generation before proceeding to decimate them—

Contrasting natures reflected on the batsmen's faces at Sydney. Bradman's (at right) tense with anticipation, McCabe's benign. One is there for business, the other recreation.

One hundred up? Or two hundred? Or three? The smile on the young Bradman's face is at once delighted and sadistic, says the author. Smears on the blade are ball redding and bowlers' blood.

the whole lot of them. Let me quote his pertinent thoughts on his own game, though he also played tennis and golf, handicap scratch, to a high standard. Noting how the clock served as a guide in many other sports, Sir Donald wrote, 'A batsman in cricket is not competing against the clock and himself. His feats are subject to what his opponents are doing—a varying set of conditions and a myriad of things of complexity.'

He says his own career covered the smaller ball and larger stumps, and much of it was under the off-side lbw rule. All this favoured the bowler. This, he says, indicates that S. F. Barnes was a greater bowler than his figures suggest . . . 'and Trumper had to bat against Barnes—I didn't'.

He proceeds with sound, thought-provoking stuff.

I think the modern era tends to have champions of other days thrown in its face, but the error is often committed of comparing only former champions with the rank-and-file of today. What about the rank-and-file of yesterday? For this reason, I often think the modern cricketer is unduly maligned. You may not think our present team for England compares with certain earlier teams, yet I am prepared to say you could find names in some of the earlier sides which would be lucky to make the grade in the present team. Are you concerned with style or effectiveness? As Cardus has written, the eagle is more beautiful to watch than a jet plane, but there is no doubt which is the faster. My view is that the champion of any era would have been a champion in any other era. But, having said that, I've no idea how you sort out Dempsey, Louis or Clay.

But I must not be side-tracked. I have to write of Sir Donald, himself, and I do so with zest because I played with and against him a lot and I can still see him in bold perspective against many of the greats I knew: Hammond, Compton, Woolley, Duleepsinhji, Hutton, Cowdrey, May, Dexter (what a pity the two latter played Tests for so short a time!), Worrell, Sobers, Weekes, Hazare, Amarnath (a lovely stroke-maker), Pataudi, Nourse, Pollock, Ponsford, McCabe, Macartney, Kippax, Jackson, Morris, Miller (up and down but certainly great on his day), Harvey, Simpson and one or two others who touched the top with infrequency. As a youngster, I once opened an innings with the Master, Jack Hobbs, in Sydney. I knew, too, Collins, Bardsley, Taylor, Andrews, Hendren and South Africa's Herby Taylor.

One's memory, then, covers a glittering field, yet I have not the slightest hesitation in saying that Don Bradman was the most remarkable batsman I knew. Moreover, there would not be a single person of his generation who would not say the same. He bestrode the cricket world as nobody before or since has done. His consistency was incredible.

Dr Grace, who had to contend with indifferent pitches, and J. B. Hobbs, were outstanding for their consistency, but Bradman stood alone. In all matches, he scored 50,731 runs in 699 innings for an average of 90·27. In first-class matches, Bradman scored 28,067 runs in 338 innings for an average of 95·14, and in Test matches he made 6,996 runs in 80 innings for an average of 99·94. Those are staggering figures and it is pertinent that 63 of his Test innings were played against England, the common enemy. It is to be stressed that he never toured India, the West Indies or South Africa, all with fruitful batting pitches. Nor did he tour New Zealand.

None of his generation, either, toured the West Indies. I flew there in 1965 and had a practice on the Bridgetown ground. The lovely pace of the pitch, its true-ness, the clear light, the fast ground and the short boundaries brought Don Bradman immediately to my mind. I thought, then, that he would have written another page in his record book had he toured the West Indies. So too, had he not withdrawn from the captaincy of our team to South Africa in 1935–6.

Of the 211 centuries Bradman scored in all matches, 41 were double centuries, eight were treble centuries and one a quadruple. He is the only Australian to have made a century of first-class centuries, a wonderful feat when it is considered how few innings he had compared to those others who passed this peak.

I see him, again, as he came to bat in his final Test innings at The Oval in 1948, on the verge of averaging a century in all Tests. Capricious fate saw him out for a duck second ball to Eric Hollies. I think the ovation given him by the crowd, all the way to the middle, where Yardley had his players grouped and called for three cheers for the retiring hero, unnerved him. Bradman was seldom unnerved.

Figures tell the undisputed story of Bradman's greatness, yet they tell only one portion of the story of his tremendous capacity. One had to bat with him, bowl or field against him, or, knowing the game and the art of batting, see and analyse his technique to comprehend the revolutionary dominance he brought to the game. On and on and on he seemed to go, batting into cricket eternity.

Bradman was not, in the sense of Trumper, McCabe or May, a classical stroke-maker as one knows the term. He was of medium build, well-muscled and supple in the wrists, yet there were no pretty passes or deft glides (in the Duleepsinhji manner) to suggest that some magical wand was weaving a spell over the field.

Some bowler, for instance, might think that he had won through to Charlie Macartney's stumps only to find, hey presto, a fiendish flick at the last fraction of time that sent the ball screaming to the boundary. So, too, with Sobers, who has his own type of magic. Bradman did not deal in such things. There was not a stroke in the game he did not play, but he was commonsense to the tips of his batting gloves.

'Are you concerned with style or effectiveness?' asks Sir Donald of me and it is a good question. He was such a genius that he could well have indulged himself in the artistic flourishes of batting, but he was too much of a realist to permit himself to do this. He knew two basic things about bowlers: none likes to be met constantly with the full face of the bat; none likes to see what, ordinarily, is good-length bowling transposed into over-pitched stuff by twinkling footwork. His fundamental thinking and love of cricket were, I am inclined to think, basically sadistic. He carried no soft feelings with him to the middle. Music to him was the crash of the ball against the fence: he delighted in seeing the figures revolve merrily against his name on the scoreboard; he loved to murder bowlers and make the opposing skipper look futile and foolish.

There were, as I have written, no deft passes or pretty glides, but every bowler, every fieldsman, every spectator in Bradman's heyday sensed that he was using not a bat so much as an axe dripping with the bowler's blood and agony. He didn't know pity. He was remorseless and a century rarely satisfied him. It had to be two or three, or even four against Queensland once when he made 452 and still didn't yield. In the middle, he was always planning, deducing and organizing with a concentration that never seemed to flag.

His dynamic and convulsive appeal to the spectator has never been equalled in my time. The roar of absolute delight that circled the ground when his magic name appeared in the vacant slot on the scoreboard was also one of anticipatory pleasure, and Bradman seldom failed his huge 'army'. I was often at the other end to him. Perhaps, with W. A. Brown, we had managed to give our side a good start against the new ball, keen bowling and fielding. If Brown had gone, I might have been 40 or so. In no time, Bradman would be past me, and in no time also the bowling and fielding would be ragged. Bradman soon had them where he wanted them—at his mercy.

He was, at the same time, aggravation to the bowler and despair to the batsman at the other end. He would take guard with a wide smile, survey the field, give his trousers a hitch, settle down and then with a piercing and shrill 'Right' he would be off to his first run off the first ball. Of this, he made a habit. In unnoticeable time, he would be 10, 20, 40, 50 and so on to the inevitable century. He dominated the strike and the batsman at the other end felt like an ineffectual goon. No matter what he did, it paled alongside Bradman's deeds. Bradman made it all seem so easy and he always regarded the clock as another enemy to be trounced.

I heard prominent batsmen of his era, cast deep into the shadows, complain that Bradman got more full-tosses and long-hops than anyone else. They were trying to suggest that Bradman was fortunate. He wasn't. The point was that bowlers were made by Bradman to bowl to him where he wanted. He dictated that. His footwork, his abounding confidence, his skill, pulverized bowlers and mesmerized them. They just didn't know where to bowl to him to keep him quiet.

W. H. Ponsford, who was the magical record-breaker until Bradman cast him from the throne, once told me that Bradman saw the ball quicker than anybody else. Ponsford meant that Bradman judged the ball's possibilities quicker than all others. And this was true. His judgment was impeccable and the coordination between his mind, feet and bat was like automation at work. His batting, his style, had many facets and it was built on footwork. He believed, implicitly, in the drive, and, often on the run, he drove in an arc from in front of point to wide of mid-on. He regarded the crease purely as a place in which to mark his guard. The keeper he ignored because he never calculated on missing a ball. Bradman was stumped 22 times in his 669 innings and most of those were sacrificial in minor games. He left 'home' like an arrant night-clubber. When the poor bowler, tired of being driven, dropped the ball short, Bradman drew back and across his wicket in a flash to slash him with pulls he learned on the concrete pitches of his country youth.

Some claimed that he was unorthodox. I don't agree. His batting was based on the soundest of foundations. He stood with the bat between his feet, an unusual stance (and one, incidentally, copied by Keith Miller), and his left hand was further to the right of the handle than is considered orthodox. This grip was doubly effective in that it enabled him to bring his devastating pull-shot quickly down to earth, the bat closing its face quickly over the ball. If he was unorthodox, it was in his outlook. Where others suspected a good-length ball of some explosive content, and were satisfied to play it defensively, Bradman sniffed contempt at it. I don't think there *was* a good length to him.

Old battles bathed in mellow afternoon light: Sir Donald perhaps showing Keith Miller the shot he might have played against Essex in 1948. With Godfrey Evans (centre) at a London dinner for Sir Donald in 1974.

His confidence was incredible. He exuded runs long before leaving the pavilion. His judgment was superb; his run-making appetite insatiable; his temperament and self-discipline unsurpassed. In Sydney, for example, he was a study when not out during the luncheon adjournment. His pads, bat and gloves would be put on the table, he would wash, take off his pants, put a towel around his middle and sit down to the inevitable light lunch he had ordered of rice custard, stewed fruit and milk. Each slow mouthful was an essay in method, in digestion, in relaxation, in cold planning and contemplation of the real feast soon to follow in the middle.

To suggest—and he missed nothing of such suggestions—that a particular bowler had his measure, was to invite that bowler's annihilation. We once played a mid-week social game at a hospital in Sydney and I had lunch at his home with Arthur Mailey, who was not at all happy that some scribe had written that morning, apropos of the game, that the veteran, who had taken Don's wicket once or twice, knew how to deal with Bradman.

'They shouldn't write this nonsense,' said Mailey, who was to play against Bradman and knew the effect the article would have upon him. Mailey was right. The Don absolutely slaughtered Mailey that day. A big crowd had come to see him and he made the day memorable for them at Mailey's expense. He hit him everywhere but into the operating theatre.

So, too, once in Sydney, with Fleetwood-Smith. Some critics had 'set' Fleetwood up and Bradman, who rarely hit sixes, purposely went out of his way that day to hit a gaggle of sixes.

Frank Tyson once suggested in Australia on television that Bradman would not have thrived against what Tyson was pleased to call astute modern captaincy but which some might describe as negative field-placing and bowling. I sensed that Tyson, who would not have seen Bradman at his zenith, was somewhat derogatory of Bradman's genius. As I was appearing at the same time, I told Tyson he would have changed his mind had he bowled against Bradman.

Tyson was apparently suggesting that the modern circle-field, negative in its concept and much used these days, would have curbed Bradman. It would have made him grin at its challenge. He knew the circle-field and he played against some astute captains. It was a matter of honour with Bradman to make field placements and skippers look ridiculous. A captain might take a fieldsman from here and put him there to cut off a flow of Bradman boundaries. Bradman invariably put the next ball where the fieldsman had been—and grinned hugely. The crowd loved this. There was no subtlety in it. It was something blatantly clear. Bradman's footwork in getting to the ball was too brilliant. He could not be confined. In his prime, he would have twisted the spokes of a circle-field in a twinkling but, perhaps, Tyson had most in mind that the slow-over approach which his skipper, Hutton, used would have eased Bradman down. In this, he was right. No batsman can carve an attack which won't come to the table.

Comparatively, bodyline did subjugate Bradman although he still averaged over 50 in the series, but that was based on physical attack—in itself a tribute to Bradman's greatness—and it was quickly outlawed. His pristine days were in England in 1930 (when Larwood played) and he made scores of 131, 254, 334 and 232—974 in the series, a century before lunch at Leeds, and all made at a fast rate.

Understandably, at forty years of age, he was well past his murderous best when he came to England for the last time in 1948, yet he contrived to make eleven centuries on the tour. Just think of that—eleven centuries in one summer at forty years of age!

Jim Laker, who once had all ten Australian wickets in 1956 at The Oval for Surrey and got 19 of their wickets in the 1956 Old Trafford Test, never once succeeded in getting Bradman's wicket in 1948. Bradman tallied almost 1,000 runs in games in which Laker played in 1948. Bradman's feet had lost their quickness in 1948; Laker still could not get his wicket.

Bradman was not a hail fellow with players of his own generation. It is to be admitted immediately that jealousy and resentment often made his position a difficult one, yet there were times when he might have assessed his standing in the game and made more of a gesture himself to his fellows. Yet, he might have reasoned, this could have sapped his purpose. His genius tended to make him a man apart, his soul immersed in batting and (it seemed) in records. He was often a lonely person in his peak years, although he might have thought that the fault was not all his.

Dr. W. G. Grace had the ample girth not unexpected on a man whose fee for touring Australia in 1891 was worth £28,000 by 1974 money standards.

Lord Harris.

A. Chevallier Tayler
1905

Mr. C. B. Fry.

A. Chevallier Tayler
1905

Spy

Why are these men smiling? England are on their way to 903 at The Oval, 1938; Bradman has just chipped an ankle bone while bowling. Uninjured, he might still have been at the crease when German troops entered Poland.

(Opposite top left) At last the England blazer fits perfectly. Dennis Amiss rests from run-harvesting around the globe at his Edgbaston home.

(Opposite top right) Lord Harris, a well-intentioned blimp, whose contempt for French novelists and indolence almost matched his contempt for untidy bowling.

(Opposite below left) C. B. Fry, who, according to Arlott, is over-suited to Elysium. There are too many other interests to distract him from cricket matches there.

(Opposite below right) The writings of Lord Hawke were 'hair-raisingly indiscreet' and the contents of his head unlike the contents of anyone else's.

Even as a young man, he was an adroit businessman. Offers chased him and he capitalized, as he was entitled to do, on his unparalleled standing in the game and with the public. He seemed to most who played under him in his early captaincy to be dictatorial and it was apparent that post-war players got on much better with him.

Pre-war, he indulged in gestures neither to his players nor his opponents. He ignored the courtesy of bidding his opponents welcome and farewell in the Adelaide dressing-rooms and once he had his innings declared against his former New South Wales (of which I was captain at the time) by an official over a loud-speaker. His vice-captain, McCabe, his number one bowler, O'Reilly, Fleetwood-Smith and O'Brien were once summoned by the Australian Board to appear before them on a charge of not giving Bradman full support against England. Some Australian officials are odd birds, not deeply immersed in a knowledge of the game, and his team thought Bradman should have gone along with them to give support.

Bradman seemingly intent on more than rival captain Hammond's chat on their way to toss at Trent Bridge in 1938. Eight years later, dialogue was scarcer.

England had won the first two Tests and we were well down to them in Melbourne in the third Test when the Board issued its summons. We then, surprisingly, got the third Test back and won it. Bradman and I were under the showers at the end of the game and the team were jollying those players who had been 'invited' to tread the carpet. 'What is all this about?' asked Bradman of me. 'Surely you know that four of your players have been carpeted by the Board,' I told him. 'You must go along with them.' 'You know what I think of our Board,' said Don. He didn't go with the players. As we had won the Test, the Board's charges crumpled limply.

Now, in a happy family life and with a charming and helpful wife, Lady Jessie, I think Bradman has mellowed. So too, no doubt, have some of his comrades of his early cricketing days. Cricket, I think, was more intense, more individualistic, and held the public stage more in those days than it does now. No other cricketer knew the blinding publicity that Bradman knew. His life was seldom private.

Perhaps he never knew that his fellows stood loyally by him in England in 1938 when our Board churlishly refused permission to his wife to travel to England when the playing part of the tour was over. Bradman had the match off, against Derbyshire, when the news of the Board's decision came to us at Grindleford. A team meeting was called and an ultimatum was given to manager Jeanes, who was also secretary of the Board, that he would have a cricket strike on his hands if Mrs Bradman wasn't allowed to come to England. Almost overnight the Board reversed its decision.

Bradman was a clever, astute captain, knowing all the moves, and he played the game to the full. He was one of the most brilliant fieldsmen ever, unerring in his screaming throw to the stumps, often holding the ball in the deep and challenging the batsman to run. He is a capital after-dinner speaker, droll in his rich humour. Spectators crowded Lord's in 1948, after his last game there, to bid farewell to the greatest batsman of his type the game has known. For all the thrashings he gave their bowlers—and they included some of the greatest of all time—the English adored Bradman.

One analyses his art again and declares, without question, that he would have been Bradman in any era of the game. He was, and is, a remarkable man. Today, from Adelaide, he holds almost as many business directorships as he still, and will, hold cricket records.

DON BRADMAN'S TEST CAREER

In a Test career spanning twenty years, Sir Donald Bradman only once finished a series with a batting average below the seventies—such was the power of Australia's run machine. He scored an average of 26·03 per cent of Australia's runs in Tests and 25·47 per cent of his side's total in all matches. Born on 27 August, 1908, Bradman got his chance in first-class cricket at nineteen years of age in the 1927–8 season. He entered the Test scene a year later, batting number 7 in his first appearance and becoming the regular number three from 1930 onwards. Here is a complete record of his 80 Test innings during which he scored 6,996 runs for an average of 99·94.

Series	First Test	Second Test	Third Test	Fourth Test	Fifth Test	
1928–9						
England (H)	18	—	79	40	123	First innings
Aus. 1, Eng. 4	1	—	112	58	37*	Second innings
1930						
England (A)	8	254	334	14	232	First innings
Eng. 1, Aus. 2, Drn 2	131	1	—	—	—	Second innings
1930–31						
W. Indies (H)	4	25	223	152	43	First innings
Aus. 4, W. Indies 1	—	—	—	—	0	Second innings
1931–2						
S. Africa (H)	226	112	2	299*	—	First innings
Aus. 5, S. Africa 0	—	—	167	—	—	Second innings
1932–3						
England (H)	—	0	8	76	48	First innings
Aus. 1, Eng. 4	—	103*	66	24	71	Second innings
1934						
England (A)	29	36	30	304	244	First innings
Eng. 1, Aus. 2, Drn 2	25	13	—	—	77	Second innings
1936–7						
England (H)	38	0	13	26	169	First innings
Aus. 3, Eng. 2	0	82	270	212	—	Second innings
1938						
England (A)	51	18	M	103	—	First innings
Eng. 1, Aus. 1, Drn 2	144*	102*		16	—	Second innings
1946–7						
England (H)	187	234	79	0	12	First innings
Aus. 3, Eng. 0, Drn 2	—	—	49	56*	63	Second innings
1947–8						
India (H)	185	13	132	201	57†	First innings
Aus. 4, India 0, Drn 1	—	—	127*	—	—	Second innings
1948						
England (A)	138	38	7	33	0	First innings
Eng. 0, Aus. 4, Drn 1	0	89	30*	173*	—	Second innings

* not out; † retired hurt; M match abandoned without a ball bowled.

England won by record 675 runs on Bradman's debut in first Test. Dropped for second Test (which England won by eight wickets), he returned to score first Test century (112 in 4 hr 7 min.) batting number six.

Finished series with average of 139·14. Shattered all previous batting records with his 334 at Leeds after coming in at 2 for 1 on first morning: 105 at lunch, 220 at tea, 309 at close. Batted for 6 hr 23 min.

With Ponsford again topped the Australian batting in a low-scoring series. After West Indies had been dismissed for 99 in fourth Test, Bradman completed first 50 of 152 in 45 min.

An average of 201·50 after batting for more than 16½ hours in series. At the crease 6 hr 36 min. in fourth Test, running out last partner going for 300th run. Did not bat in fifth Test (injured).

The 'Bodyline' series. Missed first Test because of illness but in second hit 103 not out of 191 total after playing on first ball to Bowes for first-innings duck. Fell to Larwood's bowling four times in series.

In fourth (Leeds) and final (Oval) Tests, Bradman and Ponsford dominated the Australian batting, sharing respectively in stands of 388 (fourth wkt) and 451 (second wkt) which still stand as records for Australia v England.

Caught first ball off Voce at Sydney for second duck against Allen's MCC side. Shared with Fingleton remarkable sixth wkt stand of 346 in third Test after Australia had lost 5–97 and batted 7 hr 38 min.

His finest Test innings was again at Leeds (fourth Test): a chanceless 103 in 2 hr 50 min. Injured ankle while England amassed 903–7 dec. (Hutton 364) in fifth Test and did not bat in either Australian innings.

After surviving 'catch' to Ikin when 28 in first Test went on to share record stand of 276 for third wkt with Hassett. Record fifth wkt partnership of 405 with Barnes in second Test; bowled by Alec Bedser for duck in fourth.

For the fourth time Bradman ended a Test series with a three-figure average (178·75) and for the first and only time recorded a century in each innings. His 201 in fourth Test was 37th and last double century of career.

Match-winning innings in fourth Test when he and Morris put on 301 in 220 minutes after Australia had been set 404 to win at 70 an hour. Needing only four runs for career Test average of 100, bowled second ball by Hollies at Oval.

Yon Laads are Reet Cobbers:

MICHAEL PARKINSON

As a writer, Michael Parkinson has earned numerous tags: the Bard of Barnsley, the Boswell of the jockstrap set, the Hans Christian Andersen of the sporting prints. There is more unanimous agreement that he has given a new dimension to the word 'partiality' in sports writing. Mr Parkinson is no stranger to 'impartiality'. He can spell the word effortlessly and can usually forebear from jabbing his swordstick into the rumps of those sporting word merchants who care to bring it into active service. But, long ago, he prised the word from his own dictionary, wrapped it carefully inside one of George Best's old football stockings, and tossed it into a desk drawer to moulder alongside a few of his foul cheroots and some yellowing Valentines from the MCC.

Instead of balancing the scales, Mr Parkinson has taken a stance of vigorous and endearing simplicity: Yorkshire number one, the rest nowhere. In Parkinson's lore, one ancient Yorkshireman discovered fire; another invented the wheel; a third drew up the blueprints that enabled the Egyptians to build their pyramids. Since those footling days, the Tykes have trodden a rising path towards even greater accomplishments; the pinnacle, of course, has been their deeds at cricket.

People in distant lands may not know that Yorkshiremen are the Texans of Britain. They tread the widest acres, sup the strongest ale, breed the noblest horses and comeliest lasses, accumulate the highest piles of slag and brass. Theirs is the county of the largest town halls, the toughest steel, the hairiest tweed, the broadest vowels, the staunchest miners, the funniest comedians, the most irresistible football tacklers. And, you cannot say it too often, an incomparable conveyor belt of great cricketers—the wisest, winningest cricket team of them all.

No matter how far he travels, or how much time has passed since the winds of Ilkley Moor have savaged his features, every Tyke is always a practising Yorkshireman. Amid this ceaseless, rumbling tattoo of horny Yorkshire fists beating their own beefy Yorkshire chests, Mr Parkinson has performed mightily to have become a stand-out in the ranks of White Rose boosters. Yet he is as a twig to a forest oak, a Tiny Tim to a Caruso, a coracle to an aircraft carrier compared to another fount of earthy Yorkshireness: his father John Willy Parkinson. John Willy is a wonderful man: fifty years a miner, pithy, trenchant and a club cricket captain of a wiliness to have made Brian Sellers and Brian Close seem like two of the more languid and effete members of the Drones Club. No shrewder palm ever brilliantined half a cricket ball nor more educated thumbnail excavated a canal along its seam. If Mr Stephen Potter had been lucky enough to have met him, Parkinson senior would have provided the book to complete his set: Johnwillymanship.

John Willy reveres Aussies; he thinks they are at least half as good as Yorkshiremen.

That in itself is enough for the Australian Prime Minister, Mr Whitlam, to declare him an honorary Australian and his birthday a national holiday. His affection for the enemy planted the seeds of understanding that helped his son to undertake the following article.

In an ever changing world there are but two tribes remaining with the traditional view that life is centred round strong beer, docile women and good cricket—not necessarily in that order. They are called Australians and Yorkshiremen. It is my firm conviction that, when Britain severed relations with its colonies and joined the Common Market in the mistaken belief that we could find anything in common with wogs who don't play cricket, Yorkshire should immediately have declared UDI, appointed Fred Trueman Prime Minister and signed a Treaty of Alignment with Australia.

When I was a kid I was brought up to respect and hate the Australians. I was told that they would rob, cheat and go to any lengths to win at cricket. 'Just like us' said my old man, 'us' meaning Yorkshire and not England. My lasting memories of cricket in my childhood are to do with being taken by my father to see the Australians at Bramall Lane or Headingley. There was then, as there is now, a special look about an Australian and a Yorkshire side as it takes the field. Others look rag, tag and bobtail as they come down the pavilion steps, but the Aussies and the Tykes, no matter whether they are a great side or a poor one, always resemble a powerful and intimidating body of men.

The first time I saw the Australians was just after the war and we went to Bramall Lane, rising with the birds so that we could get there three hours before start of play to ensure admittance. Even then we had to sit on the grass. If memory serves me, Hutton and Lowson opened for Yorkshire and certainly it was Lindwall who bowled the first over for Australia. His first ball was wide down the leg side and went into the crowd for four byes. The fielder at fine leg waited for the ball to come out of the crowd and became increasingly restive when it didn't appear. Finally it was handed to him, whereupon he started laughing and called over the umpire.

The ball, shining red and new only minutes before, was now as dirty and scuffed as a small boy's toecap. Some Yorkshireman sitting in the crowd had rubbed it in the dirt and removed all vestige of shine. A new ball was ordered. 'Silly buggar,' said my old man. 'He ought to have just rubbed a bit off so they didn't notice.'

That day I couldn't take my eyes off Lindwall. It was my first look at a great fast bowler and from that day on, whenever he played in the county, I went to see him. Once I cycled the thirty miles to Bradford to see him bowl at Hutton. I would have walked twice that distance if needs be to see the connoisseur's delight, the master bowler attacking the complete batsman.

Yorkshire batted and I shall never forget the Australians taking the field with fifteen thousand pairs of Yorkshire eyes on Lindwall as he went through his limbering-up routine, every man in the crowd wishing he'd do himself a serious injury. Then the roar as Hutton came to the wicket, pale faced under the blue cap, the man whose wicket the Australians prized the most, the player to whom Lindwall paid the supreme compliment of never bowling badly to him.

Hutton took guard and complete silence fell upon the ground. I swear that, as Lindwall began his approach to the wicket, one of cricket's most menacing and thrilling sights, you could hear his footsteps on the turf. He bowled the perfect ball, an inswinging yorker, and Hutton's stumps rocked in their sockets like drunken sailors. The Australians rejoiced like only they can and the Yorkshire crowd reacted to bitter, numbing disappointment with an uncanny stillness. Crestfallen, Hutton walked back to the pavilion and the crowd was so hushed you could hear him take his gloves off.

'What's tha' reckon to that then?' asked the man behind me to his neighbour as Hutton disappeared into the pavilion. 'Not much,' said his friend. 'But I'll tell thi' what, I wish that buggar Lindwall had been born in Leeds.' Raymond Russell Lindwall, for all he is assured of his place among the immortals of cricket, never knew higher praise than that.

Norman O'Neill at Lord's. The soft southerner who applauded even his snicks through slips got his just punishment: the wrath of a most vocal Yorkshireman.

Hutton b Lindwall for nought in the Leeds Test in 1953. The Pudsey man's other duck at Bradford the same season put 15,000 Yorkshiremen, including the author, into a catatonic trance.

Any comparison of cricketing stories, apocryphal or otherwise, about Australian and Yorkshire cricketers, underlines the similarities between the two tribes. By which I mean that a story summing up the Yorkshireman's attitude to the game would be equally accurate and authentic-sounding if copied word for word with 'Australian' substituted for 'Yorkshire'. As an example, let us take that archetypal Yorkshire cricket story which concerns the spectator watching his home county in action when his son arrives breathless and flustered.

"Oh, dad, summat terrible has happened,' said the youth. 'What's up, laad,' said dad, never taking his eyes from the middle. 'Everything. Our Charlie's got arrested for drunk and disorderly, mother's lost all thi' money at bingo. Granny got knocked down wi'a bus and just now our house burned down and we're not insured,' he said. 'Terrible,' said his dad. 'But I've got even worse news for thee . . . Hutton's out.'

Now that story, summing up as it does the Yorkshireman's insane love for the cricketers of his native county, would be just as accurate set in Australia and Bradman or another hero substituted for Hutton.

It is no matter of chance that one of the best stories on cricket was written by an Australian about playing in Yorkshire. I am referring to Jack Fingleton's magnificent account of playing at Bramall Lane with Bradman's team in 1938 when Yorkshire came within an inch of winning. What sets the piece apart from others is Fingleton's perception of the affinities between the two teams, the matching of a supreme pair of gamecocks.

He summed it up precisely with this passage about the team's arrival at Bramall Lane:

It is easy to mistake the atmosphere that receives rather than greets you on this ground. It seems to bristle with belligerence. The looks bore through you in cold analysis as you go to the nets before the game. At Lord's, going to the nets, one is greeted with cheery nods and smiles and often a call of 'good luck'. There's none of that at Bramall Lane. . . . The grim look of the spectators, the postures and the gestures of the eleven robust Yorkshiremen with the white rose on their caps all issue a challenge to the Australians and it runs something like this: 'We are Yorkshire. Tha's playin' wi' cricket fire laad when tha' cooms here. We're noo abaht to show tha' laad, tha's noot sa good as tha' thinks.'

One can argue with the accent but not with the article's real authenticity of mood and attitude.

It was at Bramall Lane, alas a cricket ground no more, that I saw the final starburst from that sublime player and entertainer Fred Trueman. Like the actor he was, Fred chose the setting and the occasion carefully. Bramall Lane was where he started as a young, raw tearaway and it was on the same ground twenty seasons later in 1968 that he gave us the last look of a great fast bowler and old sweat in action.

He skippered the Yorkshire side that day and, after winning the toss and contributing a typically swashbuckling and humorous innings, declared at 355 for nine. He opened the bowling himself off his long run and for the last time we were privileged to see this man being what he always claimed he was, 't'best fast bowler that ever drew breath'.

In this, his last match at Bramall Lane, he showed the entire repertoire of his talents, not just his bowling and his batting but his fielding too, reminding us that he was one of the best close fielders in the world when he dived far to his right at second slip to catch Doug Walters off Richard Hutton.

Directed by Trueman, who ran the entire operation with the panache of a theatrical impresario, Yorkshire beat the Australians by an innings and sixty runs, the first time they had beaten the tourists since 1902. It was Trueman's swansong and it was fitting he should have achieved it against a team he regarded as the dearest of enemies.

One story sums up completely Fred Trueman's attitude towards the Australians. It was on his last tour down under and Fred was becoming increasingly impatient with being told that everything in Australia was newer and superior in comparison to anything else. This, he reckoned, was the prerogative of the Yorkshireman and not the upstart Aussie. His patience broke when he was shown the Sydney Harbour Bridge.

'What do you think of our bridge?' asked his host as they surveyed the majestic structure. 'Your bridge? *Our* bloody bridge, you should say. Buggar me, a Yorkshire firm, Dorman & Long, built it . . . and you bastards still haven't paid for it.'

As a diehard Yorkshireman, I must concede that, after watching my own side play, I consider the greatest event in the sporting calendar to be the arrival of an Australian touring team. Me and my old man used to go and give them the once over, conceding them nothing except the grudging appraisal of people who can tell a cricketer's quality with all the certainty of a wine taster's palate.

Once we went to Lord's to see their opening game against the MCC. We went especially to see Norman O'Neill, who was making his first tour and who had been described as the new Bradman, or something equally absurd. We sat in the free seats, right behind the bowler's arm so that we might see everything important.

Now it should be explained that my father, like all Yorkshiremen but unlike other British cricket lovers, particularly those who frequent Lord's, believes in savouring his delights noisily. Which is to say he believes that both excellence and indifference should be given their just rewards and that, having paid through the turnstile to see a cricket match, it was his right to tell any player what he thought of him. This characteristic would make him a welcome guest on Sydney Hill. (Just how welcome readers will learn from reading David Frith's article at the front of this book: Ed.) But it does mark him down as an outcast at Lord's.

This day the inevitable happened. O'Neill, understandably nervous on his first appearance at Lord's, and with all the burden of unenviable publicity on his shoulders, began luckily. He snicked three chancy boundaries that had my old

Brian Close has led Yorkshire, Somerset and England with distinction but was a languid and effete skipper compared to John Willy Parkinson.

man groaning out loud. Not so the gentleman in front of us who, not having had the benefit of being born in Yorkshire, thought it his duty to make O'Neill feel at home by applauding every sketchy boundary.

After the fourth occasion when O'Neill's intended off-drive produced a four past third man and was applauded by the man in front of us, my father became truculent. He tapped the man's shoulder.

'Excuse me, but can tha' tell me what exactly it is tha' is clapping at?' he said. 'The stroke, of course,' said the man. 'What bloody stroke? He hasn't hit t'ball in t'middle of t'bloody bat yet. If tha' doesn't stop applauding him, he'll die of bloody embarrassment.'

Ten minutes later, O'Neill went on the back foot and played a lovely drive through extra cover, the shot of a quality player. The man in front turned to my old man. 'Do you mind if I applaud that stroke?' he asked sarcastically.

'If tha' knew owt abart t'game, tha'd be on thi' bloody feet cheering that shot,' said my old man, and sat back to get a better appraisal of this Australian who was beginning to look a bit like a good cricketer.

My favourite Australian cricketer of all time was Keith Miller. I worshipped him from afar and the greatest fulfilment of my adult life was when we both worked on the same newspaper in Fleet Street and turned out for the office team. He could be forgiven for showing little enthusiasm for the game as the cricket was at village green level, and he diverted his energies to some hearty drinking and knowledgeable appraisal of the racing papers. Thus, when we took the field for the afternoon session, the great man had already made the acquaintance of the local bookmaker who had appointed one of his minions to stand by the sightscreen and semaphore the results to his client in the middle of the field.

It was about time for the three-thirty to be announced when Miller, standing at first slip and gazing to the sightscreen, did a remarkable thing. I was crouching alongside him at second slip when the batsman swished at the ball outside the off stump and sent it hurtling towards my ankles. I had not even started focussing on the ball when Miller dived across in front of me, somersaulted at my feet, stood up and put a cricket ball in my hands.

'Thank you,' I said, unable to comprehend exactly what happened except to notice that Mr Miller, who a moment ago had been on my left-hand side staring towards the sightscreen, was now on my right-hand side and still staring towards the sightscreen. 'I wonder what won that bloody race,' he said.

What he ought to have said to me after his astonishing feat of athleticism was: 'We catch those in Australia.' He didn't, not because of his becoming modesty, but because he knew he didn't have to. He knew I'd got the message. Australians and Yorkshiremen are blood brothers, part of the same tribe and it's what they don't say to each other that is meaningful and important.

The View from Elysium:
Dr Grace in 1975: JOHN ARLOTT

Dateline: Elysium, 1st April, 1975

I knew that eventually one of the newspapers, or some publication, would ask me if I thought I could succeed in the game of cricket today. The request would have come long ago, I suppose, but that people from the Press do not often come to these exalted regions. Certainly C. P. Scott, the famous editor of the *Manchester Guardian*, was here for some years, but he spent most of his time with the statesmen and was never interested in popular sports writing. Anyway, he left when he heard the management had entered into negotiations for entry with Malcolm Muggeridge. So eventually this exclusive report was obtained by a 'ghost' with much experience of these ethereal deals who came here on a brief visitation that in no way foreshadowed his prospects of future permanent residence.

Some young readers may wonder why I should be consulted on the subject at all. Well, several people who ought to have known have said that I created modern cricket. That is not a claim I ever made for myself. My concern was with making runs and taking wickets and catches to win matches. It is a fact, though, that cricket was a vastly different game when I first scored a century at any worthwhile level, in 1864, from the one I left after my last first-class match—against Surrey, in 1908. Statisticians, who count these things—and several have paid me the compliment of counting mine—calculate that I scored 54,896 runs, took 2,876 wickets and made 871 catches in first-class cricket; in all cricket, all but 100,000 runs, more than 7,000 wickets and 1,300 catches: and in my early days the opposition in what are now called 'minor' matches was often almost as strong as in the others.

An oldun's view may be valuable now that England of the mid-1970s are struggling, not only against Australia but against the West Indies, Pakistan and New Zealand as well. This is certainly not the first time people have viewed the state of our cricket with alarm. In my time—when the Australians beat us at The Oval in 1882—*The Sporting Times* actually printed an obituary of English cricket and announced the body would be cremated and the Ashes taken to Australia.

In case you think I am out of date, I can say that I have watched cricket all over the world in some detail ever since I came up here. The gods' eye view is a splendid one; we can see exactly what the ball does in the air and off the pitch and also the line of the batsman's stroke; a much better vantage point, for instance, than a mortal's Press box. At one time it became somewhat monotonous seeing through the eyes of the celestial umpire all the time; but now we have television, we can vary the view when we feel like it, add to our information by lip-reading the players, and study the advertisements.

We play quite a bit among ourselves, too, which keeps us in touch with the new ideas. We have had some useful bowlers of the googly, the chinaman; inswing and offspin to a leg trap; we have tried the Carmody field and even—for two minutes before we abandoned it in disgust—a purely restrictive one. I have seen no development since my day that would stop me scoring as many runs as ever, though these fielders at short leg would mean that I had to give up my leg glance, which would slow my scoring rate a little.

We can whip some historically strong sides, though it took the Australians a long time to raise an XI owing to the somewhat idiosyncratic language they used to Rhadamanthus at the gate. Our games, mind you, are not always as serious —nor the dedication so intense—as I would want. Last season the best of our lob bowlers, Simpson-Hayward, who is a botanist, went to the Garden of the Hesperides for a new flower. While he was away, Digby Jephson, his deputy, popped off to Parnassus for a poem. Charlie Fry, of course, is in too many of his elements; he misses at least a couple of matches a year through his visits to Helicon. Felix, too, the best of the mid-nineteenth-century left-handers and a key middle order batsman in any Gentlemen's XI, is constantly being called away to paint battle scenes from the Trojan wars.

The matches are interesting but, in this most perfect of worlds, almost too perfect. Dionysius looks after the drink, so the champagne is all vintage and, since the umpires are immortals, they never make a mistake. This means that some of the play is dull by comparison with my time, when every county had one umpire who travelled with the team and, to say the least, always knew which side was batting. The greatest change from my young days—both here and with you folk below— is the perfection of the pitches. I have had four shooters from Fred Morley—fast left-arm—in the first over of a Gentlemen v Players match at Lord's; and, while the crowd stood and cheered when I stopped them all, I should never have made the runs I did if I had not been able to stop more shooters than I missed. I must say all this celestial comfort makes it vastly entertaining to watch the troubles your young fellers are in now.

Two things the editor wants to know are why I had such a successful career and whether I should be as successful as I was if I came back now.

The first question is the more difficult. If you have the physical equipment, start early, study the techniques and practise hard, you can play any game fairly well. I certainly had all the original advantages. Ours was a cricketing family; my mother studied the game remarkably closely for a woman in mid-Victorian times; my father and my uncle Pocock were useful club cricketers, and my elder brother Edward—E.M., whom they called the Coroner—the youngest, Fred, and I, all played for England.

The background was there—the enthusiasm and the knowledge—and from my earliest memory there was a practice wicket worthy of a first-class club in the orchard of our house at Downend. So I was born into cricket; I was strong and tall, my reflexes were quick—or they became quick through constant training—and you could say that my eyesight was sharp; certainly I never abused it by reading a lot of books like some of the young fellers used to do. I suppose, too, I had unusual stamina. In 1895, when I was almost forty-seven years old, I was on the field, batting—330 for once out—bowling or fielding all three days of a Gloucestershire match at Gravesend, when we beat Kent. That was the year I made the last 841 of my thousand runs in May, including my hundredth hundred, during the second half of the month.

You had to be fit then if you were going to enjoy everything that went with cricket. One August at Scarborough, Lord Londesborough asked four of us to shoot one morning. There was a ball the night before and no one went to bed until four. We were up again at seven—I had only time for a brandy and soda and raw herring for breakfast—we shot over sixteen miles on foot and were on the field sharp at twelve.

Even as a boy I was desperately keen: I played every moment I could, and if there was no one to play with, I just bowled at a tree trunk; if I did not hit it I had to run after the ball. From the time I was five, the family gave a considerable amount of thought to coaching. People used to joke about my brother E.M.s pull stroke—he would pick up a ball pitching outside the off stump and land it over midwicket—but that was because he used too big a bat at an early age. My father never let me make the same mistake. Although I was tall as a lad he made me continue long with a small bat; and kept me bowling from eighteen yards until I was easily capable of a length on a full-sized pitch. We practised not only through the season but before and after it. Even in my fifties, I began in the nets at the start of April or in March if the weather was fine enough. Cricket was not easy for me. It is a difficult game for anyone and I practised like a Boycott at every chance. We ran, rode or hunted at times, but cricket was our life.

I enjoyed practice; I enjoyed fielding more; I enjoyed taking wickets more still; and I enjoyed making runs most of all. Above all, it is important that I enjoyed cricket so much that, for me, it was always fun. I never in my life grew tired of it: and, until I decided to give it up, it never occurred to me that I could not succeed. It was a long run: I was fifteen when I first batted for the All-England XI; and that year I scored a thousand runs in club cricket: fifty-one years afterwards, the bowlers could not get me out in my last innings.

In my last Test match, when I was fifty-one, I batted safely enough, if only for eight and twenty, but it was because I could not bend in the field that I knew I had come to the end of my international cricket. Then there was that 74 for Gentlemen against Players in 1906 when I was fifty-eight; and the final innings, eight years after that, 31 not out on a devilish wicket in a club match at Feltham.

I have no doubt that I could do it all again—or more—especially on these far, far easier wickets, without so much strain of travelling, and with better umpiring; no bowlers so fast as Ernie Jones, Charles Kortright—he left me black and blue about the ribs more than once—Tom Richardson, W. N. Powys or John Jackson. My dilemma would be whether or not I could afford to play cricket as things are now. I gave almost all my attention to it, and it paid me well: but I doubt if it would today. My brother E.M. and I were, and are, the only qualified doctors who ever managed to play anything like full time cricket.

Because I gave so much attention to it, I never had real time for any other sport. On the last day of the Surrey v England match at The Oval in 1866, after I had scored 224, the England captain let me go over to the National Olympian Association meeting at the Crystal Palace to run in the quarter mile hurdles which I won in the then good time of one minute ten seconds. I did not take to golf until my late fifties, but if I had played it earlier, I am sure I could have done well. So, if I were a young man now, I should have to consider the best living I could make. Would it be in cricket, I wonder?

For my medical practice in a working-class district of Bristol I needed an assistant during the winter and two locums during the cricket season. There were some fairly fierce disagreements with the Gloucestershire County Club over my expenses—including this help in the practice—and more than once I had to point out that, if they could not meet them, I could not afford to play county cricket. That, in a way, was the strength of my position and a factor in my success. I did not have to succeed at cricket; I could have made my living from medicine. Cricket was, in every way, a bonus.

I always had a weakness for champagne which, as I said, is wonderfully catered for up here. My father used to prescribe a pint of 'The Widow' as a stimulant for a bowler called on for a major effort: but you cannot drink Veuve Cliquot every day on a parish doctor's stipend. Through the 1870s, until I qualified in 1879, I used to run matches for the United South of England XI. The organizers were desperately keen for me to play in the games and there was never any pretence that I did it for nothing. By present-day standards my position was more like that of Pele than of any cricketer. The arrangements were conducted in a thoroughly businesslike fashion; there was a separate legal agreement for every match and it carried a heavy penalty clause if I failed to appear to play in person. There was not anything like a full first-class programme in those days and the professionals were happy enough to turn out for me for five pounds. It was a rewarding business and five or six matches brought me in enough to cover my living expenses for a year.

Cricket stood almost alone in importance and crowd appeal in the sport of Victorian England. Football began to catch up during my time: but it was then strictly a winter game, not your present ten-months-of-the-year affair. Perhaps nothing ever impressed me more as a compliment than when, one day, after we had beaten Middlesex at Lord's and their captain, Webbie—A. J. Webbe— came up to see me off on the Bristol train from Paddington. The station master saw me to an empty first-class carriage and stood at the door. Webbie had several things to say and suddenly I looked up at the station clock and saw it was five minutes after the train was due to leave. I turned and said to the station master, 'Is the train delayed?' He replied, 'Not really, sir, but we waited her—we didn't want to hurry you.'

That was fine for the ego; but it buttered no parsnips. I could not often spare the time to go overseas, but I did make a trip to Canada and the United States in 1872; and to Australia in 1873–4 and again in 1891. The American visit was short and the cricket not too serious, but it was a chance to see the country in as much luxury as could be mustered then, and in good company.

The first Australian tour was a business enterprise which stemmed from the United South of England XI matches. I was engaged to raise the team—which did not prove as strong as I wanted—and captain it. The match guarantees were high, but the agreements stipulated that, if play finished early, we had to fill out time with single wicket games. Like most tours at that time, though, it was a considerable financial success. Conveniently and pleasantly, too, the promoters covered the expenses of my wife on the tour for what was, in effect, our honeymoon.

The second Australian visit, in 1891, was as captain of Lord Sheffield's team, at an agreed fee of £3,000—equivalent to £28,000 in 1974—plus all expenses, including a locum for the practice.

When I qualified in 1879 a national testimonial raised almost £1,500—which would be worth £16,000 now—a clock and a pair of bronze ornaments.

Then, after that great season of 1895 there were three separate testimonials which produced a total of precisely £9,073 8s. 3d that was worth more than £80,000 by present-day standards. After the Bristol parish medical services were rearranged in 1899, I felt in honour bound to resign and, at almost the same time, I was invited to manage the new London County Cricket Club at Crystal Palace. Gloucestershire decided I could not take that job and captain the county as well; and, after thirty years, we parted. The Crystal Palace venture was only a partial success; but it paid me £1,000 a year and expenses and when it ended, in 1908, I was able to retire and live on my savings.

The people near cricket knew well enough that I had taken some income from the game. It would have been odd if I had not. It is true that my young brother Fred was barred from a Gentlemen v Players match because he had taken match fees for his games with the United South XI. He was by no means the only 'amateur' who accepted payment for playing. I could have been banned, too, and for the same reason. On the other hand, I was in a strong position. Cricket was the most popular and best-supported game in the country; and, without false modesty, I was by far the best player in the country. In several seasons my batting average was twice as high as that of the next player. More important, people came to watch me play. It was no uncommon sight to see outside a cricket ground—

CRICKET MATCH

Admission 6d

If W. G. Grace plays

Admission 1/-

If that was my value, I was prepared to accept it. No one *had* to offer me money— least of all the testimonials. They were proffered and I took them in return for a moneysworth of performance. I am convinced that if I had my time over again I could do the same again in performance if I—and English cricket—could afford it. I must say that I find the reports of the financial rewards of Messrs Pele, Mohammed Ali and Arnold tantalizing reading. So . . . who knows?

From Our Cricket Correspondent: BENNY GREEN

Benny Green is a cricket enthusiast who believes the game should be served in all areas at the highest sustained level of excellence that its practitioners can achieve—with bat, ball, goose quill or microphone. As a man weaned on the bat of Compton at his zenith and the pen of Cardus (whose imagination, Mr Green avers, comfortably outstripped that of Edgar Wallace), his concept of adequacy is set rather high. His own cricketing talents were fractionally below Test standard: he scored the thousandth run of his career in his nineteenth season of club cricket. He loves cricket and loves to see the English language used with the flair of a Toscanini with a baton or a Lester Piggott with a pair of reins above a thoroughbred's silky neck. Are there cricket writers and commentators around whose talents in their fields can match maestros such as these? Please read on . . .

When I was fourteen years old I participated in my first properly organized, eleven-a-side, bails-and-umpires match. The encounter was between two youth clubs, and I remember that my own batting contribution to our victory consisted of only two strokes. Off the first ball sent down to me, an express delivery of terrifying pace and trajectory, which bounced three times before finally coming to rest at a point about three yards outside my off stump, I performed an immaculately executed leg-glance. The ball inexplicably went straight over the large and distinctly bulbous head of cover point, who was so astonished by this development that, by the time he had picked himself up after tripping over his wellington boot (I use the singular advisedly, for he was also wearing one brown suede shoe), I and my partner had crossed for two runs. The second ball I spooned magnanimously back into the hands of the stupefied bowler. A fortnight later there appeared in our club journal a match report which included the following passage:

> Green got off the mark with a crisp cover drive which completely defeated the field and enabled him to open his account with two useful runs. Now requiring only 98 for the fastest century of his career, he made a gallant and spectacular attempt to straight drive the next ball to the ropes, and was only thwarted by a brilliant catch taken by the bowler. A bright if sadly brief debut.

Thus I learned at a tender age that all sports writers and commentators are unmitigated liars and scoundrels, a conclusion unaffected in the slightest by the fact that the report had been composed by the assistant editor of the journal and that the assistant editor happened to be me.

I was, of course, perfectly justified in my cooking of the facts. Most cricket, like most of everything, is a humdrum business, and, were it not for the adjustments to reality made by the professional communicators, there would be very little left about the professional game that was bearable. Of course, sporting journalists could try actually playing cricket, but, as most performers in the media have had little exercise for years, apart from jumping to conclusions, there is probably no practical value in the suggestion.

In any case, what are the facts? Do they exist at all? Here are two samples of cricket reporting. Both are well-intentioned; both are perfectly honest; both observe the 'facts'. And yet there is no more resemblance between them than there was between the contents of Lord Hawke's head and the contents of anyone else's.

Lancashire batted first, completed an innings of 280, and dismissed Derbyshire for 236, causing them to go in again and lost two wickets for 35.

I am afraid England's heavy guns were supplied with some dubious ammunition; I had a vision of spurious shells hitting the earth and burying themselves in the middle of the wicket. They will probably explode in some innocent match in the future between MCC and Hampshire, and blow everybody sky high, scorer, pavilion cat and all.

The first of these extracts simply records the event, or rather, records the outcome of the event, and is of no more interest to the reader than the contents of one of his grandmother's telegrams. The second paints a brilliantly affectionate and communicative picture, not just of ineffectual fast bowling but also of the quaint, parochial charm of the lesser items in the English first-class cricket programme. Clearly the writer of the first item had yet to discover that the actual statistical outcome of the cricket is quite dull unless you are there watching for yourself. The second writer, on the other hand, has realized that, if the sporting journalist is to justify his existence, then he must take the facts and embellish them with all the resources of his own temperament. Unfortunately most cricket writers don't seem to have any temperaments, which explains why reading their match descriptions produces the sensation of munching soggy cardboard.

By far the most interesting fact about those two extracts is that they were both composed by the same man, Sir Neville Cardus. The Lancashire-Derbyshire cryptogram was his very first match report, before he had grasped the true nature of his function in life. The second came several years later, when he was able to distil events through his own considerable creative imagination. All this casts a

Sir Neville Cardus at 85. A man of considerable creative imagination, he advanced his writing from cryptograms to literature that was profound and beautiful.

true light (Cardus would no doubt call it the dry light of ratiocination) on cricket writing and reporting. It reveals to us the very awkward fact that, unless you happen to be a good writer with a literate mind, you can no more compose an adequate report of a cricket match than you can stand in Sir Pelham Warner's stockings without falling over. In any case, most British newspapers are not really interested in cricket anyway; they only tolerate it at all because, for three or four weeks of the year, the nation's footballers retire to have new publicity photographs taken. Somewhere in his biography of Lord Beaverbrook, Mr A. J. P. Taylor reproduces the following memo from the great man to his journalistic minions:

> Many readers hate cricket. Most of them know nothing about it. The cricket public is dwindling every day.*

We can, I think, take Beaverbrook's sentiments for those of most people who administer the affairs of mass-circulation newspapers. However, the situation for the devoted cricket-lover is less parlous than you might think, because most of the match reports published in most of the English national papers are to do with some spectral championship unknown beyond the taverns of Fleet Street and may therefore be said to have no connection with English cricket at all. There is the ghosted drivel of the cricketers themselves, which the National Health Service has been prescribing for some years as a cure for insomnia; there is the fine-old-English-port style of E. W. Swanton, which is much better suited to pieces about fine old English port; there is the nondescript baroque school headed by John Woodcock; there is the bellicose Toryism of Robin Marlar, who most Sundays dons the gorilla suit of assumed toughness; there are others in the hinterland of whose prose only the bedouin could survive.

The truth is that, in the last fifty years, there have been perhaps three English cricket reporters of any consequence: Robertson-Glasgow, Arlott and Alan Gibson, and only one capable of producing literature, Cardus. (Alan Ross might have qualified for either of these groups had he not mistaken himself for a kind of cricketing James Fitzpatrick, as in *Australia '55*, which was so hard to read that a better title would have been *Australia '555555.*)

This leaves the discerning reader with the bald match reports. I perhaps should say the reports of bald matches. Certain things in the 1970s are much as they always were. The printers still have to lay out tablets containing eleven names, as they have since Hambledon. (Although, if, in the 1980s, some firm of bra manu-

* The fact that this ukase instructing editors on Beaverbrook papers to devote less space to cricket was written on June 12, 1930, by which time Bradman, by scoring 1,230 runs in eleven completed innings, had become one of the world's most famous men, casts an interesting light on the news instinct of newspaper owners.

facturers or purveyors of cat-food persuade the Cricket Council that, for purposes of subsidy, an even number of players in a side would suit them, we may yet live to see eight or six or four or two or no-man teams competing for the Stretchcup Cup or the Pussylumps Trophy.) The main new development to test typesetters' mettle has been the appearance in Test and county teams of so many overseas cricketers whose names tend to make the match-cards look like a computer programme, as witness:

A. I. Kallicharran c Chandrasekhar b Venkataraghavan . . . o, which makes one sigh for the good-old-days of simplicity of, say:

R. C. Rought-Rought c B. W. Rought-Rought b D. C. Rought-Rought . . . o.

The truth is that much cricket writing is boring and dreary when it should be either hair-raisingly indiscreet, like Lord Hawke's, or unintentionally funny, like Lord Harris's, or poignantly anachronistic even at the moment of writing, like E. H. D. Sewell's, or madly idiosyncratic, like Albert Knight's, or profound and beautiful, like Cardus in those inspired moments when he apotheosizes George Gunn and A. C. MacLaren into fiction, or analyses through sheer power of literary sensibility the techniques of Woolley and Rhodes. The cases of Harris and Knight may be especially apposite in these utilitarian times for two reasons: first, that neither writer is much read today if at all, and second, that placed in juxtaposition, they make us realize how we tend to oversimplify the Gentleman-Player division.

Harris, a well-intentioned blimp who carted the solar topee of his patrician pretension to those far corners of the earth where the sun never used to set, appears to have believed, among other things, that there is something less reprehensible about Wisden and Lillywhite than about Balzac and Flaubert:

> It was thought that, because I occasionally took part in a game of cricket, at the outside, ten days in the year, on the private ground of Government House at Poona, I was grossly neglecting my duties. Whereas I might have been lying on a sofa, smoking cigarettes and reading French novels; and, because they would not have known what I was doing, I should have been free from condemnation.

There have also been certain anatomical differences between the British and their subject races, which might tend to make a game of cricket between the two a somewhat uneven contest:

> Where I was disappointed with the Parsees was in their fielding. I should have thought that, with their activity and what appeared to be rather long arms, they would have been specially good fields.

As for Knight, there is simply no explaining him away. A Leicestershire professional who opened the batting for many seasons, his *The Complete Cricketer*, published in 1906, remains one of the most remarkable specimens of polysyllabic rococo throughout the entire range of cricket literature. Somehow, in his travels up and down Edwardian England, Knight managed to acquire the oratorical verbosity which posterity usually associates only with those who passed through the forcing houses of the English public schools of the period. There is, for instance, his wonderfully obscure passage on cricket at Oxford:

> Matthew Arnold, musing o'er the beautiful city which did not appreciate his interpretation of the Faith of the centuries, wrote of Oxford as 'The Home of lost causes and forsaken beliefs, of unpopular names and impossible loyalties'. If this were true of the theologies, that Oxford bent not her knee to the passing Zeitgeist, but set aloft her lonely light amid the mists of Tübingen criticism, she may do the same for sport.

Then again there is his innocent assumption, in discovering the ethics of professionalism, that we are all Greek scholars:

> When we read that the town wall was breached for the victorious athlete returning to his home, one can understand the sneer of Euripides in his oft-quoted fragment. But perhaps the best indication of Greek athletic enthusiasm is conveyed by a chance remark of Thucydides describing the magnificent reception given to Brasidas, the Spartan general, after his triumph in Peloponnesia, when the crowds decked him with laurels 'as though he were an athlete'.

Best of all is Knight's pretensions to theology, which lead him to the conclusion that W. G. Grace:

> Is the occupant of cricket's Papal chair; incorporates its massive splendours, its persistence, its marvellous endurance. In the sum of his achievements, in the impersonal greatness which characterizes his ability, in the large time-view which is his possession, we feel how great is the measure of his superiority. He represents cricket as the Pope represents Christianity, not as St Francis represents it.

Whatever the then incumbent at the Vatican may have made of that breathtaking paragraph, certainly Knight wrote the only cricket textbook whose index lists Comte, Horace Walpole, Charles Lamb, the Psychical Research Committee, *Daniel Deronda* and *Far from the Madding Crowd*. What, one wonders, did Knight's fellow-cricketers make of it all? Did they scurry to their Thucydides for enlightenment on the current condition of the lbw law? Did they ransack George Eliot and Thomas Hardy in order to improve their back-play? On the contrary,

Warwickshire's Jameson and Kanhai after their world record. Of their effort, Mr Arbuthnot could say: 'They took the long handle, hit rollicking tons, grabbed the attack by the scruff of the neck.'

(Below right) A bulwark of Yorkshireness: George Hirst. Unhappily, the Aussies did not see the best of him on his 1897 tour: hot, dry conditions straightened the curve from his left-arm in-swingers.

(Below) Parkinson's choice for the Tykes' Prime Minister should Yorkshire secede from Great Britain: Fred Trueman at Sydney Cricket Ground, the lair of any good Yorkshireman's blood brothers.

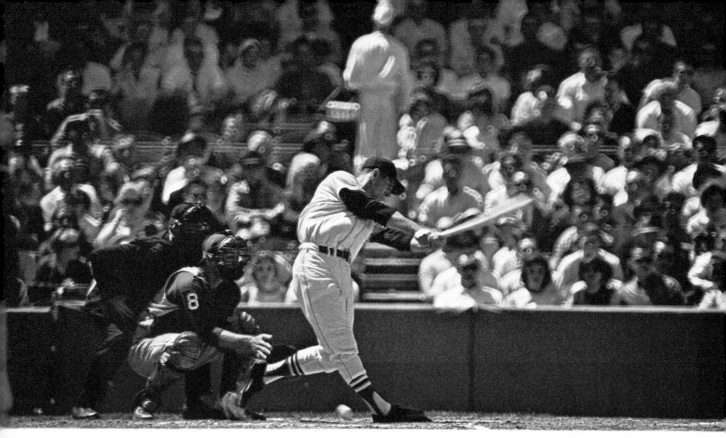

Carl Yastrzemski, a 1970s inheritor of the Boston Red Sox traditions and skills that, in the 1940s, sometimes turned Stan Reynolds's thoughts away from girls.

No mean versifier himself, Snow (bowling to Boycott in a Test trial) inspired a Brooklyn poet to write '. . . O dear John Snow with | your poet's hair so black in such a mop . . .'

it is doubtful if they read a word of Knight, or, had they done so, would have understood any of it. Certainly those intellectual paragons of the amateur tradition who went through the universities with a bat under one arm and their own head under the other were not advanced enough to follow Knight's reasoning, least of all, perhaps, the well-known author Gilbert Jessop, who once perpetrated the grammatical blasphemy that would have made poor Knight's nose bleed:

I have been to [sic] infernally busy to do much towards its publication.

Occasionally the modern era does produce books on cricket which are, in their own way, as riveting and as informed as classics of the past, but the irony is that, while the interminable sawdust-prose about the latest tour to or from one of the outposts of what used to be Empire is publicized and packaged as though it was worth reading, items like Rowland Bowen's remarkable *Cricket, a History* (1970) and C. L. R. James's classic *Beyond a Boundary* (1963), both written by men outside the freemasonry of the Press box, are rarely so much as mentioned.

Now for the good news. One genuine advance in absorbing some details of contemporary cricket has been the development of television, which, at last, releases the absent cricket-lover from the need to pollute his mind with the contents of the sports pages. Today a man can sit in his armchair and see which way the ball is moving. If he is lucky and it is a freakishly active game, he might even be able to see which way the cricketers are moving. But, if he is to enjoy his experience, what he must do is to keep the picture on and the sound off, otherwise his brain will be softened by the disingenuous drone of commentators who are terrified, almost to a man, of the blandishments of candour.

These commentators may be divided into two groups, each more disturbing than the other. First there are those ex-public schoolboys whose careers, so far as cricket at high levels is concerned, have been packed with lack of direct involvement or incident. They tend to chortle their way through the day's play as though this was Big Side and young Faversham was leading the College against the Townees, circa 1905. Instead of presenting an accurate picture of Test cricket which really is played in a tough, stern manner, they suggest nothing more than prep school prizedays or study fires at dusk.

The other group of public persecutors, growing almost by the hour, in size if not in maturity, consists of a formidable battery of ex-Test stars who sit there presenting a bogus picture of scintillating cricket, radiant sportsmanship and fastidious manners.

Two notable British exceptions include Ted Dexter, who, although he rarely risks any actual candour, conveys a certain amused patrician tolerance in his contributions, as though what he is watching is too ridiculous for words but a Radley College gentleman is expected to play the game and be polite. The only commentator I have ever heard who actually—when it applies and it sometimes does—says that the batting is feeble, or the scoring rate infantile, or the cricket dreary and the general concept of the game ignoble is Denis Compton. Often as I sit there watching him (barring the two-handed summary efforts which are unwatchable) I wonder how thankful he must be for having completed his own career just in time to avoid the modern utilitarian debacle.

The perfect solution, of course, for the viewer is to watch the picture and listen simultaneously to BBC sound commentary, at which point we arrive at last at very nearly the perfect way of conveying impressions of the cricket to those who are somewhere else at the time. The radio team varies a little from series to series, but over the years its regular performers have included at least three virtuosi and one promising youngster. As to the three grand masters, there is no need to extol any further Arlott's gift for painting word pictures, which equals that of Alistair Cooke himself. But Arlott is well-matched by Jack Fingleton and Alan Gibson. Indeed, so accomplished is this marvellous trio that when rain stops play and they are reduced to talking about what is *not* happening, it becomes a positive delight to listen to the extreme virtuosity with which they conduct an inconsequential chat packed with pearls of wisdom, with nuggets of humour, with whole shiploads of commonsense and small-talk of the most engaging kind. The promising newcomer to this group of Senior Wranglers is Trevor Bailey, who consistently deploys a fine sense of humour, which is after all not unexpected in a man who once perpetrated the hilarious joke of being at one and the same time an amateur cricketer and a paid clerk of the same county.

Mention of Fingleton raises the question of people from outside England who try to get inside England. Fingleton is by far the most accomplished and perceptive of the Australians who have attempted it so far. When he finally arrives at the Pearly Gates and has to ask Lord Harris if it is all right for him to pass through, he can always justify himself with *Brightly Fades The Don* and *The Ashes Crown the Year*, two volumes of sociology masquerading as cricket reportage. Marring them are only two blemishes: first, a slight tendency to see the Old Country as populated entirely by brave charladies and Big Ben; and second—but wait, perhaps the second fault is no fault at all. To put it bluntly, Fingleton cannot leave Bradman alone. Bradman is to him what King Charles's head was to Mr Dick, with equally weird results. How baffled were readers of the *Sunday Times* one morning some seasons ago when, starting to read how a great innings from the Australian batsman Peter Burge had saved his side after seven wickets had gone down for 178, saw this:

The game gives and the game takes away. One August day in 1948 Don Bradman walked to the middle of The Oval for his very last Test innings, not only against England, but in all Tests. The England players gave three cheers and the crowd joined in. Bradman needed only a few meagre runs to average 100 per Test innings. But a few moments later, he was wending his sad way back to the pavilion—clean bowled for nil.

What this had to do with Burge's innings in 1964 was never clear, but then, perhaps berating Bradman is not altogether a bad obsession from which to suffer. In any case, Fingleton has mellowed somewhat over the years and throws darts into Bradman's effigy with less persistence than he used to. His one-time rival for the honour of pencilling in black teeth and pimples on Bradman's official portrait, Ray Robinson, hardly ever appears at length in the English sporting prints, much to the regret of those who know *Between Wickets* and *From the Boundary*, and perhaps a little to the relief of those who know only *The Glad Season*.

I suppose an English cricket-lover's idea of a paradisial morning would be to wake up to read Cardus and Arlott in the *Guardian*, Robertson-Glasgow and Gibson in the *Times*, Fingleton and Robinson in any two other sheets of their choice. Later, on the radio, Arlott, Fingleton and Gibson would be heard squeezing jokes out of Bailey because rain had for the moment stopped play just as Compton and Dexter were counter-attacking Grimmett and O'Reilly.

In the meantime, until that comes to pass, I shall continue to search for the source of a certain fragment of cricket writing as zealously as ever the Victorians searched for the source of the Nile. I understand that once a cricket reporter at the turn of the century, worried about libelling the Lancashire throwers, but determined not to let them get away with it, opened his report with: 'Mold and Crossland opened the attack, and at three-thirty Briggs came on to bowl the first overs of the day.' Does anybody know who this anonymous Swift of the Press box might be?

The Cliché Expert Testifies on Cricket: MIKE GIBSON

Mike Gibson, the lively and imaginative sports columnist of the Sydney Daily Telegraph, *interviewed Mr Arbuthnot, the cliché expert, the day before the first Test of the 1970–1 series began in Brisbane. It was warmly received by many—if not all—of his Sydney newspaper colleagues. A very experienced cricket writer, who lives in that harbour city, considered the column should, one day, be put into an anthology. The Editor is pleased to oblige. Because of space restrictions, much material had to be pruned from Mr Gibson's piece to fit into his slot in the sports pages. Freed from these confines, it has been expanded for this book from its original form in print.*

In all things, justice must be seen to be done. Counsel for the defence has a right to speak on behalf of cricket writers, or, at least, the top layer of cricket scribes from many countries. Following the sun and cricket teams around the world, they have to work from a multitude of time zones. From certain overseas countries, deadlines to Fleet Street or home office elsewhere, are sometimes cruelly tight and demanding. Writers have to work at top pace under intense pressure. In these circumstances, it is not surprising that, now and then, a cliché leaps from typewriter or quill to lay a dusty patina on purple prose. Mr Arbuthnot is not a completely alien figure in even the highest company.

Yet, despite the tyranny of the clock, rigours of heat, the clattering bedlam of press boxes and perhaps the sports editor's choler, the extraordinary and impressive feature of cricket writing is how few of Mr Arbuthnot's favourite phrases actually seep into their copy. Phrase for phrase, line for line, cricket writers must surely maintain the uniformly highest standard of writing in countries where cricket is a major sport.

Its sustained quality is apparent by simple comparison to a lot of popular soccer writing, that roiling, bellowing, twitching, hyperthyroid outpouring that slops endlessly through English sports pages for twelve months of the year. The smooth rhythms, the charm, the informed pleasantness of cricket writing stand out in delightful relief against that polluted tide.

So, the cream of cricket writers need feel no strong qualms, pangs or blushes when Mr Arbuthnot strolls into the press box. They know that if he was let loose on the footballing fraternity he would have—to use a phrase he savours—a field day.

Mr Arbuthnot, the cliché expert, flew into town yesterday. He dropped in for a bite of lunch with colleague George Grippe and myself.

He presented a rather bedraggled figure when he came into the pub. 'It's raining cats and dogs out there,' he observed. 'Coming down in bucketfuls,'

George replied. 'Touché,' said Mr Arbuthnot, who respects nothing more than a good kickback to start the day.

Mr Arbuthnot was *en route* to Brisbane to watch Ray Illingworth's England play Bill Lawry's Australia in the first cricket Test starting today.

Cricket being a cliché in itself, Mr Arbuthnot was worried that he might need to brush up on the grand old game. 'I don't want to make a fool of myself up there,' he said.

Being a cliché-cutter of some renown myself, I could understand Mr Arbuthnot's concern. Up in Brisbane in the press box, he would be pitting phrases with some of Fleet Street's kings.

'Well, look, my friend, how about we put you through your paces, give you a quick quiz, more or less to freshen you up?' George said. 'A verbal fitness test on the eve of the match?' Mr Arbuthnot said. 'Very well,' he added, draining his beer glass. 'This'll make your hair grow curly.' 'Make you see in the dark,' said George.

Seeing he was in weight-for-age cliché company, Mr Arbuthnot tipped his brow. I could see he was going to rest on his laurels and play it by ear. He told us to have no mercy and fire away. George opened the attack.

Q. What is cricket played on?
A. Cricket is played on a pitch. When a match begins, pitches can show signs of early life, be lively and offer some assistance to the bowler.

Q. And if the pitch shows no signs of life?
A. It is sluggish, unresponsive, innocuous, drugged, doped, slow, docile. In short, it is a batsman's wicket.

Q. What will a pitch of this kind be likened to?
A. A featherbed, or a shirt-front, or a masterpiece of the groundsman's art. Some have been known to be as lively as Noah's corpse.

Q. What will precipitation do to a wicket?
A. Make it rain-affected. Then it can become full of devil, venomous, spiteful. A lot of rain will turn it into a gluepot or a sticky dog. It makes batting a nightmare.

Q. How does a game of cricket begin?
A. Opening batsmen take strike against the new ball. These opening batsmen are, I must add, a wide and varied race. They can be plucky battlers, gutsy gamecocks, consistent run-getters, reliable willow wielders or cautious accumulators of runs. Opening batsmen who score slowly are disciplined grafters, grim stonewallers, thorns in the side of the opposition. They are determined, solid, gritty and dour.

Q. And should the opening bowlers fail to dislodge them . . .?
A. They see off the new ball.

Q. Which means that they can . . .
A. Set a good foundation for the innings. They steer the ship out of troubled waters, make fighting knocks, weather the storm and survive the blitz. They have got the team off to a good start.

Q. What would you say about openers who score quickly?
A. They get the team off to a flying start. They push the score along. In doing this they take the smile off the new ball's rosy countenance, paste the pace and rouge the pickets. The attack holds no terrors for them.

Q. What about opening bowlers?
A. The quickies or speed-merchants spearhead the attack and send down hostile deliveries. They are fiery, demon, fierce, express-train and menacing. They send down vicious bouncers that make the batsmen duck for cover. The denizens of Fleet Street once christened an Australian fast bowler 'the wild colonial boy'.

Q. My goodness, all that sounds most disturbing. So, their speed is capable of making the batsmen . . .
A. Hurry their strokes, flash at balls outside the off stump or grope forward without making contact. They hang out the bat. With sheer speed, the speed-merchant can get through the batsman's defences.

Q. And when this happens . . .
A. They castle the batsmen; they send the stumps flying or cartwheeling towards the wicket-keeper. If the batsman is good enough to get a touch, he tickles the ball to the keeper or snicks it to the slips, if he gets a thick edge.

Q. Is there a term for durable pace bowlers?
A. Naturally. They are iron men who are kept on for long bowling stints. If they bowl long enough, pace men bowl themselves into the ground and often become willing workhorses who carry the team on their burly shoulders. If they bowl longer than that, they become old warhorses.

Q. How would you describe a batsman who goes for runs?
A. Oh, you mean the crowd pleasers, the cavaliers. They take the long handle, hit rollicking tons, give lusty displays, demoralize the bowling, pepper the pickets, treat bowlers with disdain. They collar the bowling, inflict severe punishment and grab the attack by the scruff of the neck and shake the very life out of it.

Q. So such batsmen have . . .
A. Every stroke in the book. They are capable of despatching the ball to all parts of the ground. Such strokes are full-blooded, hit off the meat of the bat, tucked away to fine leg, steered down to third man and flicked off the batsman's toes. They pick the gaps in the field.

Q. These shots are apt to be called?
A. Glorious.

Q. In contrast to these . . .
A. Aggressive stroke-players.

Q. Yes, in contrast to them, there are the batsmen who don't go for the runs. What would an accomplished cliché expert say of one of them?
A. He plays with a dead bat, puts up the shutters, puts a sleeper hold on the game. He hammers nails into the coffin of cricket. He is invariably compared with someone named Bailey. His bat can seem as broad as a barn door.

Q. His performances can be summed up as . . .
A. Dreary displays. He lets the bowlers dictate the terms, take the initiative.

Q. What is he most likely to do to the ball?
A. Play it gently back along the pitch to the bowler. He does this because he is lacking in enterprise, content to plod along.

Not a cliché-monger in sight. Len Hutton tells Fleet Streeters how England beat Australia at Sydney in 1954. Among the scribes: the late Bruce Harris (writing), Frank Rostron (speaking) and, at far right, the late Ron Roberts.

Q. How about the slow bowlers?
A. They are wily, cunning, resourceful and full of guile. There is one thing, however, that they are not.

Q. And that is?
A. Astute. Only captaincy is astute.

Q. What does every good slow bowler have?
A. A repertoire, which contains a stock ball, wrong 'un, bosie or googly, chinaman, faster ball and one that goes with the arm.

Q. What are slow bowlers capable of doing?
A. Good ones beat the batsmen all ends up, win the battle between bat and ball and snare their victims. Really mean ones reduce batsmen to impotence. They tempt batsmen into making mistakes. They lure batsmen out of their ground.

Q. And what can they do to make a batsman lbw?
A. Trap him.

Q. So he is lbw to what degree?
A. Palpably.

Q. Can he be lbw in any other way?
A. No, only palpably. The decision is palpable because the batsman is plumb in front; he has fallen victim to a wizard of spin.

Q. These wily men must be capable of great achievements?
A. They certainly are. They can cause a batting collapse.

Q. Which is . . . ?
A. Dramatic. They bundle out the opposition, who are sometimes dismissed cheaply, unless there is a rearguard action.

Q. You would sum up poor slow bowlers as being . . .
A. Erratic. They fail to achieve a line and length; they cannot drop the ball on the spot. Because of this, they must buy their wickets. When they lack control, they pay the penalty for wayward length by seeing the very cover flayed from the ball.

Q. What would you say if I told you a batsman was indiscreet?
A. I'd say he lived dangerously, had suicidal tendencies, walked a tightrope, trod a rocky path, chanced his arm or skated on thin ice.

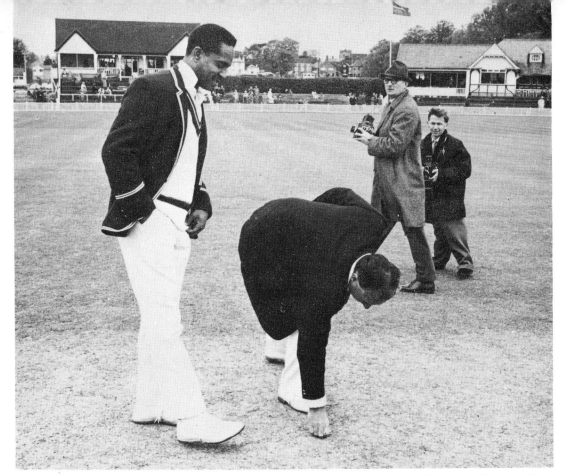

Sobers and Kenyon examine the Worcester pitch. Will it be a featherbed, sluggish, innocuous, doped or full of devil, venomous or spiteful?

Q. Is there an inevitable result to this?
A. Yes, he would throw his wicket away.

Q. If neither batsman nor bowler takes charge . . .
A. Gains the ascendancy.

Q. Gains the ascendency, what will happen to the match?
A. It will peter out.

Q. Into what?
A. A tame draw.

Q. What part do the umpires play?
A. They are the men in white, sometimes called the arbiters.

Q. What are their responses to appeals?
A. They can turn them down categorically, answer in the affirmative, ignore them studiously, send the batsman on his way, give him his marching orders, or give him the benefit of the doubt.

Q. In close decisions . . .
A. We prefer to say near things.

Q. In those cases . . .
A. The umpire has the final word.

Q. Because?
A. The umpire is in the best position to see what happened.

Q. What is happening with wickets?
A. Wickets are being taken less and less these days. Instead, they are being snapped up, grabbed, seized, snaffled and captured.

Q. What about catches?
A. Catches are still being lofted, gobbled up, spooned, plucked out of the air with uncanny anticipation, swooped on with razor-sharp reflexes, pocketed, pouched, or falling down first slip's throat and ballooned.

Q. So many people say cricket is dead. I want to know are they still hitting boundaries these days?
A. Ah, trying to trick an old hand like that. Tch, tch, tch. Boundaries are never hit. They are struck, cracked, hammered, pounded, slashed, thumped, belted, flogged and smacked.

Q. Last one, sir, have we found another Bradman lately?
A. No, not since Craig, O'Neill and Walters. There is talk of this fellow Richards, but in my opinion, he doesn't qualify.

Q. Why, sir?
A. Well, he's South African. Calling him another Bradman . . . that just isn't cricket.

Q. So instead we must be content with calling him . . .
A. A run-machine.

Q. Thank you, Mr Arbuthnot. Listening to you, one can almost hear the pleasant sound of leather on willow.
A. Thank you, Mike. Now let me at those Fleet Street boys. On this form I think I can hit them for six.

The Grand Old Limey Game: STANLEY REYNOLDS

When the first flush of morning is still on a summer day we are off. As always by train, clicking through the quiet parts of town we go, Cedric and I. Sometimes Young Ainsworth, the Oxford Blue, is with us or we are meeting Campbell and the Captain at Manchester and will take the ninepenny ride together to Warwick Road and Old Trafford. But mainly it is Cedric and me, an unlikely pair, an odd couple.

He is a groundsman, head groundsman at the lovely Lancashire county ground at Liverpool's Aigburth. He is an oldtime groundsman, trained before the war; a heavy-roller man, a marl man is Cedric, despising the insipid modern wickets created by Surrey loam. And a Yorkshireman, too. Not only a Yorkshireman, but a Bradford League man and therefore a Yorkshireman of the Yorkshiremen. And I am a wayward baseball fan, upon whose heart is engraved the names of the 1946 Boston Red Sox team; whose memory encompasses the Brooklyn Dodgers of '41, the '42 St Louis Cardinals; whose file index behind the forehead contains '27 New York Yankees of Miller Huggins—Babe Ruth's greatest year—the New York Giants of John McGraw, even the Pittsburg Pirates of, say, '09, of Honus Wagner and Dots Miller, one of the all-time great keystone combinations.

Our mythology is the same as the cricketers'. The same sort of gods, who we are all much too young to ever have seen, sit on our Olympus: Rajah Hornsby, Tris Speaker, Ty Cobb, Rabbit Mauranville, Shoeless Joe Jackson, of the Chicago Black Sox scandal, the year they fixed the World Series—baseball's Watergate; Enos Country Slaughter, Lippy Leo Durocher, Joe DiMaggio, Pee Wee Reece, Satchel Paige. We make poems in our heads out of the names of the oldtime, baggy-capped, tobacco-chewing ball players of the great days, which are always and everywhere, long ago.

But what am I doing on a train going to see a cricket match? What am I doing, whose eyes can water up, well, no, not tears, it is instead a clutching at the heart, recalling the long-ago faces on the baseball cards which came with square slabs of pink and sugary bubble gum? That was real love, chewing that bubble gum to get the pictures.

'Oh, you just want to see someone hit a ball with a piece of wood,' a lady I know said to me; her first husband had been a cricketer. Perhaps, after it has all been said, all the poetry about Lord's and the romance of the village green on a high summer afternoon, the bitter lady is right. But how odd it is to abandon the native faith and worship at a foreign altar before gods with outlandish handles, all initials and sometimes unpronounceable to a tongue at home with the plain German or simple Irish and musical Italian names of baseball. K. S. Ranjitsinhji! The Nawab of Pataudi! The Nawab of Pataudi? They'd never believe that back home outside Tonelli's Fruit Store & Ice Cream Soda Bar where, from the first green days of April until smokey autumn October, the talk was always about baseball, girls and baseball. How could a game be a game where you stopped for tea?

In the fall of the year, we talked of football and girls, and in the winter, it was basketball and ice hockey and girls. You see something right there. There is no more insular country in the world than America. It is American baseball and football, which is really just a sort of chess game played by robots, which are eccentric. We play games no one else in the world really plays. And then we call it the World Series.

Cricket, after all, is not an English mystery. It is an Australian game and as much at home in Africa or Asia or the Caribbean as in Canterbury and Hove. A world sport, international. It travels; as they say of some wines.

If I had stayed in London, I would probably never have gone beyond the dutiful tourist's peek at Lord's. The London Americans meet in Hyde Park each Sunday in season to play softball, which is a fat old Rotarians' form of baseball, played with a slim bat and a giant ball which you cannot help hitting but which will not travel very far. It's a game for failing eyesight and short breath, is softball. Then on to the pub—I wonder if they even try bitter beer?—and chat of the race for the first place in the American League between the New York Yankees and the Baltimore Orioles.

There is something basically ridiculous about a Lancashire American with a red rose stuck in his button-hole, attempting to grasp the vocabulary of cricket, but I think there is an edge of sadness around the softball players of Hyde Park desperately trying to hang on to baseball's silver cord. I loved the sight and smell of baseball, cutting lectures at the university, riding the funny old Boston trolley cars up to Kenmore Square and Fenway Park to see the Boston Red Sox play, though they were forever humbled by the Yankees. Playing the game in the street on summer evenings. Playing on sandlots, in the days before kids' baseball was organized with them all in little uniforms playing on special scaled-down diamonds. We played everywhere, and would slide into second base in the street, ripping the backside out of our jeans, which we called dungarees in those days. Not really so long ago, but different. I was sixteen years old before I wore a proper pair of spiked baseball shoes and played on a field with no broken glass. 'Sliding pads? What do we want them for? They're no broken bottles here. Why, you could go in head first to base on a field like this.' Cricket or baseball, everyone above a certain age has memories like that.

Cricket in the south: The middle-class game of deckchairs, tree-ringed grounds and cloudless blue skies.

Cricket in the north: Reynolds (with moustache) and Cedric (with buttonhole) savour northern cricket: wind-whipped, rain-dripping tents, soggy sandwiches, indifferent beer.

But I fell in love with Lancashire, with rainy old Manchester and nasal Liverpool, and that meant drinking pints of warm beer, the *Manchester Guardian*, the mystique of the Liberal non-conformist conscience, Miss Horniman's theatre, Neville Cardus, and the War of the Roses. There is a certain irony in a Boston Red Sox fan becoming a member of the Lancashire County Cricket Club. Always with the Red Sox we had the Yankees to break our hearts. And now I have Yorkshire. But, then, Lancashire never could have sold Archie MacLaren to Yorkshire like the Sox sold Babe Ruth to New York.

Even with the hired soldiery of modern cricket, there is still a local flavour about county cricket which you don't get in baseball. Clive Lloyd and Engineer may be out-of-towners and Barry Wood a true son of Osset and Yorkshire cricket, but most of Lancashire's men speak with the true tones of the valley where the Lancashire League is played, even dusky young John Abrahams, born in Cape Town, has the authentic drawl.

Cedric, the Yorkshireman, translates for me when I am among the men of Nelson, Tod or Haslingden. 'Eeee, 'e didn't 'alf tek brawd when firs' cum t' 'Aslin'den, did Dennis, eeee.' What'd he say? ''E says,' informs Cedric, 'Didn't half talk broad when he first came to Haslingden, did Dennis Lillee, oh aye!'

I feel sorry for other Americans who have fallen in love with cricket because it is the southern game they have fallen for, the pretty and romantic cricket of Kent and Hampshire and Sussex, played against a scenic backdrop, the *New Yorker* magazine's idea of rural England. Or the Lord's of the Eton and Harrow match, all top hats and Daphnes, Amandas, Arabellas, and Miss Huntington-Gore-Fitzphedrick. (Actually a lot of the girls you'll see most afternoons at Lord's are the high-class hookers of St John's Wood who use it for sunbathing.) I rather suspect this is the England and the cricket of such an unlikely figure as Mr Marvin Cohen, the Brooklyn Jewish poet, who comes to England every time the Australians are here, and who wrote of the Sussex fast bowler, J. A. Snow:

> O successor to immortal Freddie
> Trueman. O dear John Snow. With
> your poet's hair so black in such a
> mop. With your aquiline features,
> so determined and virile.
>
> In years to come, when I'm old
> and grey by the fire hearth, I'll
> chant this plaintive woe:

> Woe's curse on me
> I'll not more see
> Yesteryear's sheer Snow.
> Do your doom, wind. Blow.

I have been to see southern cricket. To Hove, to Folkestone, Canterbury, Tunbridge Wells, the Saffrons at Eastbourne, Dean Park at Bournemouth, and Priory Meadows at Hastings, where Cedric enthused, not over the day's play, but over the heavy roller, a 1928 Barford. My cricket is the northern game, the hard-nosed men of Yorkshire, the rolling yokels of Lancashire and Derbyshire. A game of grey concrete and wind-whipped rain-dripping tents; soggy sandwiches, and very indifferent pints of beer. In the summer of 1974, we went on a cricketing tour, Cedric, Young Ainsworth and myself, viewing the English summer game in the trim, suburban respectability of the middle-class south. Tents and deck-chairs, home-made pies and pasties, grounds ringed with pleasant trees, a brass band playing on the prom only a long-leg-to-wicketkeeper's-throw away, and cloudless, windless blue skies: another world it was, and a totally different game.

If I had stayed in the south, I would not have taken up cricket although, for a journalist and a former baseball writer, there is a natural fascination about a game which makes for such fine writing as Sir Pelham Warner, R. C. Robertson-Glasgow, F. S. Ashley-Cooper; Jack Fingleton on Trumper and S. F. Barnes; John Arlott on Maurice Tate on a sea-fret wicket at Hove; The Country Vicar on Ranji, Denzil Batchelor on C. B. Fry; Cardus on Gunn and Bradman; E. W. Swanton on Compton.

Or Alan Ross on fast bowling: 'There are other arts: of flight, of spin, of length as naggingly repetitive as the water-torture. But the great fast bowler's is the final apotheosis, the embodiment of a devilish joy that is at once physical and spiritual, retributive and musical, a rite, a ritual of Chinese inscrutability and subtlety, to which no calligrapher has done justice, an art form, a balletic event, a conflict reflective of national prestige, a resumé of English taste, habits, maso-chisms, a canalization of the erotic impulse, a species of warfare, the instinctual man's introduction to aesthetics . . .' Someone should write of baseball that way, but no one ever has.

As a journalist, as the father of three English sons, I was drawn to contemplate cricket. But it was only as a northerner, a Lancastrian, however bogus, that I have started learning what I could about the game until finally I mastered a rather distorted mirror image of a fast-bowling action and laced on my meta-physical white-washed pit boots and one day opened the bowling. Only to be no-balled for chucking, while my eldest boy, at square leg, giggled and smirked. It hardly seemed worth the effort of wearing out the dog and the back garden in days and weeks and months of practice while the great American novel lay fallow

Lancastrians in the Old Trafford crowd in 1972 urged their 'adopted son' Dennis Lillee to discomfort Roses' rival, Geoff Boycott. This bumper fulfilled their wishes.

and the neighbours smiled and tapped an index finger to their head. I now come round the wicket, but my fingers are too soft and white for spin. Yet, when I journeyed to Widnes in Lancashire, again in 1974, to see a touring University of California XI play, I talked such a stream of marl and Surrey loam, leg glances and googlies (which is really just baseball's knuckle ball), that the Californians took me for the genuine item until nostalgia got the better of me and I asked if they happened to know if the Red Sox looked like having any twenty game winners in their pitching stable that season.

Once, in an unguarded moment, the *Sunday Times* asked me to go to Old Trafford to write about Lillee, the Australian paceman of the day, facing Boycott, the best of English bats, while all of Lancashire sat and hoped the adopted son of Haslingden would take the Yorkshireman's head off. And *Punch*, being basically a humorous magazine, has also let me try my hand, rather like surrendering to the whims of an eccentric relative. But I am too timorous and cannot really write about the gods laughing at The Oval or Ranji flicking aside the thunderbolts aimed at his head. Actually that is what makes Cardus so good about writing about cricket; he is full of the gods and imps, all manner of magic and dark fire, the sentences crackle with poetic hi-jinks and high drama, and it is all just about a game played by Archie and Wilf, Jack Tyldesley and Jimmy Heep, names and men as common as clogs until they took to the cricket pitch and performed feats of daring and possibly even great beauty.

> Pedalling between lectures, spokes throwing off
> Sun like Catherine Wheels,
> . . . A boundary, whose grouped trees might have been
> Set up by Claude or Poussin

Alan Ross writes in a poem called Cricket at Oxford. The poetry of cricket is full of such posh images and I don't believe there is a baseball fan alive, reared up in the dust of a diamond during a rainless August with the heat and light glaring off his shirtsleeves; those cat-calling, hooting, jeering people in the bleachers who could or, indeed, would want to identify with that genteel picture of cricket.

Cricket in the north is still a people's game, for yokels and millhands, raw-boned and rough men like those weird, chaw-chewing, red-necked hillbillies who always made the best baseball players. And it fills a need, that desire to see a fellow hit a ball with a piece of wood, to see a man make the ball go where he wants it to go.

Philosophically all ball games—all games played with a ball—are much the same. Plus, cricket has Cedric and his incantations about marl and loam and the heavy roller. There may be groundsmen in baseball but I never met one, certainly I could envisage none with the priestlike devotion to grass of a Cedric. Cricket is full of surprises and I learn something new every day. Still, there are always the shades and ghosts of that other ball game which steal across the cricket square towards the end of a long afternoon and make the expatriate sigh and feel a chill.

O my Hornsby and my DiMaggio long ago!

Notes on Contributors

DAVID EDWARD JOHN FRITH

Born Paddington (London) 16.3.37. Editor of *The Cricketer* since 1972. Lived Sydney 1949–64. Third grade cricket for St George, first grade for Paddington. Publications: *Runs in the Family* (John Edrich) 1969; *My Dear Victorious Stod* (Biography of A. E. Stoddart) 1970, which won Cricket Society Jubilee Literary Award; *The Archie Jackson Story* 1974.

LESLIE THOMAS JOHN ARLOTT OBE

Born Basingstoke 25.2.14. Southampton Police Force 1934–45, ending as detective-sergeant. Joined BBC 1945 as talks and poetry producer; began cricket commentaries 1946; much TV and film commentary. Contested Epping as Liberal candidate (honourably but unsuccessfully). Author of more than thirty books on cricket. Major titles: *Fred*, *Vintage Summer*, *Concerning Cricket*, *From Hambledon to Lord's*, *The Noblest Game* (with Sir Neville Cardus), etc. Hampshireman always—lives at Alresford, surrounded by vast book and aquatint collection and with (full) cellar below.

TONY COZIER

Born Barbados 10.7.40. Educated Lodge School, Barbados and Carleton University, Ottawa. Sports Editor, *Barbados Daily News* 1960–8 (when newspaper folded). Covered every Caribbean Test since 1962 for newspapers and radio; West Indies tours to England, 1963, 1966, 1973, working for BBC 1966 and 1973; Australia-New Zealand 1968–9. Editor *West Indies Cricket Annual* from launch in 1970 and of *Caribbean Cricket* 1973 and 1974. Correspondent on West Indian current affairs for several overseas newspapers (including Eastern Caribbean correspondent for *Financial Times*) and news agencies. Has played first-class club cricket in Barbados for Carlton and Wanderers.

DICK BRITTENDEN

Cricket correspondent for *The Press*, Christchurch, New Zealand since 1946, sports editor since 1954. Served with R.N.Z.A.F. as navigator in Britain and the Bahamas during World War II. Author of six cricket books and was editor of *New Zealand Cricketer* until *The Cricket Player* bought out the magazine in 1974. Has reported tours to South Africa (1954), India and Pakistan (1965, 1969), and England (1965, 1969, 1973). A Cowan Award winner for distinguished reporting in New Zealand.

K. N. PRABHU

Born 1924. Started on *New Chronicle*, Delhi as general sub-editor. Moved to sports desk of *The Times of India*, Delhi edition. After eight-month spell on *The Herald*, Melbourne in 1958–9, returned to take charge as Chief Sports Editor and cricket correspondent of *The Times of India*, Bombay. Covered cricket in all countries except South Africa and New Zealand. Covered Indian tour of West Indies 1967, 1971, of Australia 1967 and England 1971. Played cricket, badminton and tennis at college.

ZAKIR HUSSAIN SYED

The Director of Pakistan Sports Council which is responsible for all sports activity in Pakistan. Since 1966 regular TV and radio commentator on cricket. Permanent Pakistan correspondent of *The Cricketer*. Covered 1971 Pakistan tour of England, on which he wrote the successful book *The Young Ones*. Played first-class cricket for Pakistan International Airways, Punjab and Rawalpindi division.

LOUIS DUFFUS

Born Melbourne in 1904. Doyen of South African cricket writers. Until retirement in 1970, wrote accounts of one hundred and twenty-nine Test matches, including all played by South Africa 1929–70. Tours with South African teams: England (seven), Australia-New Zealand (three); twelve internal tours of South Africa and Rhodesia with visiting teams. Also covered hockey (South African men's and women's teams to Europe and USA), tennis (Davis Cup, Federation Cup in many countries), golf and baseball. Forty-one years with Argus Group including sports editor *Daily News*, Durban and *The Star*, Johannesburg (seventeen years). Publications include *Cricketers of the Veld*, *History of S.A. Cricket*, *Beyond the Laager*, *Springbok Glory* and *Play Abandoned* (autobiography).

BILL FRINDALL

Born Epsom, Surrey 1939. Succeeded the late Arthur Wrigley as BBC's radio scorer in 1966. Devoted compiler of cricket statistics. Plays club cricket and has trundled his fast bowling in far-flung places, e.g. Geneva, Malta, The Hague, Paris, Cologne.

RICHIE BENAUD OBE

Born Penrith, New South Wales 6.10.30. Huguenot extraction. Father Lou Benaud successful Sydney grade leg-spinner. Played for New South Wales 1948–64; for Australia sixty-three times between 1951–2 (v West Indies) and 1963–4 (v South Africa). Captain in twenty-eight Tests, never lost a series. Australia's all-time leading Test wicket-taker: 248 at 27·03. Scored 2201 runs in Tests (av.

24·45) with three centuries (one in West Indies 1955 in seventy-eight minutes—third fastest ever). Only Sobers has also taken 200 wickets and scored 2000 runs in Tests. Writer and commentator most praised by players.

JAMES CHARLES LAKER

Born Bradford (Yorkshire) 9.2.22. Surrey debut 1946, capped 1947. Benefit 1956 (£11,000). Retired 1959, returned briefly for Essex 1962. Forty-six Tests, 193 wickets at 21·23 (cheaper than anyone else in England's top fifteen wicket-takers except S. F. Barnes). World record nineteen for 90 v Aust. at Old Trafford 1956, also ten for 88 v Aust. for Surrey 1956. Forty-six wickets in 1956 series—exceeded only by S. F. Barnes (49 in four Tests England v South Africa 1913–14). Took eight for 2 in Test Trial at Bradford 1950. Total 1944 wickets in first-class cricket at 18·40 (100 wickets in season eleven times). Toured Australia, West Indies and South Africa. TV commentator for BBC.

IAN MICHAEL CHAPPELL

Born Glenelg, South Australia 29.9.43. Grandson of former Australian captain Victor Richardson, elder brother of Greg and Trevor. First-class debut 1961–2 v Tasmania. To start 1974–5 season: fifty-six Tests (twenty as captain), 3922 runs at 41·70; twelve centuries including 145 and 121 at Wellington v New Zealand 1974 (when Greg scored 247 not out and 133). Also scored two centuries in Brisbane for Australia v Rest of World 1971–2. Toured England, South Africa, West Indies, India and Pakistan, New Zealand. Highest Test score: 196 v Pakistan 1972–3. Has own journalism/public relations business.

BARRY ANDERSON RICHARDS

Born Durban 21.7.45. Captain South Africa Schools side to England 1963. Debut Natal 1964. Joined Hampshire 1968, scoring 2395 runs (av. 47·90) in first full season. Scored 356 for South Australia v Western Australia (Perth) 1970–1 (325 not out first day). His 1,285 runs in South African season 1973–4 a record. Scored more runs than any other South African-born batsman; almost universally rated as world's best batsman. Four Tests all v Australia 1969–70: 508 runs, av. 72·57, two centuries.

DENNIS LESLIE AMISS

Born Birmingham 7.4.43. Joined Warwickshire 1958, debut 1960, capped 1965. Benefit 1975. Thirty-two Tests to end of 1974 season. From March 1973 to March 1974, scored 1356 runs (av. 79·76) in eleven Tests, twenty-one innings. Only Bradman and R. B. Simpson have scored more in twelve-month period—*not* a calendar year. To end England season of 1974, he scored 1253 runs (eleven matches, eighteen innings, av. 78·30), then needing 128 runs to equal Simpson's world Test record of 1381 runs in calendar year (1964, fourteen Tests). Partner in tyre business.

MICHAEL JOHN PROCTER

Born Durban 15.9.46. Vice-captain of South African Schools side to England 1963. Debut Natal in Currie Cup 1965–6. Joined Gloucestershire 1968, capped same year. Transferred to Western Province 1969–70, then Rhodesia 1970–1 (now captain). Vice-captain Gloucestershire. In 1970–1 scored six centuries for Rhodesia in successive innings, equalling world record of Bradman and Fry. Hat-trick, all lbw, Gloucestershire v Essex, Westcliff, 1972 (also made century in match). Highest score 254 Rhodesia v Western Province, Salisbury 1970–1. Seven Tests, all v Australia: three in 1966–7 and four in 1969–70: 41 wickets at 15·02 and 226 runs at 25·11, highest 48. Also skilled player at rugby, hockey, tennis, golf and squash.

JOHN AUGUSTINE SNOW

Born Peopleton, Worcestershire 13.10.41. Debut Sussex 1961, cap 1964. Played forty-two Tests 1966–73 (176 wickets at 26·18). Still considered by many as England's fastest and most penetrating opening bowler well after his last Test selection v West Indies in 1973. Shared tenth wicket partnership of 128 with Ken Higgs v West Indies, Oval 1966 (two short of then Test record). Played two seasons for Carlton in Melbourne District Cricket, 1972–3 and 1973–4. Some talent as poet.

ALAN PHILIP ERIC KNOTT

Born Belvedere, Kent 9.4.46. Debut Kent 1964, capped 1965. Best Young Cricketer of Year 1965 (Cricket Writers' Club). Coached and played in Tasmania. Dismissed ninety-eight batsmen in 1967, including seven v Pakistan in Test debut. To end 1974 England season, sixty-one Tests: 170 catches, 15 stumpings, only 34 short of Godfrey Evans's record 219 (ninety-one Tests). Two centuries in match Kent v Surrey, Maidstone 1972; 101 and 96 England v New Zealand, Auckland 1970–1. Described in 1971 by W. J. O'Reilly as best wicketkeeper he had ever seen.

MICHAEL JOHN KNIGHT SMITH

Born Broughton Astley, Leicestershire, 30.6.33. Debut Leicestershire 1951, capped 1955. Oxford Blues 1954–6 (captain 1956)—record three centuries in Varsity matches. Debut Warwickshire 1956, capped 1957. Captain 1957–67. Retired after 1967, but returned as regular in 1970. Fifty Tests (1958–72), captain in twenty-five. In 1959, scored 3245 runs (av. 57·94). Scored 1000 runs in season twenty times (including one overseas). One England Rugby Union cap. 2278 runs in fifty Tests at 31·36, with three centuries. Managing director of country club.

JOHN HENRY WEBB FINGLETON

Born Waverley, Sydney 28.4.08. Eighteen Tests, first v South Africa 1931–2, last v England 1938. In Tests: 1189 runs at 42·46, including 112, 108, 118, 100 in successive innings (separate matches, three v South Africa, fourth v England), first batsman to achieve four consecutive Test hundreds. Much battered and respected in Bodyline series. Made 2263 runs for New South Wales in Sheffield Shield at 39·70. Publications include *Cricket Crisis, Brightly Fades the Don, Masters of Cricket, Ashes Crown the Year, Fingleton on Cricket*. Outstanding writer and broadcaster.

MICHAEL PARKINSON

Born Barnsley, Yorkshire, 1935. Punishing left-hand bat, extraordinary slip field (copy supplied by M.P.). Journalist and feature writer with *Manchester Guardian, Daily Express*; features editor *Topic*. Producer *Scene at 6.30* (Granada TV), reporter *Twenty-four Hours* (BBC TV), member of presenters' team for *What The Papers Say* (Granada TV); presenter *Cinema*; executive producer *Sports Arena* (London Weekend Television); presenter *Good Afternoon* (Thames TV); host *Parkinson* chat show (BBC TV). Sports columnist *Sunday Times*. Publications include *Cricket Mad, Football Daft, Football A–Z* (with Willis Hall). Contributor to *Punch*.

BENNY GREEN

Professional jazz saxophonist, turned writer. Club cricketer. Reviews films for *Punch*, books for *The Spectator*, jazz records and performances for *The Observer*. Has written two novels and several books of musical criticism. Frequent radio and television appearances in Britain. Co-author of acclaimed hit musical *Cole*.

MIKE GIBSON

Born Sydney 27.5.40. Educated North Sydney Boys High School, obtained Commonwealth Scholarship. Briefly studied Law at Sydney University. Cadet journalist Sydney *Daily Mirror*, transferred Sydney *Daily Telegraph* 1959—still there. Worked as sports writer in newspaper's London bureau, covered Wimbledon, British Opens and other leading sporting events. Played fair tennis, awful game of Rugby League, poor cricket. Most impressive cricket performance witnessed: two-year-old son Danny clouting another child with stump at Chinaman's Beach park in Sydney. Plays ferocious game of stud poker, middling game of gin rummy.

STANLEY REYNOLDS

Born Holyoake, Massachussets 27.11.34. Educated Williston Academy, Boston University. Worked as sports writer, mainly baseball, for various American newspapers, including A. J. Liebling's old paper, *Providence Journal*, Rhode Island. Married Lancashire girl, moved to Liverpool in 1960. Reporter and columnist for *Manchester Guardian*, later weekly Arts column for *Guardian*. TV critic for *The Times*. *Punch* contributor. Novels: *Better Red Than Dead* (1964), *Thirty is a Dangerous Age, Cynthia* (1967), later filmed with Dudley Moore. In gestation: a play to be called *A Cricket Writer's Wet Afternoon*.

Index